# Chicken Soup for the Soul®

# New Moms

Chicken Soup for the Soul: New Moms
101 Inspirational Stories of Joy, Love, and Wonder
Jack Canfield, Mark Victor Hansen, Susan M. Heim

Published by Chicken Soup for the Soul Publishing, LLC   www.chickensoup.com
Copyright © 2011 by Chicken Soup for the Soul Publishing, LLC. All Rights Reserved.
No part of this publication may be reproduced, stored in a retrieval system or transmitted in any form or by any means, electronic, mechanical, photocopying, recording or otherwise, without the written permission of the publisher.

CSS, Chicken Soup for the Soul, and its Logo and Marks are trademarks of Chicken Soup for the Soul Publishing LLC.

The publisher gratefully acknowledges the many publishers and individuals who granted Chicken Soup for the Soul permission to reprint the cited material.

Front cover photos courtesy of iStockphoto.com/black red (© black red) and /Lloret (© Evelin Elmest). Back cover photos courtesy of iStockphoto.com/aldomurillo (© Aldo Murillo) and Photos.com. Interior photo courtesy of iStockphoto.com/scibak (© scibak).

Cover and Interior Design & Layout by Pneuma Books, LLC
For more info on Pneuma Books, visit www.pneumabooks.com

Distributed to the booktrade by Simon & Schuster. SAN: 200-2442

## Publisher's Cataloging-in-Publication Data
### (Prepared by The Donohue Group)

Chicken soup for the soul : new moms : 101 inspirational stories of joy, love, and wonder / [compiled by] Jack Canfield, Mark Victor Hansen, [and] Susan M. Heim.

   p. ; cm.

   Summary: A collection of 101 true personal stories, mostly from new moms, but with a few from new fathers, about getting pregnant, being pregnant, giving birth, caring for an infant, and continuing to the toddler years.
   ISBN: 978-1-935096-63-4

   1. Pregnant women--Literary collections. 2. Pregnancy--Literary collections. 3. Childbirth--Literary collections. 4. Infants--Care--Literary collections. 5. Pregnant women--Anecdotes. 6. Pregnancy--Anecdotes. 7. Childbirth--Anecdotes. 8. Infants--Care--Anecdotes. I. Canfield, Jack, 1944- II. Hansen, Mark Victor. III. Heim, Susan M. IV. Title: New moms

PN6071.P62 C55 2011
810.8/02/3068743                                              2010938809

PRINTED IN THE UNITED STATES OF AMERICA
on acid∞free paper
20 19 18 17 16 15 14 13 12 11        01 02 03 04 05 06 07 08 09 10

# Chicken Soup for the Soul
# New Moms

101 Inspirational Stories
of Joy, Love, and Wonder

Jack Canfield
Mark Victor Hansen
Susan M. Heim

Chicken Soup for the Soul Publishing, LLC
Cos Cob, CT

Chicken Soup for the Soul

www.chickensoup.com

# Contents

Introduction .................................................................... xi

### ❶
### ~Countdown to Motherhood~

1. Our Last Night, *Kimberly J. Garrow* ............................. 1
2. On the Way, *Nona Perez* ................................................ 3
3. Pregnancy: Nature's Hostile Takeover, *Andrea Farrier* ........... 7
4. The Blessed Event, *Jane McBride Choate* ................... 11
5. Making Space, *Jennifer Quasha* ................................ 13
6. A Laboring Question, *Brianna N. Renshaw* ............... 17
7. A Fine Case of Baconitis, *Cindy Beck* ....................... 21
8. Speedy Delivery, *Helen R. Zanone* ............................ 23

### ❷
### ~The Mom-mary Glands~

9. I Was a Breastfeeding Failure, *Judy Epstein* ............... 31
10. Picture Perfect, *Michelle Civalier* ................................ 36
11. Blushing Ride, *D. Dawn Maxwell* .............................. 40
12. The Dinner Surprise, *Diane Buller* ............................. 43
13. Adventures in Breastfeeding, *Mimi Greenwood Knight* ........... 47
14. Father Knows Breast, *Gary Rubinstein* ...................... 51
15. Mother Nurture, *Katrina Rehme Hatch* ..................... 56

### ❸
### ~Give Me Rest~

16. Maybe in Prison I'll Get Some Sleep, *Robbie Iobst* ........... 63
17. My Little Alarm Clock, *Laura Sassi* ............................ 67

| | | |
|---|---|---|
| 18. | Adjustments, *Dayle Allen Shockley* | 69 |
| 19. | Making the Right Call, *Ronda Ross Taylor* | 71 |
| 20. | The New Mommy Dress Code, *Erin Fuentes* | 74 |
| 21. | Getting on the Right Side of Sleep, *Dianne Daniels* | 77 |
| 22. | Burping in the Night, *Marie Cleveland* | 80 |

## ❹
## ~The Wonder of Being a Mother~

| | | |
|---|---|---|
| 23. | Two Heartbeats, One Bond, *Misa Sugiura* | 85 |
| 24. | Growing Pains, *Kim Ehlert* | 88 |
| 25. | The Drawer, *Becky S. Tompkins* | 92 |
| 26. | To Have and to Hold, *Mary Jo Marcellus Wyse* | 96 |
| 27. | Prince Charming, *Kimberly J. Garrow* | 100 |
| 28. | Forever Changed, *Michelle Sedas* | 102 |
| 29. | The First Change, *Jane Ann Miller* | 104 |

## ❺
## ~Doubts & Insecurities~

| | | |
|---|---|---|
| 30. | Mother to Mother, *Terri Duncan* | 111 |
| 31. | A Tale of Two Mothers, *Shelle Lenssen* | 114 |
| 32. | A Good Mother, *Lynn Juniper* | 117 |
| 33. | Six Days In, *Liesl Jurock* | 121 |
| 34. | Life Is Not Always Good in the Motherhood, *Julie Sharp* | 125 |
| 35. | So This Is Love, *Alyssa Ast* | 129 |
| 36. | Motherhood: Not Quite a Stroll in the Park, *Maizura Abas* | 132 |
| 37. | An Unexpected Blessing, *Aimee J. Lenger* | 136 |
| 38. | I'm Pregnant, *Ken Hoculock* | 139 |

## ❻
## ~Words of Wisdom~

| | | |
|---|---|---|
| 39. | Gestation Citations, *Melissa Face* | 147 |
| 40. | A Pot of Soup, *Catherine Ring Saliba* | 150 |

41. Expert Advice, *Cara Holman* ................................................. 152
42. The New Silence, *Danielle Kazemi* ...................................... 156
43. The Motherhood Marathon, *Denise K. Loock* ..................... 159
44. The Great Name Debate, *Victoria Grantham* ..................... 162
45. In Like a Lion, Out Like a Lamb, *Shawnelle Eliasen* ........... 166
46. What a New Mom Needs to Hear, *Sarah Sweet Newcomb* ... 170
47. A Little Hard-Earned Advice, *Maria Rodgers O'Rourke* ........ 172
48. Those Trying First Weeks, *Christa Gala* ............................. 176

# ❼
## ~Born of My Heart~

49. A Free Fall with a Soft Landing, *Beverly Beckham* ............... 183
50. A Promise, *Rachel Allord* ................................................... 187
51. The Right Choices, *Pearl Lee* ............................................. 190
52. The Match, *Kathy Lynn Harris* ........................................... 192
53. The Labor of Two Moms, *Kathleen E. Jones* ....................... 196
54. Just Like Any Other, *Dena May* .......................................... 199
55. Three Mothers, One Heart, *Kathryn Lay* ............................. 201
56. When You Least Expect It, *Debbie Schmid* ........................ 204
57. Your Son Looks Just Like You, *Sharon Pheifer* ................... 208
58. Letter to the Birth Mother, *Christine White* ........................ 212

# ❽
## ~Tough Stuff~

59. The Power of Two, *Kathleen M. Basi* ................................. 219
60. A Rough Start, *Erin Cloherty Baebler* ................................. 221
61. Will's Whole World, *Amy Bourque* ..................................... 224
62. Surviving Postpartum Anxiety, *Jenny R. George* ................. 228
63. Delivered Not by the Stork, *Lanita Moss* ............................ 231
64. He's the Same Baby, *Tina Marie McGrevy* .......................... 234
65. Jefferson's Journey, *Brandy Kleinhans* ............................... 236

## ❾ ~Giggles & Mischief~

66. The Perfect Accessory, *Dawn Hentrich* ................................. 243
67. Noah to the Rescue, *Nikki Studebaker Barcus* ...................... 246
68. Drew and the Pacifier Blues, *Leslie Boulden Marable* ........... 249
69. Confessions of an Earth Mama Wannabe, *Lela Davidson* .... 253
70. The Baby Olympics, *Judy Epstein* ......................................... 256
71. Mom on the Run, *Deirdre Fitzpatrick* ................................... 259
72. Yoga Night, *Rhonda Bocock Franz* ....................................... 264
73. A Dime Worth of Hope, *Malinda Dunlap Fillingim* .............. 267
74. Not So Small Packages, *Jess Holland* ................................... 270
75. The Gold Dust Twins, *Rosalind Zane* ................................... 273

## ❿ ~The Long Road~

76. Elliott Comes to Play, *Cynthia Patton* ................................... 279
77. A Dream Becomes Real, *Helen R. Zanone* ............................ 283
78. The Infertile Mother's Day, *Julia Garstecki* ........................... 287
79. The Day Time Stopped, *Patricia Barrett* ............................... 289
80. Unfinished Business, *Wendy Dellinger* ................................. 293
81. Out of the Clear Blue Easy, *Nicole R.C. Pugh* ...................... 298
82. The Master Plan, *RMB McManamon* .................................... 301
83. Sixteen Pink Lines, *Jamie Richardson* .................................. 304
84. Longing for a Child, *K.T.* ...................................................... 308
85. A Letter to My Unborn Child, *Tiffany Mannino* ................... 311

## ⓫ ~Second Time Around~

86. It, *Angie Reedy* ...................................................................... 317
87. Sea of Mother Love, *Shawnelle Eliasen* ................................ 321

88. I Didn't Know, *Amanda Yardley Luzzader* ............................ 325
89. New Mother, Redux, *Barbara Diggs* .................................. 328
90. To My Younger Son, *Alice Knisley Matthias* ....................... 333
91. The Outfit, *Jeannie Dotson* ............................................. 336
92. The Second Time Around, *C. Hope Clark* .......................... 339

## ❿ ~Toddler Time~

93. The Bottle Fairy, *D. B. Zane* ............................................. 347
94. First Haircut, *Tina Smith* ................................................. 349
95. ABC-CEO, *Nancy Berk* .................................................... 353
96. Sleepy, Grumpy, and Dad, *Carol McAdoo Rehme* ................ 356
97. Sloppy Mommy, Little Faces, *Julie R. Bunnell* ..................... 359
98. Flowers from an Admirer, *Sharon Landeen* ....................... 362
99. I Got a Boy, *Stacey Tucker* ............................................... 364
100. Mixed Feelings, *Marilyn Nutter* ....................................... 366
101. Playmate Dates, *Michelle Civalier* ................................... 368

Meet Our Contributors ..................................................... 375
Meet Our Authors ........................................................... 393
Thank You ...................................................................... 396
About Chicken Soup for the Soul ...................................... 398

# Introduction

*Aside from new babies,
new mothers must be the most beautiful creatures on earth.*
~Terri Guillemets

Being a mom, of course, is a life-long endeavor. Motherhood begins from the moment that test strip shows a positive result and never ends, even when our children are grown and have children of their own. However, the challenges and rewards change through each stage of our kids' lives. In the first year, we may encounter colic, teething, and toxic diaper leaks. In the toddler years, we're obsessed with safety and potty-training. In the school years, there's peer pressure and homework. And don't even get me started on the challenges of the teen years! But, for now, let's focus just on the first few roller-coaster years. *Chicken Soup for the Soul: New Moms* starts at the beginning of our parenting journey — from the announcement that "I'm pregnant!" through the very active toddler and preschool years.

Most of us define the term "new mom" as being a mother for the very first time. It's sharing the news of the first grandchild with our parents, going for our very first ultrasound (and possibly finding out whether it's a boy or a girl), and hearing that first cry as the baby emerges from the cozy cave he or she has been inhabiting for many long months. But that's just one definition of a "new mom." For me, I've always felt that I was a new mom twice! The first time was when I found out I was expecting my oldest son, who is now a young man in his twenties. I was twenty-four and had no family around. Although I had been an expert babysitter in my teens, I found that I still had a lot to learn! So, I combed the parenting books, talked to friends who were already parents, and asked a lot of questions of the pediatrician. This was new territory for me, and I did my best to get the information I needed in a pre-Internet world. Nearly three years later, my second son arrived, but I was pretty much an "old pro" at that point. I'd ushered my first son through ear infections, separation anxiety, and an obsession with Barney the purple dinosaur, so I didn't feel quite as inexperienced as I had the first time around.

Flash forward eleven years. My two boys were growing up, a preteen and a teenager, when I got some shocking news. I was going to be a mother again! So many years later, the gadgets and advice had changed. It was like I was a "new mom" all over again! I had given away all of my baby gear, so I was starting from scratch in setting up a nursery, buying baby clothes, and researching diapers. Once again, I had a lot to learn. And to add even more confusion to the situation, I found out I was expecting twins! Now, not only did I have to figure out what I needed for a baby, but I had to double it and consider all of the unique issues that arrive with twins. (You can read more about those adventures in *Chicken Soup for the Soul: Twins and More*.)

So, it matters not whether you're in your twenties or your forties, pregnant or adopting, raising a newborn or a two-year-old, or even adding a second (or third) child to the family—you're a new mom. And no one understands your joys and struggles better than other moms. Every time I read the stories in this book, I find myself nodding my head in agreement. I have had many of the same experiences, and I know exactly how the mothers (and fathers) felt in these situations. I also love the memories these stories bring up. I had forgotten what it's like to go out in public while breastfeeding, only to experience an embarrassing "leak" upon hearing a baby cry! And I realize with sadness that I really miss the days of rocking a baby through a sleepless night, even though it's accompanied by exhaustion. I know now that the potty-training days I thought would never end were just a blip in my children's many milestones.

*Chicken Soup for the Soul: New Moms* is our gift to all mothers. It is the celebration of the honor of being somebody's mom. And it is a tribute to all women who muddle their way through the trials and delights of raising a child. The truth of the matter is that we are all "new moms" because there are always new challenges and new pleasures, regardless of the age of our children. But the early years are especially years of wonder and learning, which the authors of these stories so beautifully illustrate. Chicken Soup for the Soul stories are tailor-made for new moms because you can easily read a few pages while your child is napping, playing with Grandma, or throwing the contents of his high-chair tray to the family dog. So, treat yourself to a little well-deserved "me time" and enjoy *Chicken Soup for the Soul: New Moms!*

~Susan Heim

# New Moms

## Countdown to Motherhood

*Pregnancy is a disease from which you recover
in eighteen years and nine months.*

~Carrie Latet

# Our Last Night

*A mother's joy begins when new life is stirring inside...
when a tiny heartbeat is heard for the very first time,
and a playful kick reminds her that she is never alone.*
~Author Unknown

The darkness engulfs my bulging figure as I gracelessly flop to the other side. Peaceful sleep has become a thing of the past, since somewhere in these nine-plus months I have metamorphosed into a female Buddha. Tonight's restlessness, however, is not unwelcome. It isn't the heartburn or the frequent need to go to the bathroom that is keeping me awake.

I place my hand on my stomach as you roll over and poke me with a protruding limb. The game of "try to guess the body part" has become a favorite pastime of mine. Soon, however, the mystery will be revealed, and I will be able to see with my own eyes what has been causing all this commotion inside. For such a tiny life, you sure do know how to make your presence well-known. I can hardly believe that, before long, my tiny butterfly will spread his or her wings and emerge from the warm cocoon.

I glance over at your sleeping father, who is oblivious to what is happening. "We won't wake your daddy just yet," I whisper to you in my mind. These private conversations will be deeply missed, as will the now-familiar acrobatics you perform. "No, we'll keep this our little secret for just a little while more." The increasing waves tell me this will be our last night, and I want to hold on to these final moments as mother and unborn child.

The past month I have gone from anxiously counting down to fervently praying for this moment to get here. I already feel like I have been pregnant a lifetime. It's not just my body that has been stretched to the end of its limit. I have gone way beyond the "cute pregnant woman stage" and have entered the "beached whale phase." If I hear one more time, "Are you still pregnant?" or "How far along did you say you were?" I really think I might burst! Don't get me wrong. I have loved carrying you inside me and am utterly amazed that my body has nurtured you and been your safe haven for all these months. These past days, though, I admit, I have been preoccupied with one thought: "Would you get here already?!"

Now that our journey as mother and unborn child is finally coming to an end, however, I am not prepared for this melancholy drifting over me. There is a bit of sadness mingled with my joy about what lies ahead. I long to hold you in my arms, and yet part of me still wants to carry on this special bond we share right now. At that thought, you give me a gigantic kick, as if to remind me, "Hey, Mommy, we will still have a special bond; it will just be different!"

My face lights up with a smile, and I am filled with an overwhelming sense of love and happiness. I am ready for our last night as mother and unborn child to come to an end and for our first day together as mother and newborn to begin. I touch my stomach one last time, caressing the now familiar shape of the unseen you. Then I remove my hand, reaching over to wake up your father. It is time.

~Kimberly J. Garrow

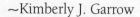

# On the Way

*Women's bodies have their own wisdom, and a system of birth refined over 100,000 generations is not so easily overpowered.*
~Sarah Buckley

Nothing smells better in the morning than good coffee brewing. Even though I don't drink the stuff, the aroma wakes me and brings me comfort as I snuggle under the covers, hugging my husband's pillow and breathing in his scent where it still lingers. I hear him in the kitchen, banging around, tinkering, puttering. He restlessly awaits daylight, anxious for the sun to illuminate the world, eager to start his day. My giant belly rolls.

"Hey, little one... you awake?"

I caress my swollen tummy, soothe my stretched skin, stroke away the discomfort. I hear a clank. Elias puts the cast iron skillet on the stove. Oh, no... I hope he doesn't start cooking. Not yet. Just the thought of it makes me queasy. Eggs and onions, his favorite breakfast, will make me hurl....

Whoever decided to call this "morning" sickness? It's been all-day sickness for me. And those doctors, they don't know anything.

"It'll only last a few weeks," they assured me, "a couple of months at the most."

Yeah, right. I've been sick for nine months. It should be called "mourning sickness" because I'm in mourning. I mourn the loss of my body, the loss of my balance, the loss of emotional stability and... my belly button. Oh, blessed event. At least it's almost here.

Ooooh, baby... That's not so nice. My belly feels like a melon ready to burst. Looks like one, too. My little one squirms, wiggles, kicks. Not that sweet, gentle nudge I usually get. No, this is more like an attempted escape. It hurts.

"Are you hungry, honey?" Elias's voice is soft, nurturing.

"Oh, babe, please don't cook anything. Not yet. I've got to go to the bathroom and then... maybe I'll have some crackers or something. If I smell eggs, I'll lose it. And nothing's worse than dry heaves."

"I'll get you one of those protein drinks. You've got to keep your strength up."

I wash my face, brush my teeth, fight back another cramp. Oh, hey, that's what this pain is: a cramp.

"Uh... I think I'm in labor."

"Really...?"

"Yeah, maybe... ouch... yeah, definitely... um... I think we should go."

"Scott's coming over for his paycheck. Get ready, and we'll leave as soon as he shows up."

I head for the front door, reach for the handle, and crumple against the doorjamb. A fierce contraction squeezes the life from me. I lean against the wall, gasp, moan.

The door opens. Scott's face pales.

"Dude, my paycheck can wait."

"Hi, Scott. Want a cup of coffee?"

"Hey, man, you better get outta here. Seriously..."

"Oh... uh... I'll call ya later."

Elias cradles me against his strong chest, supports my contorted frame, and helps me into our van—our school-bus yellow, one-ton window van. I cradle my belly in one arm, ease carefully into the seat, and sit on the edge. No way I'm using a seat belt.

The van rumbles to a start, crunches gravel, and rolls down the driveway. I glance back and notice a Hawaiian print quilt on the floor in the back of the van.

"I think I want to lie down... in the back."

I climb between the seats, crumple to my knees, and roll onto my back. Another contraction hits, and we are on our way. The van sways back and forth, around curves, down our windy mountain road. The sun peeks over the ridge, pouring sunshine onto my face and warming the morning. Around a turn and the light is gone. I see, instead, trees. The forest flies by.

"Oooh…!"

"Honey? Are you okay?"

"The pains are getting really strong."

"Hold on. We're almost there."

The trees zoom by faster, faster. The sun in my face, and then gone again. The sky outside begins to show blue, the clear crystal blue of a crisp December morning. Beautiful. Ugh, another contraction…

Relax, go with the flow, it'll be okay. This is natural, a part of life since life began. I can do this. I just need to relax and follow my instincts. Relax… breathe… relax… owwww… breathe… relax… push! I can't help it. I can't resist it. All at once, I am calm, focused, confident.

"The baby's coming.…"

Elias looks back from the driver's seat, eyes wild.

"No… Hold it! We're almost there."

"Baby's coming… I can't hold it.…"

"Really… I just saw a sign. We're almost there. You can hold it for a few minutes.…"

"It doesn't work that way. This baby's coming… now. You can either keep driving or pull over and help."

Gravel crunches. The van rolls quickly to a stop. A dormant fruit tree hangs over the windshield, filters the early morning sunlight, becomes a focal point. The side door of the van bangs open, and I feel the warmth of my husband's hands.

"What do I do? What do we do?"

"I can't stay on my back. It hurts too much. Help me up.…"

His strength lifts me. I grab the back of the driver's seat. Another contraction contorts my body, and the uncontrollable spasm wreaks havoc. Natural… this is natural… I can do this. My mother did this. My grandmothers did this. Mothers since the beginning of time did this. Squat... That's better, more normal. Breathe... relax... breathe... oh, wow... push! Push! Push! I feel resistance, tearing, squeezing.

Elias, excited, terrified, yells, "Oh, my God! I see the head!"

I pant, catch my breath, relax between contractions. One more contraction, one more big push... and it's done. A gasp. A cry. I wilt, collapse back onto the quilt, look up, utterly exhausted. My husband holds our new baby, his arms wrapped tightly around it as though afraid of losing his grip. A broad smile grows across his face.

"We did it. We did it. He's okay. We have a son."

Elias hands our new baby to me, nestles him in my arms, and covers us with the quilt. He latches on, hungry, content. Ten tiny toes, ten exquisite fingers, perfect little nose, chocolate eyes, and a really big head. He's absolutely astonishing.

"I lied to you," Elias admits softly.

"What? What are you talking about?"

"When I told you we were almost there. I said we passed a sign, told you we were just a few miles from the hospital. I thought you could hold it if you thought we were close."

"Huh," I chuckle wearily. "So... where are we, exactly?"

"Oh, about fifteen miles away."

~Nona Perez

# Pregnancy: Nature's Hostile Takeover

*Think of stretch marks as pregnancy service stripes.*
*~Joyce Armor*

It has been three years since my last pregnancy. It is a bit off-putting to be in public, surrounded by pregnant women and nursing moms, and to realize that I have aged out (or, as I prefer to think of it, "experienced out") of that club. I really thought that babies and bellies would be my reality for eternity. After all, I have spent two and a half years pregnant, five years breastfeeding, three days in labor, and exactly 38,465,342.8 hours worrying about parenting decisions I've either made, am making, or have yet to make. Being a mom isn't for the fainthearted.

No one tells you what it's going to be like, do they? I mean, I know part of that is our fault, as new mothers, because we are so convinced we know what we're doing that when a well-meaning friend tries to give us advice, we roll our eyes and snicker behind our hands at them. "Well, sure you had to use a pacifier with your baby, but mine won't have any anxiety issues, and therefore won't need external comforting." Spoken like a true preggo or newbie. Just wait until the middle of the night about three days in — you know, right after you've come home from the hospital and it's just you and Angel Baby staring at each other by the glow of the nightlight. You'll be desperately digging in the bottom of the diaper bag to find that pacifier, too, momma. Trust me on this one.

No, new moms aren't known for their willingness to take advice, but maybe that's because they feel ever so slightly lied to. Let me give you an example. When a pregnant mom asks me what pregnancy was like, I tell the truth—it was wonderful. I loved every minute of it. Couldn't believe what a magical experience it was. Would do it again in a heartbeat. Etc. This, of course, is the perspective I have about it now. You know, now that I'm on the other side of it. Now that it is becoming a memory. Now that I've reaped the rewards. I'm not lying when I say that pregnancy is awesome, but perhaps I'm also not telling the truth, the whole truth, and nothing but the truth, as I might have been experiencing it at the time.

The whole truth, of course, involves a bit of unpleasantness. It involves aches in body parts I didn't even know I had. Before I got pregnant, I was only vaguely aware of being in possession of a cervix. I had never seen said "cervix." I didn't have an owner's manual on it, had never changed its oil or had it tuned, and I certainly didn't know it could hurt. Further, I never guessed that it would become fair game for discussions with colleagues after visits to the doctor. Let's face it—it's fair game for discussion with everyone near the end, when even Great Aunt Lucy will ask how far dilated you are. (This is the same woman, by the way, who always chastised you for not acting like more of a lady when you were young, and now she's hollering into the phone to see how stretched and skewed your most private of parts has become.) By the end of it all, three doctors, ten medical students, eighteen nurses, and a cleaning lady who doesn't know how to knock before entering will all have seen the very same cervix you've still not been properly introduced to.

The whole truth also involves, shall we say, anatomical reorganization. These are similar to the theories discussed in college geology classes—poles shifting and causing wobbles and a loss of balance, new hilly eruptions and subsequent foliage cover, bulges in the equator, and the heartbreaking, gradual sinking of northern mountain ranges. Stuff just doesn't stay put when you're pregnant. Your belly button thrusts forward, as if trying to escape the disruptions to its previously peaceful domain. Your feet widen. Your organs squish and slosh (sometimes even leaking). Fact of the matter is, you even get new body parts. It's true. Look it up. (Or, if you're pregnant, just look down.)

The human body is full of strange-sounding parts. You have to wonder if the only reason some people go into medicine is because no other area of science or technology would hire them because of their funny names. They only backed into stellar careers in gastroenterology or otolaryngology because their initial interviews at, say, NASA or the National Park Service went something like this:

"I'm terribly sorry, Mister... uh... Kiesselbach, is it? Though your credentials are excellent, we can't run the risk of you discovering something truly remarkable and then wanting to name it after yourself. It's just a PR nightmare. Have you ever considered medicine, though?"

So, that's why we now have parts inside each and every one of us that sound like they're more likely to have come from a *Star Wars* movie than a medical text. I kid you not — if you looked hard enough (and knew where to look), you could find your very own Hydatid of Morgagni (didn't he rule the Mongols in the mid-1500s?), Islets of Langerhans (makes you want to vacation there sometime, doesn't it?), Space of Moll (right next to the Black Hole of Moll), and White Line of Tolt (every bit as spectacular as the White Cliffs of Dover, but not nearly as crowded).

Anyway, these funny little innards are silently working away inside you all the time. But your Montgomery's Tubercles only kick into gear when you're pregnant and breastfeeding. They're actually little bumps around your nipples that secrete a special oil to keep things properly lubed for breastfeeding. Montgomery originally described these glands as "a constellation of miniature nipples scattered over a milky way." Very poetic. Most women, however, describe them as just another part of the hostile body takeover that is pregnancy. Oily bumps. On your breasts, no less. Great. Unfortunately, they go perfectly with those dark hairs you sprout on your upper lip and the unexpected gift that is urinary incontinence. You see why pregnant women don't exactly fall for my "everything is beautiful" explanation of motherhood?

No, one cannot deny that there are some parts of pregnancy that aren't all glowing beauty. Here's the thing, though: That doesn't all magically go away when you give birth. That first post-baby look in the mirror is quite a shock. Your breasts sag. Your belly is floppy. Your stretch marks shine. Your leg hair is thicker. You see parts you haven't seen in nine months, and they're not pretty. Worst of all, you're convinced you're never going to be the same again. And I've got to level with you here—you won't. Sure, things will get better. Heck, you might even get back into your old clothes and look just as smokin' as you did before, but you will still be forever changed. You will regard your body with new respect. You will cherish the memories and honor the sacrifices it has made. Those aren't stretch marks—they're battle scars, and you've earned 'em, momma—just like you've earned a special membership into the exclusive Mommy Club, and the right to tell expectant mothers the same truth about pregnancy you heard all along—it's absolutely wonderful!

~Andrea Farrier

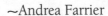

# The Blessed Event

*I'm not interested in being Wonder Woman in the delivery room.
Give me drugs.*
~Madonna

My husband and I prepared for the arrival of our first baby with the attention of a general preparing for an invasion. We did it all: Lamaze classes, nutrition classes, even a pregnancy bra fitting, not an easy task for a girl who had been brought up to be modest at any cost.

No amount of preparation, though, could equal the reality of giving birth.

Two hours into labor, I promised to devote myself to good works if I survived.

My husband held up a wedding picture for me to focus on. I ripped it to shreds and snarled, "I want drugs."

"But, honey," my hapless spouse said, "we decided we were going to have a natural birth."

I grabbed him by the neck of his hospital gown. "You have it natural. I want drugs."

With my promise that I'd take a contract out on his life if he ever laid a hand on me (translation: got me pregnant) again ringing in his ears, he meekly asked the nurse for painkillers.

At six hours, I vowed celibacy for the rest of my life as the back pains hit. You know the ones I mean — the kind that make the Inquisition rack seem like a session with a masseuse.

By the tenth straight hour of agonizing pain, I changed my mind and decided to skip the hit man. I'd do it myself. I fantasized about ways to do in this man I'd promised to love and cherish. First, though, I'd make him suffer.

Twelve hours into labor, I heard my husband excuse himself to go have breakfast. Seriously? The monster abandons me in my hour of need and goes to have breakfast? Death was too good for him.

In between screaming, I plotted. Suffering took on new meaning.

The doctor had yet to arrive. Alone with the nurse from Hades, I felt an uncontrollable need to push.

"Get this thing out of me!" I yelled.

"Pant, honey," the whey-faced nurse with ferret-like eyes encouraged.

"You pant."

"We don't have to be unpleasant," she chided.

"We don't have to be anything," I snarled through gritted teeth.

She snagged a doctor unfortunate enough to stroll into the room.

"I'm not an obstetrician," he whined. "I'm a proctologist."

With my last ounce of strength, I roused myself and grabbed him by the neck of his green scrubs. "I don't care if you do nose jobs," I said in a voice hoarse from screaming. "I want this thing out of me, and I want it out now."

He stuck his head between my legs and held out his hands just in time to catch a nine-pound squalling scrap of humanity—a beautiful daughter.

Eventually, I forgave my husband and allowed him to touch me again. The pain of giving birth must have faded for I endured it three more times. Each brought a miracle.

Thank heaven for drugs.

~Jane McBride Choate

# Making Space

*In pregnancy, there are two bodies, one inside the other. Two people live under one skin.... When so much of life is dedicated to maintaining our integrity as distinct beings, this bodily tandem is an uncanny fact.*
~Joan Raphael-Leff

For twelve weeks, I felt nauseous—from the moment I woke up to the moment that sleep rescued me. For a girl accustomed to popping a pill and feeling better, this was unacceptable. I could not believe that morning sickness was so common and yet people still decided to have babies. Then, as if God (or the gods/Mother Nature/whatever you want to say) was laughing at me, at around nine weeks, the migraines started to kick in. As a long-time sufferer, I should have known how horrible they would be, but I had never experienced them in pregnancy before. Pregnancy migraines happened every day. For four months straight. Sometimes, they were just low-grade throbs as I climbed the stairs. Sometimes, they were ocular migraines causing blurred vision in one eye. And then there were the full-on migraines that required a dark, quiet room for hours—sometimes even days. My dream of having a child had turned into a nightmare.

Every day I reminded myself that I wanted this. I chose this. I actually tried to get pregnant. Plus, others had done this—many times. I had dreamt about having my own little girl one day, and now the dream was coming true, but the reality had no relation to my fantasies. My child, no bigger than a grain of rice, had taken over, was tormenting me, and she was a long way from even being born. Bedridden from the migraines, depressed at the shutdown of my regular life, teary from the hormones of creating a girl and her reproductive system, I morphed from a happy woman into an angry vehicle for "my husband's" baby. Some days I was so lonely and sick that I wanted to die.

After I passed the twelve-week mark, I brought others into my "joy." All the myriad of congratulations left no room for my variety of complaints and honest misery. Having a baby was a miracle, they said. What I was feeling would pass, they added. For me, this was not passing, and there was no joy. What I wanted was not to be pregnant again. I wanted my body and my life back.

I read book after book about pregnancy. I wanted answers, help, and advice. Only one book was honest and identified my deep misery as something that "some people" experienced. Initially grateful, the honesty kept going. The writer was so honest about every part of the process, I felt terror like I never had before. I simply couldn't do this. This wasn't going to get better. I couldn't have this baby. I lay in bed wondering how I was going to get myself out of this one.

After five months, relief came slowly, like the rising sun after years of rain. A cute bump was forming between my ever-widening hips. I was headache-free for three days running. I wanted to eat again—and, I mean, I really wanted to eat. At last I could rejoin the world. Active until I had been invaded, I decided to try prenatal yoga. Friends had loved it, the books recommended it, and I wanted to do something marginally athletic after the past months of torpor.

At the start of the second class, the yoga teacher asked us to sit with our legs crossed, rest our hands on our bellies, close our eyes, and try to feel at one with our baby, make a connection with our baby. I closed my eyes. I put my hands on my belly. I waited. I felt no connection. I waited again. There was still no connection. In my belly was a troublemaker. My life as I knew it was over. My little girl had taken over. After class, I felt horrible. How could I feel this way? It had to stop. What was I doing to our "pre-birth relationship?" I was a bad mother, and my baby hadn't even been born. Yet my feelings wouldn't stop.

I waddled to prenatal yoga three days a week. Along with the exercise, I liked the camaraderie of the women. I liked watching them — us — all grow bigger together. The ones farther along were visions of the future to the ones a few weeks behind. There were the days when "an announcement" was made. Someone we had seen two days earlier had had her baby. Joy spread among the class. Who would be next? Another day brought a first-timer, someone with a flat tummy. We all smiled at her, knowing what other people passing her on the street probably didn't know. Being a part of other women's pregnancies was helping me move through mine. I was not alone on this journey. When my little girl kicked, a trickle of joy crept through me. Hope began to surface.

Although we practiced the same poses, different teachers used different words to help us into them. A variety of soothing words would ease our wobbly bodies into position. One day when a teacher was explaining how to get into Warrior 1, a standing pose, she said, "Reach your hands out. Reach forward like you are reaching to the future and reach back like you are reaching into the past, but keep your body centered right in the middle. Centered in today." Her words worked like magic. My twisted-up thoughts were always moving forward, backward, inside-out, and upside-down. Somehow, her simple words straightened me out. I left class clinging to feeling centered for as long as I could.

Another day, another teacher had us in triangle pose. We were standing, our legs wide, one arm on our knee and one arm reaching toward the sky. My belly was big enough now, and I was twisted in such a way that I looked like I had a basketball poking out of my left hip. I was wondering if my fat ankles were going to be able to hold me through this one. It seemed like a lot to ask. As the instructor told us to look up toward our raised hand, she said, "Keep your heart open. Try to open up your shoulder as much as you can. Make some space. If you are able to make just a little more space, you'll find your breathing will be easier."

Suddenly, I felt like an old oak tree from which hundreds of noisy black crows had just taken flight. Make space. If I made some more space, then I would be able to breathe easier. Trying to stay balanced, I struggled to get my shoulder back. I opened up my chest, took a deep breath, and stretched. I could feel my body open. Then my mind took over. That's all I needed to do. My baby hadn't taken all of me away. Maybe she took a lot in the beginning, but I was back, sort of, in a new way. I simply needed to make a little more space. If I made space in my heart, my mind, my body, and then my life, it would all be okay. My baby just needed a little bit of space.

I left class convinced that even I could handle that.

~Jennifer Quasha

# A Laboring Question

*The power and intensity of your contractions cannot be stronger than you, because it is you.*
~Author Unknown

I had to ask. I knew the answer. I knew the question was preposterous, but I couldn't help hoping. "Can we just leave her where she is?" I panted in exhausted pain.

I was in the final throes of labor. For the past forty-five minutes, I'd been enduring strong contractions. Lying on my side dressed in a thin cotton gown, staring intently at the logo on the hospital bed, contraction after contraction wracked my body. As my stomach clenched, I finally understood why all the media and literature stressed breathing during childbirth. The pain of my contractions was so incredible, my entire body froze tight, including my lungs. So I gripped the bedrails tightly and focused on breathing.

I was too overwhelmed with agony to pay attention to the clock, and before I knew it, the moment had come. I was maneuvered into position, and the doctor said the magic word, "Push!"

It was all I could manage just to breathe during the contractions, and now she wanted me to push too?

I've always thought of myself as a strong person. I run long distance and do my best to stay in shape. But my body was now completely weak, and my mind was giving up. I asked myself, "How can I end this with the least amount of pain?" The solution seemed simple enough: stop pushing and let the baby live in my tummy forever. Now I recognize how absurd the idea was, but at the time it seemed completely rational. I began to contemplate an entire lifetime of walking around with a huge swollen belly and aching feet. It didn't sound like a bad idea at all compared to the idea of more pushing.

This was my first baby. I thought I knew what to expect. I thought I could handle the pain without drugs. I thought giving birth was comparative to running a marathon. I thought a lot of things that ended up being wrong. First, childbirth was nothing like running a marathon. The fatigue was similar, but I'd never felt like my stomach was being turned inside out while running. Even the combination of every side stitch I'd ever had while running didn't compare to the pain of one single contraction. Second, I figured delivering a baby would be painful, but manageable; after all, it was a natural process women had been doing forever. I'd heard countless personal accounts of labor from different women while I was pregnant, and not one of them had said they didn't go through with it.

I went into the delivery nervous, but confident. The moment the contractions started, I felt my confidence slip slightly. This didn't feel at all like I had expected. As the contractions came faster and faster, and the pain became greater and greater, I did what I always do in times of personal struggle: I prayed silently, "God, give me strength."

I turned to my husband, Dan, who had been by my side from the beginning, and we shared a look of bewilderment. It seemed we'd both had a different idea of what labor was going to be like.

"I don't think I can do this," I told him between contractions.

"Yes, you can," he replied automatically. He didn't sound very sincere, and his eyes kept flicking back and forth between my feet and my head. It was obvious he was preoccupied. He tried to comfort me, to cheer me on, but his words lacked conviction. Lucky for him, I understood. His presence, while not a balm to my pain, was a balm to my heart.

At this point, the nurse who was assisting in the birth piped up with a cheerful "You can do it! Just keep pushing!" Her words quickly went in one ear and out the other since she'd told me earlier that she had never had a baby. What did she know? I dismissed her as easily as I would an annoying gnat.

As labor continued, my prayers grew more frequent and desperate.

"Oh, God! How can I possibly do this?"

"This can't be natural!"

"Please, God, make it stop."

"God, I'm sorry for complaining about not being able to bend over! I promise I'll live the rest of my life upright if you just let me keep her inside so I can stop this awful pushing."

Finally, after an hour of pushing, I gritted out, "I can't do it!"

The doctor responded blandly, "You can do it," as if my comment was something she'd heard millions of times before. She was sitting at my feet looking utterly bored, like she was wishing she had brought along a nail file to pass the time.

I completely disagreed with her diagnosis. That's when I asked, "Can we just leave her where she is? I don't mind staying pregnant the rest of my life."

But apparently the answer to my question was so obvious that no one even bothered to respond. My memories of everything but the pain are fuzzy at best, but I'm pretty sure my husband even had the nerve to roll his eyes at me!

In spite of my certainty that I'd given everything I had, I pulled myself together, just like I did at mile 23 of my last marathon when I thought I couldn't possibly continue another three miles. I dug down deep within myself to find the strength God gave me and kept pushing until my beautiful baby girl was born into the world.

The moment she was in my arms, the pain faded to nothingness. All I felt was amazement at the tiny angel resting on my chest. I looked at my husband, and we shared a moment of pure joy. We'd done this. With God's help, we'd created and delivered a miracle.

Once again, I was moved to pray, "Thank you, God, for helping me find strength at a time when my body and mind had given up."

And, thankfully, a few days after being home, I was also able to pray, "Thank you, God! I can bend over again!"

~Brianna N. Renshaw

# A Fine Case of Baconitis

*"Lisa honey, are you saying you're never going to eat any animal again? What about bacon?"*
~Dan Castellaneta, The Simpsons

Pregnant with my first and only child, I did the typical things—threw up as soon as I got out of bed in the morning, threw up at lunch, and threw up when anything smelled stronger than a saltine cracker. One sunny Sunday morning before I knew I was expecting, I decided to cook bacon. Bad, bad move. By the time the bacon had crisped in the frying pan, I'd raced to the bathroom more than once.

Please understand that I'm a bacon lover. My heart sings at the sound of bacon crackling in the hot grease of a frying pan and at the smell of the meat's smoky scent wafting through the house. It takes me back to Saturday morning breakfasts long ago, when life seemed to be a ribbon-bedecked gift, waiting to be opened.

So, it's understandable that in my state of prenatal ignorance, I decided only one thing could cause me to feel that sick at the smell of bacon: an advanced disease. Something with a weird medical title, such as Second Stage Pork-inoma or Third Degree Baconitis.

The morning following the bacon fiasco, I felt fine. Odd disease, that Third Degree Baconitis—one minute my stomach felt great, the next I was driving the porcelain bus. Being late for work, I didn't have time to ponder the oddity of the symptoms. However, I'd learned my lesson, and there would be no leftover bacon for me that morning. Instead, I grabbed a handful of grapes and an opened, now fizzless root beer. When I got to the workplace, where I developed film for a cancer research company, I topped off my breakfast with a custard doughnut that sat on a plate on the receptionist's desk—last week's leftover doughnut.

It didn't take long before I lay curled up on the cold, linoleum floor in the darkroom, holding my nose with one hand to block the acrid scent of photo chemicals—a smell that only made the nausea worse—and rubbing my stomach with the other.

"This Third Stage Baconitis is advancing rapidly," I muttered to myself through gritted teeth. "I have to make an appointment immediately to see a doctor." Then I jumped up and dashed to the bathroom.

Several weeks later, the doctor confirmed it. No, not Third Stage Baconitis, but a three-month pregnancy. I walked out of her office elated. Now it all made sense. No disease, no treatments involving chemo or radiation, just six more months of waiting for a baby—a cute, sweet baby to fill our lives with joy.

I was so happy I didn't even wait until we arrived back at our little nest to tell my husband. I told him in the car... and then we drove home faster than the wind so I could go throw up again.

~Cindy Beck

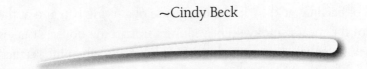

# Speedy Delivery

*Just as a woman's heart knows how and when to pump, her lungs to inhale, and her hand to pull back from fire, so she knows when and how to give birth.*
~Virginia Di Orio

"I think I am in labor," I told the nurse on the other end of the line.

"Ma'am, if you were in labor, you would know it." Her tone was short and snippy.

"All right," I said in a quiet, noncommittal way and hung up the phone. She was the nurse, after all. She must know better. Not to mention I had already called her two times that night. The problem was that I couldn't articulate how I was feeling. I was just uncomfortable.

This was nothing like my first pregnancy. Why didn't someone tell me that no two pregnancies are alike? Maybe they did, and I just didn't listen.

I lay back down on the couch. I tossed and turned in bed so much that I decided to move to the living room so I wouldn't wake my husband. I fell back to sleep. It was a restless sleep. Then I had the dream that I had to pee but couldn't find a bathroom. (Please tell me I am not the only one who has that dream.)

Thank goodness it was disturbing enough to wake me. I waddled to the bathroom. I peed... and peed... and peed.

"Boy, did I have to go," I said into the quiet apartment as if someone were listening.

I had never peed that much in my life. It seemed quite odd to me, but I was not calling that nurse again tonight. I still had two weeks left in my pregnancy, and I just needed to suck it up and get through it.

Again, I headed back to the couch. No sooner had I laid down, I wet myself.

"My water broke!" I shouted into the empty space around me. "I am going to call that nurse and give her a piece of my mind."

However, as soon as I stood up, it stopped. Maybe my water didn't break. There was so much doubt because my first pregnancy had me sloshing in my shoes. I couldn't call the nurse. I was not giving her a good laugh at my expense.

I paced around the apartment. "What to do? What to do?" I knew what I had to do. I had to call the cranky nurse. I would be cranky, too, if I had to listen to some woman rambling at three o'clock in the morning.

"Hello?" I said into the phone, hoping she wouldn't recognize my voice.

"What's wrong now?" The nurse sighed into the receiver. I could picture her rolling her eyes and thinking I was a crackpot.

"Well, you see... Well, I think..."

"Are you having contractions?"

"No," I said feeling embarrassed.

"Did your water break?"

"Not really." I didn't want her to know that I, a grown woman, had peed my pants.

"Then you are definitely not in labor," she said in short puffs of air.

Just as I was about to hang up, water gushed down my leg. Gushed, not trickled.

"My water just broke. And I am in labor!" I said to the nurse in a self-righteous sort of way. "I will be there in a few minutes." I slammed the phone down on the hook.

"John. John. You have to get up. My water broke." He began to stir when I got my first real contraction. I doubled over the bed, trying to blow the pain away. The sight of me shot him out of bed.

"How are you? Do you need anything?" Men sure have a way of asking stupid questions at the worst times!

"Go get the neighbor so she can stay here with Zach while we go to the hospital."

"Oh. Yeah. Right," he said as he pulled on a pair of pants. Just then, another contraction hit. It had been less than two minutes since the last one.

"You better hurry!" I said as I panted through the contraction. John ran out the apartment door before he could get a pair of shoes on. I moved around slowly trying to get my things together. I slipped a pair of leggings on under my nightgown. It had to be good enough because another contraction hit.

John and the neighbor came running through the door. John swung my bag over his shoulder and grabbed me by the elbow to lead me down the hall as if I was some old lady he was walking across the street.

We lived on the fourth floor, and there was no elevator. I took a deep breath and prepared myself for the eight flights of stairs below me. I had a contraction on every flight. I could see fear on John's face.

"We need to move a little faster," he said to me.

"Are you serious? You want me to move faster?" That was as possible as asking me to run a marathon in my condition. "Men!" I huffed under my breath.

As we walked out of the apartment complex, John ran ahead to open the car door. I stood on the front porch blowing away another contraction. Something had changed. Things felt very different.

"Honey," John said in his sweetest voice, "you need to get in the car."

"I can't get in the car," I cried. It felt as if the baby might fall out right on the porch.

Again, he took me by the elbow, almost dragging me to the car. "You have to get in the car!" he shouted. Looking into his eyes, I knew what he was thinking. It was the same thought I was having. We couldn't deliver this baby here.

I forced myself to get in the car. For reasons unknown to me at the time, I could not sit in the seat. So I put myself in a half-laying, half-sitting position. Thankfully, we only lived seven buildings away from the hospital, and it was the middle of the night. John sped the whole way, never stopping at the stop signs.

A couple of buildings away from the hospital, I screamed, "I'm pushing! I'm pushing!"

All he could do was scream back, "Don't push! Don't push!" He pulled into the emergency entrance honking and going the wrong direction. He slammed on the brakes and ran out screaming for help. "My wife is having a baby!"

Two orderlies strolled out of the entrance. The first one opened my door and peered in. The shock showed on his face. "Ma'am, stay right there," he said as the second one raced back inside.

"I am not having this baby in a car!" I exclaimed. He reached down to help me as I pulled myself out of the car. The second orderly came barreling towards us with a wheelchair. Was he serious? Did he expect me to sit down in that thing? I did my best to get in the chair as I rolled my eyes at him.

Just inside the doors of the emergency room, my legs went stiff with another contraction. My feet hit the floor like a pair of brakes and stopped the chair from going any further. One orderly lifted me from under the arms while the other grabbed my feet. They placed me on a gurney.

My leggings were slipped off to assess the situation, and there was my beautiful, healthy daughter. There was no time for gloves, IV or a doctor. Because of the special circumstance of her delivery, they rushed her to the nursery while I was moved to an examination room.

Meanwhile, the orderly began to apologize. "I am so sorry. You don't know how many dads we get that come running in all panicked. Usually, they have hours left in the labor process."

"It's all right," I said. "It worked out beautifully in the end."

Thank God for stretch pants...

~Helen R. Zanone

## Chapter 2

# New Moms

## The Mom-mary Glands

*A pair of substantial mammary glands have the advantage over the two
hemispheres of the most learned professor's brain
in the art of compounding a nutritive fluid for infants.*

~Oliver Wendell Holmes

# I Was a Breastfeeding Failure

*Could we change our attitude, we should not only see life differently, but life itself would come to be different.*
~Katherine Mansfield

I was an abject failure. Sitting on the living room couch, my pajama top open and the shades down at 4:00 in the afternoon, I was crying hysterically. My baby was crying hysterically, too. In fact, it was impossible to tell which of us was crying harder. As the tears rolled down my face and onto his, I held him cradled next to my breasts, which—apparently—did not work. "It's supposed to be so simple!" I wailed. "Cows can do it!" But not, apparently, me.

I had tried and tried, and so had he—on our own, with experts, and with awkward, bulky equipment—and we were both getting nowhere. Only thirty days a mother, and I had failed him at the most basic level: mother's milk.

I stood at a fork in the road. One way was recommended by all the experts as the healthiest, safest, best way to nourish my child. The other was the choice I was about to make. Over and over in my head, I heard those lines of the Robert Frost poem: "Two roads diverged in a wood, and I—I took the one less traveled by, And that has made all the difference." What if it did make "all the difference," and the road I chose was the wrong one?

•••

This was not what I'd planned. I was going to breastfeed. I had always been on good terms with my breasts—they'd gotten me plenty of dates in high school—and I assumed they'd work as God intended.

Plus, I believed all the experts: Breastfeeding is the easiest option—no bottles to sterilize or wash. It's the cheapest—no formula to buy; the healthiest—all the antibodies and nutrients your baby needs, miraculously blended for every stage of a young life. And it's psychologically best for you both, as well. Just clap baby to bosom and bond.

There are just a few things the experts left out:

Number one: It is far from easy.

Number two: You have no idea what you're doing. The primal breastfeeding scene consists of a new mother nursing her baby, when someone walks in and asks, "Is the baby getting enough?" New mother then goes ballistic because that's precisely what she's spent the last twenty-four sleepless hours panicked about herself.

Number three: It hurts! My toothless infant, six hours old, clamped down on my nipples hard enough to make me scream. Then he began sucking hard enough to give me bruises. Over the next few days, my nipples scabbed and cracked so badly they bled. Convinced this was horribly wrong, I begged for a lactation consultant. "Oh, no," she said, "if you can uncurl your toes after the first thirty seconds, you're doing it right."

On top of which, you must repeat the process every two hours.

Whose idea was this? Nine months of increasing sleeplessness and "discomfort," which means pain, capped off by either labor or major surgery—or, sometimes, both. Then, just when you could sleep for a week, you have to breastfeed?

For me, this is sufficient proof that God is not a woman.

It's just so improbable! Everything else that comes out of your body, you get rid of as quickly and as hygienically as possible; this, you give to your baby?

In fact, breastfeeding was the biggest disappointment of my

life—even worse than finding out that the chocolate Easter bunny is hollow.

Of course, we'd had more than our share of problems. At two days of age, my baby developed a case of jaundice that kept him in the hospital under lights (and needing extra milk) while I was sent home without him. Then I developed an infection and fever that put me into Intensive Care for a week, while the baby went home without me. Then, two days after I went home the second time, the baby got an unexplained fever and had to return to the hospital for a spinal tap and long weekend of intravenous antibiotics. The Emergency Room nurse actually said "You again?" when I carried him in.

All told, my baby and I had been together only eight of his first twenty-one days. I had rented a machine and pumped all through my ICU stay. But I hadn't pumped enough—foolishly choosing to sleep, instead—and by the time we got back together, his demand for milk was zooming just as my supply was packing it in.

So we went to consultants, who told me not only was I not making enough milk, but my baby didn't suck correctly. To fix both problems at once, I had to wear a contraption every time I nursed him. I hung a flask of formula around my neck with angel-hair-pasta-sized tubes leading from it, which I had to tape to myself so the ends would stick out just beyond my nipples. It was like those "beer hats" they wear to baseball games—except I was the beer... and the hat.

My first attempt was a disaster. I needed someone else to hold each tube in place while I grappled with the baby. The second time was even worse, resulting in the scene on the couch.

It didn't help that public opinion was virtually monolithic. Every book, every article, every piece of literature—even the back of the formula can, for heaven's sake—all started off the same way: "Of course, breastfeeding is best. But..." It didn't matter what they said next because I knew what they meant: "But if you don't care what happens to your baby, go right ahead."

The truth was, I didn't really have much choice left at that point. Yet I still couldn't bring myself to face it. I felt so horrendously guilty.

Sitting in that darkened living room, all I could see were scenes of my baby's ruined future, like the one of us at a shopping mall when he's six months old. He's screaming his head off with hunger while I rummage through the diaper bag, desperate, because I've left all the bottles home. Or the scene two years later when he's the clingiest kid in his playgroup, pacifier dangling from his lips night and day, because he never got enough oral gratification. Or the one, twelve years after that, identical, except the pacifier has become a cigarette. And all because, on this day in his young life, I couldn't take it anymore.

I wanted to scream with anger, misery, and frustration. But someone else was already doing that, and I was supposed to be the grown-up in his life.

I took off the harness and went to fix him a bottle.

•••

It was a huge relief knowing he was getting enough to drink. And our relationship instantly became healthier. My breasts shrank in importance back to being just part of my anatomy, as feeding him became just one of many things I did, along with burping him, changing him, and playing with him—all things I hadn't even thought about before. I'd been so fixated on the baby in those dismal futures that I couldn't see the one right there in the room with me. In fact, it wasn't until I gave up and went to bottles that I realized he sometimes might be crying because he was wet, or lonely, or bored, and not for my breast at all.

Turns out, that fork in the road wasn't Robert Frost's, after all. It's more like one in the road near me, where it doesn't matter which branch you take because they come back together again down the hill. And that's what happened with me and the breastfeeding mothers I knew. After eighteen months, I could already see the differences between us erasing, as we all tried to wean our babies to cups. If anything, I felt I had a bit of an edge. At least for me, it was just a question of whether he drank from a bottle or a cup; it was nothing personal.

As for convenience — yes, I had to wash a lot of bottles. But I never did forget to bring them, and they had a convenience all their own. I was able to feed him in his car seat without pulling over. And when I splurged and met the other moms at the coffee shop, I could leave him in his stroller and hold his bottle with one hand while eating my own pre-cut food with the other.

Best of all, when he came running and asked me to pick him up, I knew it wasn't because I was dinner — even if he did then ask me to open the refrigerator door and get out the milk!

~Judy Epstein

# Picture Perfect

*I love that I'm someone special and that I feed him. I'm the milk cow!*
*~Gwen Stefani*

During my pregnancy, I learned everything about breastfeeding. I was so knowledgeable, it didn't even matter that I had never actually breastfed a baby. After all, I had taken a class, extensively highlighted the breastfeeding chapter of *What to Expect When You're Expecting*, and explored techniques and positions online. My natural instincts would fill in any gaps. It was going to be a beautiful thing.

Then I had my baby.

None of my research had produced any articles on how breastfeeding feels similar to having your nipple ripped off by a rabid kitten. It truly is shocking how it's possible to shred skin without the presence of teeth. Yet, the experts in my books insisted that if done properly, breastfeeding does not hurt. My son and I looked just like the mother and baby in the example pictures, except that lady was smiling gently at her newborn, while I was stuffing socks in my mouth to muffle my screams.

Clearly, something was wrong.

I finally decided that my baby needed to open his mouth more if we were ever going to achieve a state of breastfeeding euphoria. However, it is difficult to find a doctor willing to surgically implant a hinge in an infant's jaw, an unfortunate discovery, as that was the only way my child was going to open his mouth wide enough to satisfy the experts on the Internet. After a long series of smashing my breast into his little face, then immediately whisking it away, my son declared me to be insane with one exasperated look and began to scream. And scream.

I didn't think it could get much worse.

Then I got mastitis, which is clinically defined as a breast infection, in my case from a clogged milk duct. However, I suspect it may actually be a condition created by the formula industry, as it produced so much pain that I was soon waving my huge white nursing bra in the air and begging for someone to bring me a bottle.

My breasts were bruised, bleeding, and now bright red. I began to wonder if my gritted teeth and hysterical crying during each nursing session would cause my son to suffer permanent emotional scarring. Deciding to give my war-ravaged body a break, I sent my husband to the store to buy a breast pump.

After sterilizing every molecule, I went to work on pumping sweet relief. I cranked up the vacuum as high as I could tolerate and proceeded to spend a stimulating fifteen minutes staring at the wall. I couldn't wait to see how much milk I had produced. It was like a game show — *Pump That Breast!*

I barely squeezed out an ounce.

The other side managed an ounce and a half.

I wasn't sure how much my son was actually eating since it had all been taken directly from the source at that point, but I was pretty confident that two and a half ounces of breast milk weren't enough to build a person. I promptly concluded my breasts were defective and began to cry. And cry. Entering a state of emergency that was in no way caused by postpartum hormones, I attempted to increase my milk production by pumping after every nursing session. This left me approximately seven minutes between each feeding.

Then streaks of blood showed up in my son's diaper.

Since my diet had already been whittled down to bread and water to accommodate my baby's many food allergies, the pediatrician determined he must be swallowing my blood. He ordered me to start using lanolin cream on my breasts, unsavory as it may seem.

Lanolin is a greasy fat taken from sheep's wool before it's washed. The sheep use it as a natural water repellent, which is lovely for them, but I found it to be sticky, oily, and totally unfit for my bundle of joy.

Of course, after a few weeks of breastfeeding, I would have coated my baby's mouth with axle grease to stop the pain. I quietly packed away my ego, made a quick call to my stockbroker, and relieved the local convenience store of their lanolin supply.

Evidently, lanolin is code for magic in a tube. It doesn't specifically list magic as an ingredient, but it must be in there because it immediately solved all of my problems, namely chapped skin, cuts, and general tenderness. And, because its oily nature left stains on my clothes, it also prompted my mother to help with my laundry.

Magic.

With my mastitis finally gone and a trusty tube of lanolin in hand, I tackled my son's latching issues once and for all. This may be interpreted to mean I gave up trying to stuff my entire breast into his mouth and let him grab onto me however he saw fit. I'm sure the experts would not have approved of his preferred technique, but we trudged along anyway.

Then one day, I realized that nursing no longer hurt. I was actually smiling at my happy, growing-like-a-weed baby while I fed him.

It was finally a beautiful thing.

Our breastfeeding relationship was going so well that my husband decided he wanted a piece of the action. Resisting the urge to initiate him with a quick bite, I pulled out the breast pump once again and prayed to the wall. The ding of the timer rewarded me with an eight-ounce bottle of breast milk and the knowledge that I was indeed an effective dairy manufacturer.

The bottle was handed off to my husband, and I headed off to bed for a nap. I could finally stop worrying about my breasts and focus my attention on more important matters.

Like the consistency of my son's poop.

~Michelle Civalier

Reprinted by permission of Off the Mark ©1995

# Blushing Ride

*Mother knows breast.*
*~Author Unknown*

The windows were rolled down and the wind was blowing in my hair as I cruised down the freeway in my company car. I had the music playing and was feeling good as I streamed through traffic. All was well until the moment I heard the tenor sound of an eighteen-wheeler's horn cruising by. The driver was honking and smiling with gleeful delight at my semi-exposed breasts!

It all started so innocently. Having been bottle-fed myself and suffering from many allergies and asthma, I decided that when I had my first child, I would try breastfeeding to see if it worked for me. I desired to load up my daughter with those wonderful antibodies I had been told only existed in mother's milk.

In the hospital, I listened studiously as the nurse explained the "latch-on technique." It didn't come easily to me or my daughter, Kristen. I kept shoving the nipple into her mouth, trying to coach her to latch on, suck and get that good stuff that is supposed to be released in those initial feedings after birth. All the books said this was what good mothers did. So, even though my own mother frowned upon this method (being a product of the bottle-feeding era), I pursued mastering this technique.

With private coaching on breastfeeding from the pediatrician, I became a professional as my six weeks of maternity leave flew by. By the time my leave was over, I could inconspicuously whip out my breast and feed my baby with the best of them. Then came the realization that once I returned to work, the feeding system I had spent so much time mastering and my daughter now loved would no longer be a regular part of either of our lives. So I moved on to the next stage — the breast pumping stage. If I couldn't be there myself, by golly, my milk would be.

I invested in a breast pump. Now this is nothing like the real thing: having your baby suckle on your breast, relieving the uncomfortable build-up of milk and letting those good-feeling hormones release. No, this was downright institutional, but I was committed to making it work.

Once again, I called our pediatrician — a mother of six at the time — to be sure I was masterfully trained on the technique. I began pumping one breast at a time and treasuring every single drop of milk I could get. I would carefully pour each ounce into the measured-line bags that were available and freeze them. Those bags of milk were treated like umbilical cord fluid in my home. I was determined to leave an ample supply for my daughter during the day.

Imagine my surprise when I returned to eight- to ten-hour workdays only to discover that my breasts would become engorged and painful if they weren't nursed and pumped on a regular basis. This most likely would not have been such a challenge had I worked a traditional job and could lock an office door somewhere, plug in a pump and refrigerate the milk. But I was in sales — outside sales at that — and driving up to 100 miles per day. Luckily, I have always been a resourceful person.

Because of my allergies and asthma, I discovered the great convenience of the AC car adapter, which plugged into the cigarette lighter and provided home-style electricity so I could give myself breathing treatments. I soon discovered the adapter worked equally as well with breast pumps! So part of my daily routine now became parking in supermarket parking lots (I worked in food sales), wearing a nursing bra and loose blouses, and pumping my breasts in the car between sales calls. I found this a very discreet and efficient way to pump and store milk. By this time, I had learned to pump right into the little plastic bags and store them in a cooler.

Better yet, as time went by, I became a "double pumper" and could do both breasts at once! Continuing to wear loose blouses, I could easily and discreetly reach under my blouse, attach the pumps in a "lick-and-stick" fashion, and kick back in the parking lot. This great technique cut my pumping time in half!

I was even more excited when, while pumping and parking one day, I realized my hands were completely free during this process so there was no reason I couldn't drive and pump at the same time in order to shorten my day and get home sooner. In my mind, this was an ingenious idea. So I buckled in and started to drive. Looking down, everything stayed in place. This was great! I could now drive while pumping both my breasts! This went on for quite a while. So you can imagine my shock when I shared this glorious thing I was doing with the pediatrician during a well-check visit for my daughter and she looked stunned! I wasn't breaking any laws after all, and I was hands-free. It was a great system.

That was until that dreaded day on the freeway when the trucker drove by. There I was in full pumping mode, windows down, music on, pump pumping, hair blowing in the wind, when I heard the screech of an eighteen-wheeler beeping and riding alongside me. My blouse had blown up, giving any elevated passerby full exposure to my milk-filled breasts in motion, flailing in the breeze, milk being excreted and all.

In complete embarrassment and shock, I was completely paralyzed. I couldn't rip off the pumps and have milk squirting everywhere while I tried to maneuver a vehicle at sixty-five miles per hour. I certainly had no control over the trucker's great view of the situation—he had an elevated vantage point. So, in horror, I smiled at the trucker and exited the freeway in embarrassment. Luckily, I had already pumped enough that day to last my daughter for my next day at work—when I returned to pumping in the parking lot, parked in a corner under a large tree, and covering myself with a blanket.

~D. Dawn Maxwell

# The Dinner Surprise

*Breast milk: the gift that keeps on giving.*
*~Author Unknown*

"I have some good news for you!" My husband's promising words on the phone stopped me from setting the table for dinner.

"What?" I barely waited for him to finish. I could stand some good news. I was tired. I was tired from my infant's wide-awake eyes at 2:30 in the morning. I was tired of the snow that pelted our Midwest home. I could self-diagnose: sleep deprivation with an increasing case of cabin fever.

"We have a dinner next Thursday." His words brought hope and happiness to my tired and weary soul. The occasional business dinner often brought with it starched napkins and waiters waiting on me! This event would take place in the atrium of a music building at a local university. The more I heard, the more my heart longed for the evening. I hung up and called my parents to ask about babysitting. Five minutes later, my bases were covered.

Then reality took over. What would I wear? Post-pregnancy pounds left few options. Of course, eating my toddler's favorite crackers—graham, cheese, and just plain—didn't help. My doctor may have said my weight was "in check" at my six-week appointment two weeks before, but I still preferred sweats to blue jeans (as if I could choose).

I had neither the time, money, nor energy to take a two-year-old and her baby brother to shop for a new dress. Three days before the dinner, I built up enough courage to open the closet door and conjure up something to wear. I knew my options: the royal blue dress with full skirt or the silk-like (so what if the tag said 100% polyester) emerald green with V-neck. First, I tried the blue. With my nursing chest, it was too tight. Knowing that it was my best option, I held my breath, literally, and tried the green. I couldn't believe it. It (almost) fit! Digging through my drawer for something with the words "tummy control," I called my husband at work.

"I have good news and bad news!" I told him. "Which do you want first?"

"Good," he responded.

"I can wear my green dress for the dinner." The words rushed out of my mouth.

"What's the bad news?" he questioned.

"I won't be able to eat anything." There was silence at the other end. I had married a smart man who chose his words carefully.

"I'm sure if you can wear it, you can eat." His words gave me more hope for my tired body.

When that Thursday came, my mom and dad arrived early, bringing dinner for them and their grandchildren. I walked down the stairs wearing my green dress, high heels and jewelry, and my two-year-old asked, "Mommy, are we going to church?"

"I've got to get out more… I've got to get out more…" played over and over in my mind.

Those words wouldn't leave until we got in the car, and my husband leaned over and said, "Husband and wife, not mommy and daddy."

At the dinner, there were cloth napkins. Waiters in white shirts and bow ties served us. I actually ate some dinner and dessert without blowing out my support pantyhose! The dinner conversation with my husband's boss and his wife, plus two other co-workers and their spouses, was more casual than the surroundings.

"How is that baby?"

"What does his sister think of him?"

Baby? Thoughts of him sleeping in his crib began to travel from my head to my heart. A warm sensation on my left side signaled that I needed to think about something else.

None too soon, one of the singers for the evening's entertainment began. Ah! I could relax. But relax is just what my milk did. Drop by drop, I sensed a damp, and then wet, nursing pad. Moments later, when I saw the wet spot forming on my green dress, I hunched over the table a bit. This was not the night for perfect posture, I quickly decided. Next, I reached for my black clutch purse and strategically laid it close in case I needed to bolt!

With my husband seated to my right and the rest of our party with their chairs turned toward the stage, I was determined to enjoy a free night out with my husband. As soon as the second singer began his first song, the right side of my dress began to get soggy. I slowly crossed my left arm in front of my chest and put my right hand up in a Rodin's "The Thinker" pose. I leaned forward even more.

Eventually, the concert ended, and the men left the table for the coatroom. I was almost "home free." Gentleman that he is, my husband wanted to help me with my coat. Still seated at the table, I tried to take it, but he wouldn't give up. He held it open by its shoulders. Trying not to make a scene and thinking that speed was the best solution, I quickly stood. I spread both arms apart and pushed them into the sleeves. When I looked up, a co-worker's wife was staring at me wide-eyed. At least it wasn't the boss! Safely in the car, I poured out the details to my husband most of the way home.

The next afternoon, I pulled up to the drive-thru window at the dry cleaners with the coat I'd worn the night before. "It has a couple of spots that may need to be treated," I said.

"Do you know what they are?" the high school-aged boy at the window asked.

"Breast milk," I responded quickly and drove off.

I turned around and looked at my two cherubs in their car seats. The baby was sleeping while his sister waved a doll in a pink and white dress. One more errand and then we'd head home to start dinner.

Yes, it was good news that I could wear that green dress, I reflected. The other good news was that I wouldn't see the co-worker's wife until the Christmas party eleven months away! But the best news of all was that I got to go home to eat dinner with my husband and kiddos, pick up toys, give baths, read books, and listen to my two-year-old say her bedtime prayer. No more cabin fever for this breastfeeding mom!

~Diane Buller

# Adventures in Breastfeeding

*There are three reasons for breast-feeding: the milk is always at the right temperature; it comes in attractive containers; and the cat can't get it.*
~Irena Chalmers

I should have known I'd be breastfeeding-challenged the first time I nursed. My husband, David, and I graduated cum laude from our Lamaze class. We practiced and rehearsed till we could pant with the best of them. I had a fantasy in my mind of the perfect delivery, where David held my hand, dabbed sweat from my forehead, and whispered encouraging words in my ear. The midwife crooned, "One more push, Sugar," which was a breeze since I'd kegeled three hours a day for seven months. Then out into the delivery room air would emerge a perfect pink boy or girl who'd take right to my breast, nursing lustily, while David captured the whole thing on video.

Instead, I awoke in my eighth month in a puddle of blood. We drove frantically to the hospital where I was knocked out and an emergency C-section ensued. At least, that's what they told me several hours later when I awoke in a drug-induced stupor. But my lactation counselor was there, so at least the breastfeeding part of my fantasy could come true. My perfect little bundle was a girl, and she was a beauty. (The prettiest one in the nursery, my mother-in-law informed us, and kept dashing back when a new baby was born to make sure we maintained our status.) Even though Haley was three weeks early, she was plump and healthy, and had the good sense to look like her handsome daddy.

The counselor helped me get her arranged at my breast, but neither Haley nor I knew what we were doing, and the drugs I'd been given were so strong that I wavered in and out of consciousness. Finally, I conked out, dead to the world.

"No problem," my lactation guru announced. She nestled Haley up to my breast (where I'm told she finally figured out what to do) and told my husband, "Here! Hold this." Then she left.

I have pictures of Haley's first breastfeeding experience. They look nothing like the ones in the books. I am passed out, head flopped to one side, spittle drooling from my mouth. David is holding Haley with a befuddled won't-someone-help-me look and, sure enough, Haley is nursing. After reading and memorizing all those books on breastfeeding, I have to live with the fact that my husband got to breastfeed our baby before I did.

Our third day in the hospital, David ran home for a shower, and my sister stayed to take care of Haley and me. I was still pretty drugged and asleep more than I was awake. After one particularly long nap, I awoke to discover the Boobie Fairy had paid me a visit. During one seemingly innocent nap, my breasts had quadrupled in size and were exploding out of the top of my nursing gown. I was afraid to move. My sister was dozing in a chair next to Haley's basinet. All I could do was whisper, "Pssst, Denise, get the camera. Quick, get the camera!" I wasn't sure if they'd be there when David got back, (or even if I was awake at all) so I had to get a picture to preserve in our family history: the day Mom had bodacious ta-tas.

Little did I know that wasn't the biggest they'd get. For the next few weeks, dressing was a challenge. Even the clothes I'd bought a couple sizes too big had a hard time fitting over my morphed mammaries. But I liked having boobs, even if they did belong to someone else. Haley caught on to nursing, and I began to see breastfeeding as the miracle it is. So, when David, Haley and I were invited to visit my sister for the weekend, I jumped at the chance. She'd breastfed four kids, and I figured I could pick up some tips (plus snag a nap or two while we were there).

Everything went fine until Saturday evening when we dressed for church. An overabundance of milk had not been a problem for me, so I'd never opened the box of breast pads they'd given me at the hospital and hadn't thought to toss them in the suitcase. But when I looked at the sheer white blouse I'd packed to wear to church, I realized I was taking the chance I might be standing in the pew with two puddles of milk on the front of my blouse for God and everybody to see. There wasn't time to run to the drugstore, so my sister conceived the brilliant idea of cutting two mini-pads into little ovals and fitting them inside my nursing bra. A pad is a pad, right?

My Kotex-turned-breast-pads were a lifesaver when, halfway through the service, my breasts decided it was party time. What we hadn't considered was that the pads were scented. As the breast milk soaked the pads and I smiled at how clever we'd been, perfume was covering my breasts unbeknownst to me. When poor Haley woke to nurse that night, she didn't recognize that funny taste—and so began one of the longest nights of my life. She'd latch on to nurse just long enough to trigger my milk production. Then she'd pull away and cry. My breasts would expand. She'd latch on again, more letdown, pull away, BIGGER breasts. Latch, grow, cry. Latch, grow, cry. I didn't want to wake my sister, so I sat there lactating and hurting until dawn when Haley finally wore herself out crying and fell asleep, hungry and miserable.

Sleeping was not an option for me. By the time my sister woke up, I could barely stand the pain in my breasts. She got me into a hot shower where it looked like I had two whale spouts shooting out of my chest. It was hours before we put two and two together and figured out what we'd done.

Breastfeeding has been as eventful and surprising as the rest of motherhood. There's only so much you can learn in books and so much more you have to discover for yourself. No author could put into words the way I feel when I watch my Haley sleep or when she reaches a wobbly hand up to touch my face. No one else could tell me how much more I'd love David when I see how he loves our daughter or the sheer joy of sitting around for hours talking about nothing but her. Like motherhood, breastfeeding is one of the most rewarding, exhilarating, exhausting, confusing, amazing, life-giving things I've ever done. I wouldn't have missed it for the world.

~Mimi Greenwood Knight

# Father Knows Breast

*Breast Feeding should not be attempted by fathers with hairy chests,
since they can make the baby sneeze and give it wind.*
~Mike Harding, The Armchair Anarchist's Almanac

For seven and a half months, Erica and I had been preparing for the arrival of our first child. Her preparation consisted of simultaneously transmogrifying her body into a birthing and milk production machine. Mine was learning to take poorly worded instruction manuals and assemble nursery furniture so that it somewhat resembled the pictures.

When Erica asked me to attend the breastfeeding class, I immediately agreed, but also silently wondered how it would be of any value. Didn't I lack the necessary prerequisites? Wouldn't it be like me asking Erica to accompany me to a class on how to put off cleaning the garage? But, in a sense, I was the ideal candidate to assist her. After all, who had spent more time contemplating my wife's breasts than me?

The class was rich with interesting information. When the teacher said that much of the milk does not just come out of the center of the nipple but out of little holes around it, I would have been less shocked had I learned I was living in *The Matrix*.

I also took notes on the nursing lingo. The most important thing, I learned, was "the latch." They taught us that the milk at the beginning of a feeding, known as the "foremilk," was lighter than the creamy "hindmilk" at the end. A "lactation consultant" is an expert who can help when the feedings aren't working. They make house calls. A "dreamfeed" is when you attempt to feed an already slumbering baby. It serves as a "preemptive strike," which could keep the baby asleep longer. How, I wondered, do other species of mammals endure without these classes?

They advised us that, for the first month, Erica should do natural feedings and not pump for bottle feedings since the baby could suffer "nipple confusion." However, after a month, Erica should begin pumping right away so the baby could get used to bottles, too. Breast milk could be refrigerated for twenty-four hours or frozen for six months.

Sarah was born at 5:43 a.m. and, as we had learned in the class, we had her attempt her first latch a few minutes later. Though it takes a few days for the milk to "come in," these initial attempts enable newborns to ingest a substance new mothers produce called "colostrum," which contains a lot of vital nutrients.

Sarah went to the nursery, and we tried to rest for what we figured would be the last time for a while. Throughout the day, we went to visit Sarah in the nursery, and I'd also retrieve her from the nursery and bring her back to our room. Everything was going fine until about 11:00 on that first night when a nurse wheeled a crying Sarah into our room.

"We can't keep her in the nursery while she cries. She's waking up the other newborns," the nurse said.

I couldn't believe what I was hearing. Keeping newborns happy was their full-time job, for crying out loud.

"What should we do to get her to stop?" I asked.

"Well, since you have on your chart 'breast milk only,' there's really nothing we can do for her. Have you considered supplementing with formula?" She dared to use the "F" word? To us, "supplementing" was a fancy word for quitting. Though we knew that some mothers have no choice, we wanted to at least wait until Erica's milk came in before abandoning our plan.

We were told that the hospital's lactation consultant would be in at 9:00. For the next ten hours, we were on our own. We frantically tried to get Sarah to latch, but it wasn't working, and she continued crying. In desperation, we took out a book we had purchased about breastfeeding. In chapter two, they described several different "holds." There was the "cradle hold," the "cross-over hold," and the "football hold." The descriptions of the holds proved no more helpful than the assembly instructions for the nursery furniture. But like the furniture instructions, there were pictures. So calling on my newly developed skill of making things look like the picture, I held the book at the appropriate angle as Erica and I worked together to attach part A (Sarah) to part B (Erica's breast).

The nursery incident wasn't the last time that we were encouraged to give up nursing. Some of the pressure came from my own family. When I was born, in 1969, my mother didn't breastfeed me. She says it wasn't the style back then. This was also when they didn't realize that smoking and drinking during pregnancy might not be good for the developing baby.

"How long is Erica planning to nurse?" my mother asked.

"She's hoping to make it to six months."

"Six months! Doesn't it hurt?"

"Got Milk," for us, was more of a mandate than a catchy ad campaign. When Erica's milk came in, Sarah had her first real feeding. We were relieved to see the strong latch. After about twenty minutes, she stopped sucking. I looked at Erica and asked, "Did she get any?" Erica answered, "I don't know." Unlike bottle feedings, where you can easily see how much was ingested, you could never be sure how much milk the baby got. The only way to tell if she drank was to wait for wet diapers.

When they came, we were thrilled.

We decided to let Sarah feed on demand rather than try to enforce a feeding schedule. Every few hours was time for another thirty-minute feeding.

After two weeks, Erica noticed her wrist was in a lot of pain. She went to the doctor where she was diagnosed with something called "de Quervain's tenosynovitis," a condition you get from holding a baby with a bent wrist. I developed my own wrist problem from holding Sarah while rocking her to sleep. I decided to keep it to myself.

After a month, Erica began pumping in addition to the feedings. This meant I had my first opportunity to feed Sarah. Most parenting books describe the pleasure a father finally gets when he can give his baby a bottle. And her first few feedings were like that. But then she decided she didn't like the bottle as much as the breast. So we went through a series of nipples to find one that Sarah might agree to. I experimented with "orthodontic," "angled," "vented," "slow flow," and even one called "breast flow." While I struggled to get Sarah to take these different bottles, I knew I couldn't give up and say, "Erica, can't you just feed her?" Erica was going back to work in four months, and Sarah had to learn. With a lot of patience and begging, and after a few days of practice, Sarah was able to easily drink from either the breast or the bottle.

Erica, always the planner, pumped enough milk that we began storing four-ounce bags in our freezer. This did not mean, however, that the pressure was off. This stash was not to be used haphazardly. Each time we used a bag of milk, it didn't mean Erica got a break. She still needed to do an extra pumping so her body didn't think that nursing ended and shut down production. After six months, we reached our original goal, but we kept going. At eight months, we started supplementing with formula. We also started occasionally using our frozen reserves. This combination resulted in a weaning process that took twelve more months.

When Sarah began speaking shortly after her first birthday, most of her words were phonetic approximations. "Buh" was her way of saying "book." "Elmo" was her clearest word, though "Big Bird" was "Dee Dee." She called herself "Ya Ya." One word that puzzled us was what she'd say when she wanted a feeding—"Yide." Erica eventually figured out where it came from. Halfway through each feeding, Erica would ask Sarah, "Do you want the other side?"

When Sarah was two, six months after her final feeding, she was sitting on Erica's lap. Sarah smiled at Erica and said, "You smell like 'Yide.'"

Erica replied, "That's right."

Then Sarah said, "Yide is good," and then added, matter-of-factly, "but I drank it all up."

Our twenty-month journey to give our daughter a healthy start in life was not always easy. But the closeness it helped us build with Sarah and with each other will not soon expire.

~Gary Rubinstein

# Mother Nurture

*Grown don't mean nothing to a mother. A child is a child.
They get bigger, older, but grown? What's that suppose to mean?
In my heart it don't mean a thing.*
~Toni Morrison, Beloved

There are milestones in life when we think, "Now, I am really a grown-up." Maybe it is college or marriage or once we become a parent ourselves.

When my husband and I drove our first baby home from the hospital, I looked at Gavin nestled deep into his car seat and thought, "This is it. All he's got is us. Are we really allowed to take him home and take care of him?"

There would be no more nurses to take over during the night or to answer questions. I was a little hesitant, but my husband was more than anxious for the three of us to be home as a little family: Mom, Dad, baby... and mother-in-law.

I had invited my mom to stay with us for the first few days, not knowing what to anticipate. I was pretty sure I would need her there or was supposed to have her there or, if nothing else, simply wanted her there to dote over my beautiful newborn.

Ironically, my first night home was Mother's Day—and what a day it was. I had been warned about the perils of pregnancy; I had read many books about impending motherhood; I had even taken both a birthing class and a breastfeeding class. But nothing prepared me for the day my milk would come in. For me, that occurred on my first Mother's Day.

And it was awful.

My hormones were changing and I was a teary mess. I had two huge, heavy bricks where my chest once was… and a baby with what seemed to be the teeniest mouth. And the loudest cry.

For hours, it was a team effort—my husband and me trying to get milk from my engorged bosom to the empty tummy of my little one. It hurt almost as much as labor! And it was all up to me. I was the sustenance for this new life. I was all he had. I was his mother.

I crawled into bed that night crying, knowing there wouldn't be much sleep. My husband sat down next to me and expressed his own discouragement because he, too, felt responsible and helpless. He was the dad and spouse and felt it was his job to somehow "fix the problem," yet he didn't know what to do and hated watching me suffer.

After he drifted off to sleep, I crept back downstairs, where my mom was snuggling baby Gavin on the couch. I cried. And cried some more. My mother, with four grown children and a lifetime of experience, must have been a tiny bit amused knowing that this was just my First Night, only the very beginning for me. But instead of saying so, she instinctively nurtured, calmed, and tended her child. Me.

Late into the night, she encouraged and consoled me. She warmed towels in the microwave, wrapping them around my aching chest. She was ready with a hot towel before the last one had cooled. As I relaxed from the attention and the heat, so did my baby, and we eventually nursed!

Tonight, (almost) three babies later, I am the queen of multitasking—preparing dinner, building a fort out of blankets, and typing this story even as my husband calls to tell me he will be working late. And I think to myself, "Now, I am really a mother. Fully grown." Right?

I grin to myself and shake my head.

Since that first Mother's Day, I have phoned my mom hundreds of times for advice, reassurance, recipes, and often just to brag about my little ones to the only other woman on this earth who cares about my life and my babies as much as I do.

You see, I've learned that just because you become a mom, it doesn't mean you're ever grown up enough to stop needing a mother of your own.

~Katrina Rehme Hatch

## Chapter 3

# New Moms

## Give Me Rest

*People who say they sleep like a baby usually don't have one.*

~Leo J. Burke

# Maybe in Prison I'll Get Some Sleep

*Come Sleep! Oh Sleep, the certain knot of peace, the baiting-place of wit, the balm of woe, the poor man's wealth, the prisoner's release, the indifferent judge between the high and low.*
~Sir Philip Sidney

How could I do it? How could I ever hurt him? I was a child abuser headed for the slammer. The big house called to me. Even as I considered putting on the dull gray jumpsuit and becoming a number for the rest of my life, I knew my mind was not thinking clearly. Slammer? Big house? I never used these words.

I needed sleep!

John would be home in a half-hour, and he could make the decision to call the police or not. I decided to sit and rock my two-month-old and wait. Little Noah continued his non-stop crying. He used his Pavarotti range, from whimpering like a hurt puppy to screaming like those dinosaurs that spread their neck muscles out like peacocks right before spraying their poisonous spit. My baby was not happy.

Of course, colic didn't help. Noah's birth was peaceful, but soon afterward his lungs collapsed. After a diagnosis of pulmonary hypertension, we were given a choice: heart/lung bypass or an experimental drug that had proven effective for several other babies. We chose the drug.

Following seventeen days in the NICU, Noah came home happy, healthy and ready to use his lungs. When I took Noah to the pediatrician to ask about the almost constant crying, the doctor's expression scared me.

"He's like this... all the time?"

On this particular day, I knew his tears communicated a wish for a non-abusive mother who possessed at least a bit of skill with a newborn.

At thirty-six years old, my ultimate dream lay in my arms. For most of my life, I'd prayed to have the honor of the title of Mother. Noah was my gift from God.

And yet, I had hurt him.

I eyed his little head once again and tried to remember how the bruises came to be. One tiny brown bruise the size of a dime cursed the top of his head. A gentler pinkish one lay on his cheek. How did it happen? Maybe I had hit his head on a door or wall when I was walking through our apartment with him. Maybe I had blacked out from lack of sleep and dropped him. But wouldn't I remember either of these?

If a court-appointed hypnotist came to me during the trial, he/she would be able to get to the truth. But did I want to know the truth? Could I deal with it?

Suddenly, I heard Jack Nicholson's voice from the movie, *A Few Good Men.*

"You want the truth? You can't handle the truth!"

He was right. I couldn't.

It would be so nice to sleep, just for a little while. The night before, Conan O'Brien's late-night talk show had once again made my schedule. He'd even commented, "The only people who watch my show are nursing mothers and prison inmates."

It occurred to me that I could continue watching his show after the trial.

Twenty more minutes until I confessed my crime to my husband. Noah stopped crying, but didn't go to sleep. These moments were rare and wonderful. His little eyes looked at me with a wonder so expressive and yet so blank at the same time. Was he trying to be forgiving?

He would not have to testify against me, but his bruises would. In his little mind, was he trying to breach the gap with unconditional love? I felt the connection. My little man, for whom I would do anything. My heart hurt with love… and guilt.

If only I could close my eyes for just a little while. Five more minutes.

Oh, come home, John!

Keys jangled, and my heart leapt.

John entered with his computer bag over his shoulder and lunch pail in his hand. I was up and thrusting the show-and-tell of my felony in his face.

"I abused our son do you see can you believe it I should not be allowed to be a mom John how can I do this and raise a healthy member of society it just won't work if you want to call the police do at least in jail I will get a good night's sleep I am so sorry."

Tears poured out at this point.

"Robbie, let's sit down for a minute."

He gently took Noah and led us to the sofa.

"Hey, buddy, Dad's home."

John looked over our boy to examine the evidence.

"Do you see John the two bruises I have no idea but I hurt him and he has been crying most of the day I mean why not he has me for a mom and I am headed for prison for hitting my boy and I do love him I do but I just can't be a mommy."

"Are you talking about the brown spot and the pink one, honey?"

"Yes."

John cradled Noah in his right arm and took his left hand to my son's face. He gently rubbed first the brown bruise and then licked his finger and repeated the action with the pink.

Each disappeared.

"I'd say Coke and gas medicine."

I went numb. The jury had returned with a not-guilty verdict.

My guilt disappeared, but strangely another emotion filled its place. I began to glare at my husband.

"Robbie, why don't you go sleep for a couple of hours? I've got Noah."

Tears came again. Ah, sleep.

I stumbled to my bed and slept.

I did not dream of gas medicine or the slammer. I didn't dream of a kind husband who saw my need and met it.

I only dreamed of a little man who was worth every moment of sleep deprivation.

~Robbie Iobst

# My Little Alarm Clock

*An alarm clock is a device that wakes you up just in time to go back to sleep.*
*~Author Unknown*

I used to awaken ahead of my clock
Rub eyes to the beat of its tickity-tock
Then reach for the spot to shut off its first beep
Before my clock jangled me out of my sleep.

This pattern has changed since I got my new clock.
I simply adore its delightful tick-tock,
But now I have trouble awaking before
It rouses me up with its sweet little roar.

The moment the morning birds make their first peeps
My clock comes alive with soft gurgles and beeps.
With motherly love I arrive with great speed
To tend to my new little clock's every need.

It's true, I admit, since I got my new clock
I'm sometimes exhausted and can't even talk.
To care for my timepiece keeps me on my toes,
Bedraggled and frazzled with no time to doze.

My new little ticker is often quite wet
And gets all wound up if its needs are not met.

It jangles and beeps with a mind of its own
At dawn, noon, or dusk with a deafening tone.

But even though sometimes it's still hard to tell
Just why my alarm clock is ringing its bell,
Or waking me up in the dark of the night,
I still whisper thanks as I hold my clock tight.

Although my old clock once allowed me to snooze,
That option no longer is one I can choose.
I still wouldn't trade my new clock for the old
For the joy this clock brings is more precious than gold.

~Laura Sassi

# Adjustments

*Never being number one in your list of priorities and not minding at all.*
*~Jasmine Guinness*

Monday morning, 6:30. It is the kind of August morning that promises rain. I am tiptoeing through the kitchen like a burglar, carrying a basket brimming with dirty laundry. My two-month-old daughter sleeps peacefully in the other end of the house. Her early feeding done, I am determined to get a headstart on the day—something I haven't done since bringing her home from the hospital. Besides, it's been a week since I opened the clothes hamper; things are getting a bit smelly.

Being a mother is amazing. I love my child so fiercely, it's frightening. But there's another side to motherhood. Until my daughter's birth, I never knew the true meaning of the word "tired." I never realized how little sleep you can actually exist on. The days creep into the nights, leaving me exhausted and wondering if I will even live to see her start school.

With heavy hands, I load the washing machine, sneak into the kitchen, and put on a pot of coffee. In the darkness, I sit waiting for the brew to finish. I am exhausted. The living room resembles a garage sale. It's been weeks since I looked at a newspaper, listened to the news, heard my favorite song. My world revolves around a plump little girl named Anna Marie who makes great smacking noises, and smells of baby powder and cotton gowns, and, occasionally, something a lot less pleasant.

As I gulp down the last swallow of coffee, I have one wish: three hours of uninterrupted sleep. But just as I set the cup on the table, Anna Marie announces herself with great gusto. I can't believe she is awake again. Didn't I just put her down?

I rush to her bed, scoop up my bellowing angel, change her soaking diaper, powder her little behind, kiss her rosy face, and then settle into the rocking chair in the corner.

Holding her close, I am awed by her beauty, by the way she slaps my chest with her tiny hand while gulping down her breakfast... or is it lunch already? She is perfectly content. All of her needs have been met.

Suddenly and without warning, I have selfish thoughts. When am I going to have all of my needs met? When am I going to get a good night's sleep? Or get the house cleaned? Or eat a decent meal, let alone cook one?

I am somewhat surprised by my feelings, but since I seem to be on a roll, I decide to tell God exactly what I'm feeling. "Motherhood is a constant demand of my time," I say out loud. "I'm a person, too! I need things, too! Like rest. And sleep. And, right now, a big shoulder to cry on!" I'm afraid to say more, afraid I'll end up bawling, and that would only upset my now sleeping angel.

But then, as gentle as the summer rain splattering against the window, the thought comes to me: God gave me this child. My job is to look after her. Nurture her. Care for her. Teach her.

At once, I marvel. Slumped in the curve of rocking chair, I suddenly see the beauty of myself. I am much more than an exhausted body in a baggy housecoat; I am the keeper of a child. This revelation soothes me, refreshes me.

I look down into the face of my precious baby. From somewhere deep inside, I feel a stirring, an intense longing to be God's greatest babysitter. Wholeheartedly, unreservedly, I embrace this hallowed assignment called motherhood.

~Dayle Allen Shockley

# Making the Right Call

*A mother is one to whom you hurry when you are troubled.*
*~Emily Dickinson*

"I won't need any help," I told my mother as she visited me in the hospital after I had delivered my first child, a healthy baby boy.

"Are you sure?" she asked. "I can take some time off work."

"I'm sure," I said.

And I really was certain that I could handle a newborn. After all, I'd graduated from college, owned a house, taught elementary school. Plus, I was married, so my husband would be there, too. How could I possibly need any more help?

"Let me know if you change your mind," she said.

I smiled. Not likely, I thought. I knew what it was like to be around babies. I'd had a lot of babysitting experience, most recently with my nephew who was almost three years old. Just because my sister had needed help right after he'd been born didn't mean that I would. And, although I tried not to show it, I felt that needing help was a sign of weakness.

The afternoon we brought our newborn home, everything started out smoothly. Sure, my body ached in places — and in ways — I'd never experienced before. But I was coping. I just needed some rest. I hadn't gotten a lot of sleep in the hospital because of the unfamiliar noises and the baby's feeding schedule. But now that I was back in my own home, I expected to sleep better, and things were going to go just fine. My husband and I could handle this baby on our own.

I fed the baby, changed his diaper, and gently placed him in his bassinet. Then I sat in a nearby rocking chair, waiting to relax. But the baby didn't fall asleep. Instead, he started crying. He seemed to have his own agenda.

Thus, my husband and I began playing "take the baby and try to figure out what's bothering him" tag team. Unfortunately, despite all of our prior babysitting experience, this activity continued throughout the night. It seemed as if the moment I got a few precious seconds of sleep, the baby would cry again, waking me up. We swaddled him, we changed his diapers, we fed him, but he still didn't sleep more than a little while. By the middle of the night, I started to wonder if maybe, just maybe, we might benefit from a little help.

I was exhausted, and my body hurt. As the dark hours passed, I began to realize that my true weakness was believing I knew everything about babies when clearly I didn't.

At dawn, I decided to make a phone call. "Mom, I've changed my mind. Can you come and help?"

"I'll be there soon!" she replied.

I looked at my husband and breathed a huge sigh of relief.

Mom arrived on our doorstep carrying an overnight bag and a homemade cake with a special chocolate candy icing she'd baked the night before. Grandma to the rescue! She glided through the door, set the cake on the table, picked up the baby and rocked him to sleep with the confidence of an experienced mother. All the while, she assured us that what we'd just gone through was perfectly normal on a first night home from the hospital. But not to worry, she was now here to help us with the baby day and night until things got easier.

And before my husband and I took a well-earned nap, the three of us ate the most unusual breakfast—pieces of cake.

Three decades have passed since that morning, and now I'm expecting my first grandchild. My daughter-in-law is a nurse, so she probably won't need any help. But I have all the ingredients for a cake with chocolate candy icing ready—just in case.

~Ronda Ross Taylor

Reprinted by permission of
Martha Campbell ©1988

# The New Mommy Dress Code

*It's not easy being a mother. If it were easy, fathers would do it.*
*~From the television show* The Golden Girls

The first time I showed up to work wearing two different shoes was a clue as to how drastically life had altered. After the initial embarrassment brought on by my colleagues' discovery, I laughed. "Ah, I have finally arrived in the land of Mommyhood."

Many more wardrobe malfunctions occurred during the following weeks. A missing belt, lipstick on only the top half of my lips, mismatched earrings, and hair that was not brushed top the list of memorable moments.

My co-workers and I also laughed at my ingenious remedy for sleep deprivation. Five-minute power naps in my car, prior to work, became a higher priority than applying eye shadow in the mornings. Thankfully, sympathetic women would tap on my window to alert me that it was time for employee meetings.

My once pristinely manicured fingernails began to break as soon as all the nail polish chipped away. After wearing nail polish every day since middle school, I was surprised by the ugly color of stained yellow that was left underneath. When I prioritized the activities of daily living, I concluded that manicured nails were not as vital as meals, a paycheck, clean clothes and whatever sparse amount of sanity I had intact.

Somewhere between the sleepless nights and harried juggling of new lifestyle changes, I learned that there were many things I could do without. Instead of styling my hair each morning, a ponytail holder became my most beloved accessory. Clothes that required ironing or dry cleaning were donated to a local shelter for domestic abuse.

Along with fluctuating weight changes came my new best friend—pants with drawstrings. Sure, I was not an appealing sight for a while. However, my disheveled appearance allowed more time for what I truly craved—a little extra shut-eye before the alarm.

I once heard a woman commenting on her "placenta disease." She claimed that since childbirth she had not been able to think clearly due to the fact that half of her brain cells must have exited her body along with the placenta. Since I did not actually give birth to my child, I cannot blame physiological responses for the fact that I have been so preoccupied with the welfare of my little one that I once forgot to brush my teeth. (Thankfully, I worked with a part-time dental assistant who had spare tubes of toothpaste and a toothbrush.)

Nor can I ascertain that all people lose their minds and their sense of fashion when they have children. My husband, for instance, has never forgotten to button his shirt or worn two different colored shoes. So the answer must lie in the fact that, as women, we are wired differently. The men in our lives can happily scoot off to work with all their clothes perfectly coordinated despite the screaming children in tow. However, we sympathetic women want to do more than drop the children off at childcare. We want to find out why they are crying and somehow make it all better. Amidst the nose wiping, hugging, and comforting, we occasionally forget small items such as the car keys we locked in the house.

As the years have passed, my sleep has increased exponentially, along with my brain function. (However, my husband might disagree with the latter statement.) I've dusted off the high heels that were lying dormant in the back of my closet and started color coordinating again. The fast-food lunches I was consuming, in an effort to preserve time, have slowly been replaced by more healthy choices. I've even begun occasionally painting my nails, despite the fact that the polish does not last long due to increased amounts of laundry and dishes that necessitate hand scrubbing.

However, my empathy for other new moms is drastically altered. Now, when I see a fellow unkempt comrade doing battle in the frozen food section of the grocery store, I no longer muse, "What is she wearing?" Instead, I offer to pick up the teddy bear that was hurled face first onto the tile floor. Occasionally, my eyes meet my fellow sojourner's, and I give the smile that universally signifies, "It's going to be alright. I've been there, too."

~Erin Fuentes

# Getting on the Right Side of Sleep

*There was never a child so lovely but his mother was glad to get him to sleep.*
*~Ralph Waldo Emerson*

My exhausted mind scrambled for something to sing as I paced back and forth across my daughter's room, trying to get her back to sleep. After softly crooning every tune I could think of, I was at a loss. My eyes had seen 1:00 a.m. pass on the clock too many times over the past three weeks, as well as 2:00, 3:00, and 4:00. They were so tired they would have gladly closed at any time of day, if only my baby would stop crying.

All babies cry, of course, but what made this situation so frustrating was that Alyssa had always been a good sleeper. From the time she was born, she found sleep easily. She preferred to rest on her right side. As a newborn, my husband or I would lay her in her crib, and she would turn her head to the right and fall asleep. As soon as she could move herself, she rolled up onto her right side to enjoy peaceful slumber. On the rare occasion that she rolled to the left, we knew she wasn't quite ready to call it a night.

Our blissfully quiet nights continued until Alyssa was five months old, and my cousin got married at Disney World. We packed up the baby, our two-year-old, a double stroller, and a million diapers, and headed to the "happiest place on earth." When we landed in Orlando, a never-ending parade of grandparents, aunts, uncles, cousins, and other wedding guests jumped in line to hold the littlest member of the family. After a week of late nights, an irregular schedule, and constant overstimulation, my little angel just couldn't settle down.

Three weeks after the trip, she still woke up every hour during the night. I was so exhausted that I could barely think. I considered setting up a bed for myself in her nursery since my eyes were so blurry with fatigue that every time her cry beckoned me, I crashed into the hallway wall. My stubbed toes thought a temporary bed in the nursery was a good idea, but the little bit of reason left in my brain warned me that it wasn't. So every hour I stumbled down the hall, hoping the rest of the family would sleep through the wailing.

Night after night, I prayed that she would sleep. I begged her to stop crying. I pleaded with God to quiet her and to give us all some rest. Nothing changed. Each night was a repeat of the one before. Exhausting. Frustrating. Nerve-wracking.

One night, I finally had a revelation. Instead of wishing that Alyssa would stop crying, I hoped I would have a better attitude about the situation. It occurred to me that even though pacing her room in the middle of the night was not how I had dreamed of spending time, it was an opportunity to hold and cuddle my baby uninterrupted. It was a chance for me to be the most important person in the world to her — her comforter, her soother, her mother.

Amazingly, as soon as I started looking at my midnight visit to her room as an opportunity, I felt my shoulders relax and my breathing slow. The anxiety that normally built as I rushed through the dark to her room was replaced by a sense of peace. She sensed it as well, and immediately started settling down.

We spent three weeks of torment fighting to get her to sleep. As soon as I dropped my end of the battle, it took only three nights before she rolled onto her right side and fell fast asleep. For the entire night.

I realized that, as a mom, I have an amazing impact on my children and the way they experience the world. My stress becomes their stress. My peace becomes theirs, as well. So does my joy, my faith, my ability to trust, my willingness to love. Eventually, they will grow into mature people who make their own choices, but while they are young, they follow the example I set before them. Sometimes, I need to remember to stop trying so hard and just roll to my right so we can all relax.

~Dianne Daniels

# Burping in the Night

*Sometimes the most productive thing one can do is sleep.*
*~Author Unknown*

In the fog of new motherhood, when sleep finally comes, it is a welcome friend. After arriving home from the hospital with our first daughter, I soon found this out. Waking up every two hours to change the baby, sitting in the rocking chair to nurse the baby, burping the baby, and putting the baby back in her bassinet became my nightly ritual. I would just be dozing off when she would wake again, screaming angrily. Then I would drag myself out of bed and do it all over again.

I soon realized it would be easier for me to just bring Hannah to bed with us to nurse. After she had finished nursing, my husband or I would lay her on her tummy across one of our chests and pat her back until she burped. Sometimes, we just let her stay in that position until she had fallen asleep again, and we would doze off ourselves. Other times, one of us would drag ourselves out of bed and put her back in the bassinet.

One night shortly after Hannah's birth, I had actually managed to fall soundly asleep. I awoke in the middle of the night to my husband asking, "What are you doing?"

"Burping the baby," I answered sleepily.

A rhythmic sound had awakened him. Thump, thump, thump. At first, he had assumed I was burping the baby.

But my husband didn't remember hearing Hannah wake up.

Thump, thump, thump. The sound continued. He looked over to see me rhythmically beating my own chest.

"Where's the baby?" he asked.

"She's right here," I started to say. But then I realized that I couldn't feel a baby. I couldn't see a baby. Where was the baby?

I frantically jumped out of bed and ran to find her sleeping peacefully in her bassinet in the next room. Relieved, I went back to bed.

My husband was laughing hysterically. I was still getting over the shock of what had happened. I really had thought, for just that brief moment when I awoke, that I was burping Hannah.

Finally, I had to laugh, too. It was funny. In fact, it was downright hilarious. And it was just the kind of comic relief we needed to diffuse the stress of new parenthood.

The nightly ritual would continue for many more months, but never again was I caught burping myself during the night.

~Marie Cleveland

## Chapter 4

# New Moms

## The Wonder of Being a Mother

*God could not be everywhere, so he created mothers.*

~Jewish Proverb

# Two Heartbeats, One Bond

*Children and mothers never truly part—*
*Bound in the beating of each other's heart.*
~Charlotte Gray

While I was pregnant with my first son, I read that when some pregnant women first hear their babies' heartbeat in the womb, they cry with wonder and joy at the sound of that new little life inside them. Not so for me. This whooshy heartbeat—this new life—in my womb was a wonder and a mystery, for sure, I thought, but not worth getting all emotional about. Which was par for the course, really. I have always been much more comfortable with matters of the mind and soul than those of the heart and body. Cerebral and exalted—I'm your girl. Touchy-feely wonder—no thanks, find someone else.

Not surprisingly, I saw infancy as a short, exhausting stage that I'd have to get through before beginning the real business of raising a child. I looked forward to reading *Harry Potter* books together, going on family camping trips, and visiting my friends and relatives overseas. I looked forward to conversations about God and about how to make the world a better place. I did not look forward, necessarily, to nursing, cuddling, and rocking my little baby to sleep.

In fact, I had never been a big baby-lover. I had never felt the urge to kiss a baby's head, fragile and tender and covered (or not)

Two Heartbeats, One Bond : The Wonder of Being a Mother  85

with downy curls; never felt the need to stroke a baby's hand, with its miniature fingers, impossibly tiny fingernails, and dimples where the knuckles should be; never felt a desire to hold the weight and warmth of one of those soft little bundles in my arms. When it came to babies, all I felt was awkward.

So it was that my newborn son took me completely by surprise. I was ready for the hormonal, sleep-deprived delirium of the first few weeks. I was ready for the new capacity for worry and joy that I felt in my heart. I was not ready for the overwhelming physical bond I felt with my son. If his face was anywhere near mine, I felt compelled to kiss it. I just couldn't keep my lips off him—his petal-soft skin and sweet marshmallow cheeks drew me right in. I was constantly patting his soft, round little bottom, stroking his compact little back, playing with his silky baby hair. I loved the shape of his sweet pink lips and the squishiness of his bread-dough thighs. I loved the warmth of his tiny body snuggled up on my chest when he napped.

I had expected a connection of the heart, but I hadn't expected to feel that connection in my body. I hadn't expected to feel quite so… attached to this baby of mine. But, really, how could I not have felt attached to the child who was in fact actually attached to me through that cord in the womb? How could I not feel a bond with the one whose heartbeat depended for so long, literally, on the beating of my own heart? We had shared life. It was no wonder. And yet it was—and is still—a wonder to me.

Now my two sons are three and seven years old, inquisitive, rambunctious, and rail-thin. They ask endless questions about how things work and why people are the way they are. We've visited family in New York City, Chicago, and Tokyo, and gone to museums, concerts, and plays. I enjoy this more cerebral relationship with them—the one I had anticipated when I was first pregnant—but I still feel powerfully, irresistibly drawn to their little bodies. They are rarely still long enough for a good cuddle; I have to settle for tousling their hair as they run by, drawing them in for hugs when I can catch them, and kissing their flushed cheeks at night while they sleep. But sometimes, in the middle of the night, one or the other of my boys creeps into bed with me and my husband and snuggles up close to me. I put my arm around my child and feel the rise and fall of his body with his breath, feel his trust and his innocence curled up beside me, safe in the bond between us. And though his heartbeat no longer depends on mine, I realize, my heart still beats for him. What a wonder. What a joy.

~Misa Sugiura

# Growing Pains

*As a parent you try to maintain a certain amount of control and so you have this tug-of-war... You have to learn when to let go. And that's not easy.*
~Aretha Franklin

Today, Ryan and I are on a mission. We have just arrived at the baby mega store. I unbuckle the straps from Ryan's seat and lift his squirmy body from the car. Side by side, we begin a slow, meandering walk from the car to the store as Ryan stops to inspect every rock and sidewalk crack along the way. Today, we are in search of a potty, the one item that we have not yet purchased after two years of frequenting this popular retail establishment. Ryan has recently displayed some interest in potty-related matters, and I intend to take advantage of this apparent window of opportunity.

Once we are inside the store, I lift him into the shopping cart. He holds his half of the smoothie we are sharing in one hand and a bag of Goldfish in the other. While he settles himself and his snacks in the seat, I sneak a long look at him, knowing he will soon grow impatient and command me to get moving. I notice his pants are hiked up above his socks, and his wrists are peeking out from the cuffs of his long-sleeved shirt. He is growing again. It is time for new clothes—again. Since we are already here, I take a detour to the clothing section. As we approach the adorable shorts and T-shirts hanging loftily from miniature hangers, my eyes begin to skim the racks. I scan them quickly—0-6 months, 6-12 months, 12-18 months—and then I stop, feeling foolish. This is a baby store. These clothes are for babies. Ryan, who is now over two years old, is not a baby. My head knows this, but it takes my heart a while to catch up.

I pause to wait for it—there—the tidal wave that crashes over me. My breath catches in the back of my throat, and my heart gives a familiar squeeze. I stop the cart and wait patiently for the sensations to pass. No need to panic. It's just another episode of motherhood growing pain: his growing, my pain.

Since becoming a mother, I have been surprised by many things. One of them is this: The biggest moments are actually the small ones, the ones that sneak up on you, arrive unexpectedly, and stop you in your tracks. The big milestones, such as giving birth, first steps, and birthdays, are important, too. But what I hold most dear are those tiny moments, bright seconds in time flung together to shape the constellation of motherhood.

I remember so clearly the first of those moments. It was several days after Ryan's birth. After numbly kissing my husband goodbye as he left for work, I headed upstairs with Ryan to change his diaper. As we entered his room, we were greeted by the happy colors and whimsical dancing stars on the walls, bright with early morning sunshine. The room still felt new. Bookshelves were neatly arranged with matching, brightly colored baskets and stiff-spined books. The dresser was orderly, containing carefully folded newborn clothes and tiny diapers. The sweet smell of Dreft detergent lingered in the air.

"Good morning, Peanut," I cooed as I gently lowered Ryan onto the changing pad. I knew from the baby books I had been diligently reading that his eyesight wasn't well-developed yet. But the bright alertness and curiosity in his eyes convinced me he was carefully studying my face and features. I unsnapped his onesie and tenderly placed a hand on his belly as I reached for a diaper. His arms and legs flailed about, a windmill of extremities over which he had not yet mastered control.

With a start, I noticed the small, dark stump of his umbilical cord had fallen off. It had been cast aside to reveal a tiny belly button underneath, a perfect "O" of surprise, fleshy and pink. I leaned forward to place a kiss there, pleased with the newly revealed landscape on his small body to explore. Suddenly, I burst into tears. The clear, salty drops made their way down my face, hesitated slightly on my quivering chin, then fell and pooled delicately into that new crevice on his body.

Had anyone else been there, I could have used any number of excuses for my bizarre behavior: hormones, fatigue, sleep deprivation. But I knew it was none of those things, and I was grateful to be having that odd moment in private.

Bewildered, I gathered my son in my arms and sought the solace of the rocking chair nearby. As I rocked with him, my mind retreated to examine my recent unexpected burst of emotion. The event was a normal rite of passage for a newborn. I should have felt relief. But, instead, a cold sorrow took hold of my heart.

I thought about that perfect belly button, closed and sealed off to the world. I remembered how that place used to connect him to me. Through that connection, I was able to provide for him, nourish him, and protect him. It ground him to me, made him a part of me. Then, mere minutes after his birth, a flash of cold metal severed the cord and he was set free, a task that had been joyfully delegated to my husband by the nurse and doctor. No one had asked me if I was ready, if I was prepared to let go. The physical connection between my son and me was broken. He became his own living being, a separate person, his own person.

My eyes welled up again as a new and unfamiliar pain formed inside my gut, a hurt so visceral that I could not identify the exact source. Slowly, the thought came to me: He is leaving me. Only days old, and he is already leaving me. He will always be leaving me. My first motherhood growing pain.

In the aisle of the baby store, I lean on the cart and wait patiently for the pressure in my chest to subside. Soon, I am able to take a deep breath, collect my thoughts, and move on, back on track to the potty aisle.

After two years, I have become more accustomed to these heartbreaking moments of motherhood. They still hurt and take my breath away, but I am not blindsided the way I was with the first one.

Although often unexpected, when it occurs I can identify that pang, stop and briefly feel the pain, then move on. Some moments are filled with sadness and longing, but others contain great pride and joy.

I finally locate the potty aisle, release Ryan from the shopping cart, and allow him to examine the selection. After careful deliberation, he decides on the Elmo potty. He appears to be quite pleased with his choice as he chatters to Elmo and Big Bird on the box on the way to the checkout counter. After I make the purchase, Ryan reaches up to me with a free hand and leads us to the store exit. Silently, I say goodbye to the baby store as we leave. The doors close softly behind us as we step out into the warm sunlight of the late spring afternoon.

~Kim Ehlert

# The Drawer

*A baby is a blank cheque made payable to the human race.*
~Barbara Christine Seifert

I don't open this drawer often. I don't like to be reminded of my truncated dreams. Who would have believed that my future would be so hijacked? There in the back of the drawer, stashed behind the pencils, paper clips, and rubber bands, are the luggage tags — pristine, unscuffed, never used. I haven't even filled out the address card in them. And there's the mini-lock I bought for that new suitcase I fully intended to take to Europe. The lock and key are still in the hermetically sealed package, looking out at me reproachfully. And when I pull the drawer out all the way, I see the sandwich baggie of old luggage keys that I used when I was younger.

What had happened? I majored in a foreign language in college and couldn't wait to take off for a life of adventure after graduation. A new country, new people, new culture — it was all intoxicating in its allure.

And it turned out to be all I had hoped. I was single, unattached, free to follow my wanderlust and tackle the challenges. I had family and friends back home, to be sure, but no strangling ties to interfere with my new hedonistic life of freedom, joy, and learning. Exploring the land, my new city, the different food and weather, even the foibles and follies of trying to do my job in a foreign language went to my head like new wine.

Who can explain the feeling of waiting for your breath to come back the first time you see the grandeur and feel the eternal solitude of the Alps? Or the hallowed hush that swallows you inside Notre Dame Cathedral as your eyes involuntarily rise up to the shimmering red, blue, and gold figures in the stained-glass windows that millions before you have also marveled at? It was as if God's own hand had painted them from a divine rainbow to last not just years, but centuries.

I remembered driving down a highway in Greece, guessing from the map that Mount Olympus should be somewhere in the vicinity, and looking slowly up the distant landscape at that one mountain peak cresting over the clouds—and realizing that this was, in fact, the mystical place of all those famous legends. Surely Zeus himself was up on that hazy summit wielding his thunderbolt even in this modern age.

Strauss waltzes piped through the parks in Vienna where music truly sings to the soul, as Vienna serves up Austria's legendary composers to transport the foreign visitor away from modern distractions—classical culture free for the taking out of the air.

The old European tastes, new to this American culinary novice, woke up taste buds I never knew I had. No wonder the decadence of the chocolate and cherry Schwarzwälderkirschtorte brings visitors from around the world to the Black Forest, and the smell of Wiener Schnitzel drizzled with lemon is enough to start you booking a trip to Austria. And those lamb-stuffed tomatoes roasted in sweltering public ovens in Dubrovnik and souvlaki handed out by street vendors in Athens.

Living in other countries offered new sights, sounds, feelings, and tastes that simply couldn't be experienced just from reading books or watching movies. How lucky foreign travelers are, I realized.

But to everything there is a season, and I returned to my homeland older, wiser, and full of precious memories.

I had every intention of returning to those carefree days of hiking and exploring in Europe as soon as I could afford to. But what happened? My peripatetic traveling future was waylaid—by you, my firstborn child.

When you were born, I fell in love again—much different from my love for your father. I learned in one shocking moment why mothers are so fiercely devoted to their children, as if this is our chance to create something of real value for the world.

Suddenly, the majesty of the Alps and the chateaus on the Loire faded to gray behind your baby blue eyes and the halo of your golden curls. The first Mother's Day gift I ever received was a little booklet of poems from your dad, and one about babies said, "You are my Paris and my Rome." It hit home with a pang. How could I give up my prized freedom to roam the glorious world just to be a mother?

How, indeed? I did, and with joy. Maybe it takes time to learn that traveling and new experiences become much more valuable when you share what you have learned with others. Parenting is not just providing food and shelter, lessons in how to behave properly, and even plenty of love. It's sharing who you are and how you came to your life views with your children so they can grow along with you—the feel of that cold chill down the spine inspired by some inexpressible beauty. It's a vital legacy and challenge, every bit as important as teaching them the alphabet and not to use double negatives.

So, as you grew, I showed you pictures of Notre Dame's rose windows. I read you Greek myths so that some day the sudden sight of Mount Olympus rising over the clouds would take your breath away, too.

I played Strauss waltzes and other composers' works of beauty and genius, so you could expand your little musical brain and appreciate the mellifluous amid the cacophony of life.

I recreated the Schwarzwälderkirschtorte and Schnitzel and lamb-stuffed tomatoes in my own kitchen to help give you a sense of adventure in food, so you wouldn't grow up on just hamburgers and French fries but could take a gastronomical trip around the world in your own home.

And I taught you as much of my foreign language as I could, in the hopes that you would grow up understanding the importance and joy of learning about other people and cultures. You deserve no less.

In that desk drawer of unfulfilled travel dreams at home, along with the unopened lock package and unused luggage tags, is our family's pocket birthday book, well thumbed and becoming yellowed with age. There are magic markers, most long out of ink, used for many a school project. And notes from teachers, sports team rosters, old carpooling schedules—souvenirs of a very different adventure than I had intended to continue when I was young and footloose. But it was one of an even greater value—for you and me both. It wasn't a sacrifice—it was a gift, a hand-off from mother to son in that great relay of life. There is simply too much to be seen and experienced by each person in a lifetime, so we need to give the next generation a head start on the wonder.

Yes, Paris and Rome will always be there—but you couldn't wait.

~Becky S. Tompkins

# To Have and to Hold

*Who fed me from her gentle breast*
*And hushed me in her arms to rest,*
*And on my cheek sweet kisses prest?*
*My Mother.*
*~Anne Taylor*

In my son's darkened room, a wet slurp breaks the night's silence every few seconds. Seated in my rocker, shoulders heavy, body weary, I gaze down at Aidan cradled in my arms. The soft glow of moonlight illuminates my eight-month-old's creamy round face as shadows fall around us. His eyelashes fan his cheeks, but his mouth moves with urgency. It's my second visit to his room tonight and, again, he's hungry. Amazingly ravenous. My body aches for sleep—for more than four consecutive hours of rest—but I am not upset being here. Though my bed calls to me in the next room, warm and inviting, I choose to be the one who comes to Aidan each time his cry breaks the night's stillness. No, I'm not upset one bit. Rather, I cherish this time alone with my baby. It is ours. He is mine, and he needs me as much as I need him.

As Aidan rests in my lap, nursing, my mind travels backward through the day that has passed and then forward to the day ahead. My little guy has been army-crawling across the living room and kitchen floors all week. A new milestone. Stealthy and curious, Aidan is like a soldier on an urgent mission, uncovering hidden treasures—buttons, errant outlet covers, stale bread crumbs—as he scoots across carpet and hardwood floors alike. His baby fat is practically melting off his body. During the day, and ever since I've known him, Aidan is hardly still.

"A cute little Tasmanian devil," I say to my husband, Tim, one evening.

"A tornado," he replies.

"But we love him," we agree.

Nevertheless, he tires me out. All day, I long to hold him, to nuzzle his baby-soft skin.

Now, however, aside from those slurping, wet lips, he is perfectly still. A soft lump of baby love. To hold. To kiss. To snuggle all I want. The nights give me this gift.

During waking hours, Aidan is no cuddler. He never has been, even as an infant. Always, he has looked to the floor, to his toys, to the world beyond my arms with energy for exploration, an air of independence that I simultaneously admire and dislike. Never one to sit perched on my hip, or to wrap his chubby legs around my torso, I've had to use my muscles to keep him in my arms at home, at church, or any store where I've felt brave enough to lift him from his car seat. But now, asleep, Aidan is soft and limp. A welcome change. I must savor these moments in the middle of the night, when Aidan still depends on me for nourishment. He's unaware that while I provide him milk, he nourishes his mother's soul.

I know these nightly feedings are numbered.

I lift my son onto my shoulder and thump his back gently. He has fallen into a deep sleep after nursing, and the chances of a burp, I know, are slim. But I hold him close, his tiny body on mine, breathing in his sweet milkiness, savoring this embrace, one of the few when he doesn't twist and turn, fighting me to get down. To do his own thing.

And I stay this way, closing my eyes, leaning back against the rocker for another twenty minutes, maybe more.

Because holding him is delicious.

The next several months bring sunshine and warmth to the Northeast. Aidan, fully mobile now on hands and knees, crawls hurriedly across the carpet toward his stack of books.

"Aidan," I say, "do you want to read a book with Mama?" I scoop him up to the couch along with *Oh My Oh My Oh Dinosaurs!* and plant him in my lap. "Dinosaurs happy," I begin. "Dinosaurs sad." Aidan sits for the book, amused by one of his favorite authors, then squirms and wiggles his way back down to the floor.

Aidan pauses as if deciding what to do next, then scrambles for his alphabet-singing bus. "T says tuh, T says tuh, every letter makes a sound and T says tuh." Aidan giggles, smiling up at me.

I sigh, smiling back. Well, at least it was a few minutes of closeness.

By the time Aidan begins to walk at fifteen-and-a-half months, he is rather svelte, lean, and no less curious about the world around him and his new view of it. Reading books during the day becomes more of a rarity. Before bedtime, he begins to prefer the couch cushion next to me as opposed to my lap in the rocker. My big boy, I think. Too big for his mama to hold.

A few months later, I suggest the rocking chair, and Aidan flatly rejects me.

"Couch," he states, bounding across his room.

"Look at this," I say to Tim as my husband joins us for the bedtime routine. I raise my eyebrows, indicating the space as large as the Gulf of Mexico between Aidan and me on the couch.

"Hey, buddy, can you make room for me?" Tim asks.

"Come cuddle," I say, trying to coax Aidan a few inches closer to me so that Tim can sit down. I want to drape my arm around our boy.

Aidan obliges, scooting over, and I quickly pull him close. Engrossed in the story of Curious George, Aidan absently drops his head onto my chest. I glance over him at my husband and smile. Grateful for this moment. Wishing I had my camera.

Sad that his baby stage has so quickly begun to recede, I accept the new arrangement as we sit side-by-side, night after night, one book after another.

But about a year later, at two-and-a-half, Aidan surprises me.

"Sit in lap," he says, sliding down from his big boy bed, two hands on my knees before I know it. We've already read books both on the couch and in his big boy bed. Now he wants to sit on my lap in the rocker? Perhaps it's a ploy to stay up a little later. Aidan is no stranger to such tactics.

"Mmmm," he murmurs, settling on my lap, all thirty-two pounds of him. I wrap my arms around him as he leans back against my chest.

A ploy? I'll take it.

I open the book he has brought me and hardly notice the words on the page as I plant my nose in his hair, delivering kisses to his temple.

I love this boy so incredibly much. It is all I can do to focus on the story and to make my voice somewhat animated for my attentive audience.

Tonight, my young son chose me. And that has made all the difference.

~Mary Jo Marcellus Wyse

# Prince Charming

*You know when you have found your prince because you not only have a smile on your face but in your heart as well.*
*~Author Unknown*

Some day, my prince will come... The words that enchanted me as a little girl were echoing in my head — transported from childhood days into my now adult world. Was it truly only moments ago that we had met? It didn't matter — here I was, lost in the blue eyes of a stranger, and yet it felt like we had known each other a lifetime. He, too, seemed to be mesmerized as we silently gazed at one another.

He was dark, and oh so handsome — just as the storybooks foretold. I couldn't take my eyes off him — he was perfect. There was something beyond his outward good looks, however — an inner beauty that shined through.

Our hands touched, and my heart literally jumped for joy. Even though there were no woodland creatures surrounding us, or birds whistling a merry tune above, the moment was magical all the same. The question "Do you believe in love at first sight?" danced dreamily through my mind.

I reached over and softly kissed him; I couldn't help myself. There was something so powerful and beautiful happening here. Up to this point, there had been no words exchanged. None were needed; the two of us were content just being with one another. I suddenly broke the silence, however. My heart had already made a declaration, but my lips needed to make a proclamation as well or I would surely burst keeping the words inside.

"I love you, my sweet prince, my newborn son," I whispered tenderly into his ear.

Yes, I believed in love at first sight—and happily ever after, too.

~Kimberly J. Garrow

# Forever Changed

*The moment a child is born, the mother is also born. She never existed before.
The woman existed, but the mother, never.
A mother is something absolutely new.*
~Rajneesh

On March 9, 2004, the day my first child was born, I became forever changed. As I held my newborn baby, I recalled a moment, nearly two years before, when I was hospitalized for a second time in my life for depression. As I stood waiting to be discharged, I vowed to get better, to never return physically or mentally to that place. It was on this day that I made a promise to myself to do whatever it took to overcome this debilitating illness so that I could one day be a depression-free new mom.

As I built my new life, I went to counseling, twice a week at first, and less frequently over time. I worked on my counseling exercises at home. I read uplifting books, exercised, ate well, and began to interact again socially with others. I started a new, part-time, low-stress job where I felt I was making a difference. Months later, to my delight, I became pregnant. And for nine months, in preparation for first-time motherhood, I continued to improve upon my mental state of mind.

Then the day came when my baby, Diego, was born. It was like a scene in a movie. The doctor set him upon my chest, and I looked in awe at this tiny creature who moments before had been nicely snuggled within my warm womb. I soaked up his essence, the tiny fingers and toes, the soft, damp skin, and something inside of me clicked.

My old self faded away, and a new person emerged: "Michelle the Mother." At that moment, I knew in my heart that those turbulent, depressed years were in the past. I was now a mother, responsible for taking care of a helpless, innocent baby, and I wholeheartedly accepted this job. My focus was now on providing the most wonderful environment I could for this precious one that God had entrusted into my care. I knew then that I would love this baby with all of my heart and soul, and that I would continue to keep my mind healthy so I could be the best mother possible for him.

As the days passed, I sang him made-up songs. Cheerfully, I woke up in the middle of the night to feed him. I gently rocked him when he cried (which was often!). I had fallen completely in love with my angel. Many of my family and friends saw the change within me. My mom said my face looked different. I "glowed." "Michelle the Mother" was a title that suited me well. But as much as motherhood had changed me, and as happy as I felt, I knew that I was predisposed to postpartum depression. I vigilantly kept a check on my state of mind, doing whatever I could to stay healthy, allowing me to remain a depression-free new mom.

Becoming a new mother has proven to be the most positive, life-altering experience of my existence. While there are times when those clouds of depression still threaten to overwhelm me, my love for my children propels me forward. My two angels have rekindled my inner light and left me forever changed.

~Michelle Sedas

# The First Change

*It sometimes happens, even in the best of families, that a baby is born. This is not necessarily cause for alarm. The important thing is to keep your wits about you and borrow some money.*
~Elinor Goulding Smith

"This will be like the first time—all over again," said my obstetrician. I couldn't believe it. I was pregnant. Despite four miscarriages between our first two children, a mystery flu that only hit me in the morning led my husband to say, "You don't suppose you're..."

He couldn't—and I wouldn't let him—finish his thought. We were in our forties. Our two children were almost sixteen and eleven, and I was finished as a room parent. I knew that I was going through the "change of life," but it turned out to be greater than either of us could imagine—Pampers style.

Having a baby in your forties—or anytime after the attic collection of baby paraphernalia has been passed on—is truly a wonderful blessing from God. But it's one most couples would say they would pass on. I felt that I had more in common with an unwed teenage mother than I did with many of our friends.

"Congratulations! We're so happy for you. Thank goodness it's you and not us!" was a typical response. "Boy, I don't envy you guys paying for diapers and auto insurance for a teenage driver all at the same time," said lawyer friend Frank.

I know that if the maternity top was on someone else, I would have said the same things. We would encounter the "Dreaded Ts" of parenting—teething, terrible twos, and tuition for college—all at the same time. And then we'd be doing that third "T" of tuition all over again at retirement age.

But how often in life do you learn about survival through something wonderful? I looked for the positives that we didn't have in the first round of parenting. There were many. For instance, even while I was pregnant, there were benefits of built-in maternity fashion consultants who were better than any mirror—and more honest than any husband would dare. "Mom, if you wear those green pants with the pink top, it will remind people of a watermelon." And this time, I knew that I needed to care for myself and not give in to cravings for a Big Mac or M&Ms—at least not often.

Expenses were far lighter, too, even though we had given away everything baby. True friends share laughter, tears, and attic collections. We restocked our house and Grandma's with big-ticket items of cribs and high chairs, and shared the bounty with a friend expecting twins.

Upon arrival, blessed is the babe who has a house full of arms to hold her. There were advantages for whoever held tiny Elizabeth. "Help with dishes? Oh, I wish I could, but I'm holding the baby." Running out of diapers was never a worry with a newly licensed sixteen-year-old son in the house. He offered every day to drive to the store.

As time went on, it gave us a more mature relationship with fledgling children to depend upon their help. We survived exhausting times when our teenagers adopted my husband's mantra: "If you see something that needs to be done, just do it. Don't wait to be asked."

Junior parents felt firsthand the commitment involved in raising a child. I woke up energized because the baby slept through the night. "She didn't wake up until 4:00 a.m.," I said brightly at breakfast.

"That's through the night?" they asked with horrified expressions.

Learning tolerance is an ongoing lesson in any family, but there is far less anger toward a far younger sibling. My husband had another saying: "Lizi-ness is the price of laziness." English assignments ended up on the floor if a book bag was left by the stairs. Brown sugar was once dumped on top of homework left on the kitchen table. The siblings asked, "Will she ever grow up?" But I knew the answer from the first round of parenting.

Did I have less energy? Undoubtedly. My wise, ninety-year-old friend named Elizabeth—one of our baby's namesakes—told me, "Increased wisdom will compensate for decreased energy." I realized the truth the day I rolled a block to get the attention of a nine-month-old ready to crawl out of sight. She crawled back to me as I shook a can with more blocks. A younger self would have chased after her. I marveled that it took forty-three years to outsmart a one-year-old. Oh, there were still days I would have traded all of that wisdom for a wee bit more energy, but I learned, too, to always look for the blessings in the little things.

This time around, I never tired of playing peek-a-boo. I held this tiny child endlessly. I dropped everything to read to her. We took long, leisurely walks and made comparative smells for every flower we encountered—not just the roses. As she's grown older, I've taught her to cook and sew without losing my patience, at least not too much.

Life is all about changes and how we adapt, appreciating each moment no matter how hard. In this miracle of starting over as a new mom, I was taught the wisdom that is usually reserved only for grandmothers.

~Jane Ann Miller

# Chapter 5

# New Moms

## Doubts & Insecurities

*What lies behind us and what lies before us
are tiny matters compared to what lies within us.*

~Ralph Waldo Emerson

# Mother to Mother

*She never quite leaves her children at home,
even when she doesn't take them along.*
~Margaret Culkin Banning

It was a cool spring morning in early April. I sat at Momma's kitchen table clutching my precious baby girl to my chest. It was to be my first day back at work since her birth, and the thought of leaving my baby was tearing me apart. I had waited so long to have a child and now was considering leaving her for a majority of the day, five days a week. What in the world was I thinking?

My mother, a parent of three, had never worked outside the home when we were growing up. Momma had so many talents and was incredibly intelligent. She could have accomplished much in the career world, but instead devoted her life to her family. Because ours was a one-income family, this meant that we experienced some financial constraints. Of course, the only one truly aware of the monetary burdens was Momma. She was the one who did without, not us. I took it for granted that Momma would always be at home when I needed her.

Now, here I was, a new mother leaving my child so that my new family could have a certain degree of financial freedom. All of a sudden, I felt so incredibly selfish. I wanted to be as selfless as she had been. At that moment, I decided that I would eat hot dogs when I wanted steak, I would stay at home rather than go on shopping expeditions, and would be content to spend summers around town instead of at the beach or in the mountains. But a little voice in my subconscious lingered. Would I really be able to do that? What about that college diploma hanging on my wall, the one that I had worked so hard to earn? Would I really be happy if each day was a struggle financially? And if I was not content with the direction of my life, what kind of mother would I be? The conflicting range of emotions was truly making me a little crazy!

As the tears streamed down my face, my mother walked across the room and gently pried that little girl from my arms. I cried even harder and stammered that I just could not do it. I could not leave my baby. She needed me too much. I would just have to learn to deal with the struggle. Perhaps I would go back to work when she was older.

My mother, always wise beyond her years, smiled gently as she cradled the sleeping baby in her arms.

"Honey, this baby is always going to need you, even when she's a teenager. Time isn't going to change that. In fact, she may need you then even more than she does right now. That's what happens when you become a momma. But you are leaving her with someone who loves her just as much as you do, and she's going to know that you love her no matter where you are. I'm going to make sure of that. That's why you can go."

And with those words, I pulled myself up from the chair and walked toward the front door. My heart had never felt heavier.

All day long, I thought of my precious baby. I called at least a dozen times to check on her, and each time Momma patiently assured me that all was well. Yes, she had eaten well. Yes, the diaper rash looked better. No, she had not cried. Yes, she had slept well except that the ringing of the telephone kept waking her up.

By the time my workday had ended, my arms ached to cradle my precious baby. I raced to Momma's house and ran through the front door where Momma was waiting with my little girl. I clung to her and hugged her tight. All was right again in my world.

I worked the entire time my daughter was growing up and eventually added a son to the nest. It was never easy to leave my children, but I was blessed to have a mother to watch over and protect them just as I would have. Those two youngsters are now teenagers, and Momma was right. Though bottles, diapers, and strollers have long since been put away, they do still need me, probably even more than when they were babies. After all, I am the one holding the car keys.

~Terri Duncan

# A Tale of Two Mothers

> *Motherhood has a very humanizing effect.*
> *Everything gets reduced to essentials.*
> ~Meryl Streep

So, I had to go to the Winco for groceries. This is not an odd event; usually we do the grocery shopping once a week or so. On this particular Saturday morning, it was me and my daughter, eight-month-old Lana. We'd had a rough night. Lana was fighting a cold and needed some love in the middle of the night, so my good buddy Sleep and I didn't meet up until far too late.

I'm usually not one to care much about what I look like at the grocery store, but that morning I set the bar especially low. I noticed as I was getting dressed that a spot of baby spit-up had dried on my jeans. I didn't bother to comb my hair and just threw it back in a ponytail. The right shoulder of my coat had bits of baby snot ground into the corduroy, and a giant red pimple had taken up residence below my left nostril. Let's just say my appearance was far less than appealing. But I didn't really care. I am a very goal-oriented person, and the goal of that moment was to get the groceries, not strut in a fashion show. Or so I thought.

As I hauled Lana, my purse and the re-usable shopping bags into the store, I noticed another mom doing the very same thing. Our actions were similar, but we couldn't have been more different. She was gorgeous in her fresh make-up, curled hair and trendy designer cardigan. Her denim capris were fitted and showed the world that post-baby weight was certainly not a problem for her. And her shoes, oh, her shoes! Her shoes are what really got my attention. She wore gorgeous, expensive-looking, strappy sandals with very high heels. She looked like a mom ready for a magazine photo shoot.

As I struggled with getting the baby seat situated on the shopping cart, Photo Shoot Mom breezed by me, having no trouble snapping her little girl in the cart. She looked at me, and we both gave each other a quick smile. I noticed her little daughter looked as if she just crawled out of a babyGap commercial. Her outfit was clean and pressed, and shiny blond curls framed her round, angelic face. She was adorable. Certainly not as adorable as Lana, but very lovely nonetheless. Photo Shoot Mom glanced at Lana, but instead of smiling, like most people do when they see her round cherub face, she kind of grimaced.

I looked at my daughter and saw why. Lana's runny nose was working overtime. She made it worse when she reached up with both hands and smeared snot all over her face. I dug through my purse for a tissue and cleaned up my baby as best as I could, but alas some had already dried on her chubby cheeks. Even the neck of her pink coat was decorated with dried snot. I imagined the judgmental thoughts this other mother must be thinking of me. I was a terrible wife because if I couldn't be bothered to look decent in public, how disheveled must I appear to my husband on a daily basis? And I was a terrible mother because everybody knows you must certainly lack proper parenting skills if your baby has a dirty face and clothes in the aisle of the grocery store. At that moment, I would have heartily agreed with what I thought she was thinking of me.

Apparently, Photo Shoot Mom and I "do" Winco in the same pattern, as it seemed I followed her from section to section. The whole time, she happily chatted to her babbling daughter. I fumbled with my list and dropped the coupons. My normally easygoing daughter was fussing and crying. Neither a binky nor a bottle would make her happy. A few other shoppers gave me sideways glances when Lana's cries grew especially loud. To top it off, she sneezed a few times, making her face an even bigger snot mess.

I kept watching Photo Shoot Mom and started to wonder about

her. What kind of a life did she lead that she could look so lovely and well-rested on a Saturday morning? Surely she lived a life of leisure, and had a personal stylist and an entire domestic staff at her disposal. Surely she was not up at all hours in the night, rocking and comforting her sick baby. Surely her life was easy, and she glided through her days effortlessly. If, indeed, envy is a dragon with emerald eyes, my scales were starting to show, and my blue eyes were turning green.

Photo Shoot Mom and I checked out at the same time and walked across the parking lot to our cars. She loaded her groceries and child into her car, and I did the same. We both drove away, she presumably to her castle on the hill.

I had about a forty-minute drive home to dwell on the two very different mothers spending a portion of their morning at the Winco. I am ashamed to admit that I spent the majority of that time stewing in envy. I was jealous, plain and simple. I was mad that her charmed life appeared to be so easy, whereas I was struggling with mine.

A sound from the backseat jolted me out of my self-imposed pity party. In the mirror I saw Lana turn her head from one side to the other and then contentedly sigh as she drifted back to sleep. Even in her dirty coat and snot-smeared face, she was so beautiful. Right then I wanted to pull the car over and weep. How in the world could I ever be envious of anybody? There, in the backseat of my car, was more love and joy and happiness than some people experience in their entire lifetime.

I was humbled by an eight-month-old baby girl. Lana, beautiful, sweet, lovely Lana, was content to snuggle in her seat. Her desires were simple. She was happy to be held and rocked and fed and loved. She didn't know envy yet. I needed to be a good example for her so she wouldn't know about jealousy for a very long time. I also needed to take a lesson from my daughter and be pleased with what I have and with who I am. Sometimes, I forgot that I am blessed beyond measure, and I'm grateful for the tiny teacher in the backseat who was there to remind me.

~Shelle Lenssen

# A Good Mother

*There is no way to be a perfect mother, and a million ways to be a good one.*
*~Jill Churchill*

"Please, God," I prayed earnestly, over and over, "if I can't be a good mother, don't let me have a baby." I was in my late twenties, married for a decade by then, and I had no idea what a good mother looked like.

My husband and I had never tried to get pregnant, coming up with one excuse after another in answer to the inevitable question from friends and family. We were busy. We wanted to buy a house first. We wanted to buy nice cars first. I wanted to grow my hair out first, so I could put it in a ponytail at the hospital. (I actually used this gem of an excuse repeatedly.) In truth, I wasn't even sure I wanted to be a mother. I certainly didn't want to be the kind of mother I'd known.

My childhood had been a painful experience. My mom, afflicted with untreated mental illness and haunted by demons from her own past, slid into frequent black rages, and I was her particular target. She spat bitter criticisms in my face, slapped me, called me names. I was deeply wounded by her behavior and unable to adjust. Emotionally, I permanently withdrew from her.

When I turned eighteen, I married and fled as far away as I could to the other side of the country. All of my own anger and hurt finally spilled out, and I slid into a dark depression. Years passed as I fought my way through, and my heart slowly mended. But I kept putting off having a baby. And I started praying that prayer. "Please, God, if I can't be a good mother…" What if there is a bad-mothering gene? What if I, too, am incapable of loving my child?

Finally, my husband and I decided that it was now or never—we would try for a baby. Then I had three miscarriages in a row. The doctors drew blood and ran tests, but they couldn't find anything wrong, and I was left to wonder: Is this the answer to my prayer? Does God know I wouldn't be a good mother? Maybe it was for the best. Yet each time it happened, I sat in the bathroom and sobbed as though my heart was breaking.

Just after our sixteenth wedding anniversary, I once again became pregnant. This time, the pregnancy held. Our son Cameron arrived in the spring of 2006 after an excruciatingly long labor. There were complications at the end, so my first half-hour with the baby passed in a grey fog of pain. I tried to focus on him, but I was not in the glowy, teary "new mom" bubble that I'd heard so much about. I did not feel a magical, mystical connection the first time I saw him. No matter. I was happy he was here, and he was healthy. The bonding would come in time. At least, I hoped so.

We brought our baby home, and from the beginning, I floundered. Cameron had been a model citizen at the hospital—sleeping and eating on cue, blinking his still-smeary eyes placidly at us—but during our first night home, he started screaming and kept it up all night. My husband and I fumbled around, stiff with shock. Toward dawn, I called our pediatrician's hotline in tears. The nurse assured us that the baby was fine; he just needed to adjust. He isn't the only one, I thought.

The act of breastfeeding, which surely should have been simple and instinctive, turned into an apparatus-filled production. Cameron didn't gain much weight during his first weeks, and I panicked and ordered a breast pump. My days turned into an endless succession of pumping and feeding and washing bottles and tubes. The process threatened to consume my life. But when people suggested I start giving Cameron formula, I refused, even when I got a painful infection. I couldn't let him down, I thought. I had to give him the best.

Oh, how hard I tried to do everything perfectly! A beautiful, sunny summer passed by outside as I remained indoors, oblivious to everything but Cameron's unceasing needs. Every time I heard him cry, I sprang into action, racing to fix whatever was wrong. I obsessed and fretted over everything. I drove my husband crazy with my worry, my efforts. Once, in a moment of frustration, he asked me, "Why is this so hard for you? Women do this all the time." But I could not relax. There seemed to be no end to my stress and confusion.

In my previous life, I had been a successful businesswoman. Now, my beautiful suits hung abandoned in the closet, and I felt stupid and helpless. In the small spaces of time between feeding the baby and washing laundry, I sat on the couch and hugged Cameron to my chest, anxious and weak with fatigue. This was supposed to be the easiest, most natural thing in the world, I thought, and I was doing everything completely wrong. I was overwhelmed. Every ounce of my being pulsed with a desperate request: God, help me.

And God heard the prayers that I could not speak. My baby flourished. As the long months passed, I eventually began to relax, and grace stole in. One day, Cameron looked at me with those big blue eyes that exactly matched my own, and he smiled. Another day, I started to hand him to someone else, and he reached his chubby arms back to reclaim me. "You're his buddy," my husband told me. Such a simple thing but, oh, how it soothed my heart. And, every day, I felt it growing, that mysterious bond that I'd worried so much about. By the time a year had passed, I knew it for sure: This child was wound all through my heart by an unbreakable force.

And something else flowed quietly into my soul: I was a good mom. People said it to me, over and over, but finally I recognized it, too. I saw it in the way I put my baby's needs before my own, the way I cared for him with tenderness no matter how demanding he was, no matter how exhausted I became. Looking back, I even saw it in all my ridiculous efforts after he was born, the way I'd nearly killed myself trying to do everything right.

I understood then that you can give love that you never received, and occasionally you get a second chance at something that seemed lost forever. I could be what I had never known or dreamed. I could be a good mother.

~Lynn Juniper

# Six Days In

*Children reinvent your world for you.*
*~Susan Sarandon*

I'm trying to do up the buttons on this white knit snuggly for my six-day-old son, Lucas. The fire alarm in our building is blaring, his little face is scrunched up and red as he screams, and I cannot seem to pull the clear plastic button through the knit hole. My hubby, Kevin, is on the floor trying to coax our cats out from under our bed into their carriers. I finally get one button through and bite my lip to withhold my coming tears as I see there are seventeen more to go.

Lindsay, our midwife, gently touches my shoulder. "Do you want some help?" I stand back, hands shaking, and nod furiously without making eye contact. She scoops Lucas up and rocks him in this figure-eight motion, humming him quiet. I watch, stunned, as he gurgles away while she lays him back down and expertly buttons him up.

"Okay," she says firmly. "You get a bottle, formula and some diapers together in case this takes a while." I jump up, relieved to be told what to do and wish, not for the first time, that she would not be leaving after his checkup. I throw everything into our fancy diaper bag that won't zip up. Lindsay places Lucas into his stroller because I can't manage to bend with my fresh C-section scars. We all shove through the front door into the apartment hallway, and just as Kevin goes to lock the door, the fire alarm stops.

I want to fill the silence with my own screams. Does every single thing about having this baby have to be difficult? The colorful images I had of a home birth, nursing easily, dressing him in babyGap, and going for walks in our designer stroller have each been replaced with gritty black-and-white depictions of my failure. And any time I take a moment to think, it all washes over me. So, I keep going, keep trying to figure it out, to get something right.

As Kevin schleps our stuff back inside, Lindsay hands me Lucas. I sit back onto the couch and let him lie in the space between my breasts. I breathe in his scent — I feel like I've known it forever — and rub his back methodically. She is watching me, probably checking that we've bonded after I refused to see him on my hospital bed after the C-section. She needn't worry.

"So, how much sleep are you guys getting?" she broaches when Kevin joins us.

"Oh, you know how it is," he says. I kick him so he does not reveal that we are taking turns watching guard over Lucas because he won't sleep on his back. He'll only sleep on his tummy (risking SIDS) or on our chests.

When Kevin's parents arrive, the midwife demands that we ask them for help. I know she is right, but I hate having to ask. I manage to sputter, "Can you please watch him while we sleep?" And they are eager to do so.

I can't sleep, though. My mind races every time I lay down — back to being in labor and being hooked up to so many machines I could not move, by my "failure to progress" and resulting C-section. I hear Lucas cry outside my bedroom, and every inch of me wants to go to him, but I resist, mostly because I don't have the energy to make small talk. Eventually, I drift off and catch an hour and a half of sleep before they wake me.

He is hungry. But instead of feeding him, I go into the kitchen, slide the door shut (wishing there was a lock), and pull out the industrial-size breast pump we've rented. I meticulously dry each bottle and suction cup as I review the diagram in the manual again, take a deep breath, and start the process.

A month ago, I told my pro-breastfeeding friends that I would try, although formula was fine with me, too. Six days in, after nursing Lucas easily for two days, I'm now desperate for my real milk to come in. The nurse's voice from the hospital still rings in my mind. "Your baby is hungry, and you don't have any milk." I'm taking blessed thistle and fenugreek herbs like my life depends on it and pumping every three hours, praying each time for a few more drops.

When I am done, I go into the living room with a bottle full of formula topped with Mommy-milk and hand it over to Kevin's mom. Lucas is pecking at her, and she is excited to be able to help. I watch his little mouth chug the bottle, and his eyes fill with this drugged look of relief. I have to turn away.

I wait until they are gone before I allow myself to cry. I take Kevin's place in bed and finally let tears stream down my face. I know my hormones are inducing more than my fair share of sadness, but this knowing does not help. I am crying in a way that I never have before. Sobs reverberate throughout my body, hurting me from the inside out. After more than an hour, with Kevin trying everything from leaving me alone to hugging me to showing me Lucas' little toes, he gets worried and calls my mom to come over. I would not normally want to see her in this state, but I don't argue with him.

She starts to cry when she sees me bawling, reaches in her purse and pulls out tissues for both of us. I can barely talk but manage to hiccup, "I-thought-I-could-do-it-but-I-can't." She tells me she knows how hard it is, that I have been so strong, and that it will be okay. And maybe because she's my mom, I believe her. Or maybe it's because I know she knows—she's been through two C-sections, as revealed by the scars on her abdomen. Or maybe it's because I know I have no other choice. She holds me, and I cry and cry. Though I am drained, I feel renewed.

That night, I sleep four hours, the longest stretch of sleep I've had since the night I went into labor. At 3:00 a.m., I pump again, and a whole ounce is produced. During my shift of watching Lucas, I start writing about his birth and these first few days. I cannot stop. And in the morning, when I wake, my milk has come in. Kevin and I laugh in relief—our first laughter in days. When he pulls me into a hug, I feel my breasts are sure to burst.

We set up my nursing pillow on our rocking chair, and I scoop Lucas up into my arms. I open my robe and worry he will have forgotten how to latch on, but he hasn't. He drinks and drinks away, and his eyes fill with satisfaction. My eyes fill with tears, but the sadness is gone. As he drains my milk, I feel myself filling with something new—hope that we will get through this.

~Liesl Jurock

# Life Is Not Always Good in the Motherhood

*My mother had a great deal of trouble with me, but I think she enjoyed it.*
~Mark Twain

Today, I put my princess in a fleece onesie, stuck Pledge Grab-Its on her belly, sent her into my bedroom to collect dust bunnies and thought, "Isn't it about time for her to start pulling her weight anyway?" These kinds of thoughts run through my mind on any given day. I will not be winning Mother-of-the-Year anytime soon, but today was a good day to be a mommy. I am thankful there were no messes to clean up, boo-boos to mend, or tantrums to tune out. The reality is that my "I love being a mommy" days are pretty few and far between, and I often wonder, "Why do I feel like a bad mommy when I so much as hint that I am not enjoying every moment, or when I force my children to do things others deem ridiculous for one fleeting moment of laughter in an otherwise merciless day?"

And then it hit me. What many people consider a flaw in my design, I rank rather high on the short list of traits I love about myself. Some say I tend to over-share. I see it in raised eyebrows, looks of disdain, and judging smirks as I unabashedly relate that it took a full thirty seconds to discover the princess munching away on a bag of silica gel beads. Or that when my darling two-year-old angel told me he was going to do a magic trick and "disappear Sissy," he meant it literally, and it was probably no longer a great idea to leave him alone in a room with her for an extended period of time.

Sometimes, I feel as if an entire chapter was intentionally left out of my copy of *What to Expect When You're Expecting*. Missing was the probability that I would likely be made to feel "less than" if I did not enjoy every minute of motherhood. As much as I adore my babies, I have come to believe it is a fairly thankless job I have undertaken, at least in the early years. I exist to meet the needs of another human being and get very little in return. I am stretched to my limits, pushed to my breaking point, and then asked to give just a little more. It is difficult, but in ways I never imagined, and I am simply not afraid to admit it. What I have found truly ironic as I navigate through this journey to another planet is that the more "real" I am about my daily failures and unsavory parenting techniques, the more "me too" responses I receive. I believe people are drawn to imperfection, if for no other reason than they recognize their own weakness and find comfort in the weakness of others.

There is something beautiful in the reality that I do not have it all figured out, and I think that beauty is found in the words of a loving God who does. Romans 12:15 states, "Rejoice with those who rejoice, and weep with those who weep." I am called to relate to my sisters on the most fundamental level, stripped of pride and soul exposed. I am called to feel their pain, laugh alongside them, and comfort them in this daily battle we call motherhood.

Life is not always good in the motherhood, and so I have learned to laugh. I am forgiving of moms who do not constantly boast of the rewards of being a mother. I recognize that those rewards often do not surface until much later. I am not afraid to admit that I have dust bunnies. I temper stories of success and moments of joy with moments I care to forget. Chances are, when I am on my 375th cry of, "I swear, you are going to be the death of me," there is a good chance thousands of other mothers are mumbling the very same thing at that very same moment. What mommies do is no small feat. I soak up every fleeting moment of contentment, and share the little things that make me smile (babies do make the best Dustbusters) and the huge things that make me wish there was a vineyard in my backyard.

And if I intend to give myself any chance at all, I ask God daily to be my guide because I cannot do it without Him. And when I feel like the worst mommy ever, I give myself the grace He gives me and recognize that tomorrow is a new day and a new opportunity to do some spring cleaning. I would like to believe my Heavenly Father is actually pleased with my ability to laugh at myself on occasion and would venture to guess He, too, spends countless hours laughing at His children.

~Julie Sharp

# 35

# So This Is Love

*I saw pure love when my son looked at me, and I knew that I had to make a good life for the two of us...*
~Suzanne Somers

I became a mother entirely too young, which caused constant turmoil throughout my pregnancy. Many important people in my life turned their backs on me. The entire pregnancy was consumed by a crushing tension, so thick you could almost taste the bitterness. I dreaded the day I was to bring my baby into the world because I knew I was not prepared. I was not only not prepared, but I wasn't sure I wanted to be a mother. I didn't even like kids. But I knew I had to step up to the plate and take responsibility for the serious lapse of judgment I had made at only seventeen years old.

My pregnancy never felt real to me. Becoming a mother never felt real to me. I spent my pregnancy wondering when the maternal instincts would kick in—if they would ever kick in. I worked as hard as I could throughout the day, trying to prepare for my baby's arrival, and I spent my nights wondering if I was making a mistake.

July 18, 2005 was supposed to be a day like any other. After a long and complicated pregnancy, I went to my eight-month checkup expecting to go through the usual routine. I should have known otherwise because I had a heavy and uneasy feeling when I awoke that day. As my doctor's visit began, the nurse did the normal ultrasound, but something quickly became different. The nurse stood up and quietly said, "I will be right back." I became extremely nervous to the point I was shaking because she had never left the room before. As the doctor walked into the room with the nurse, my skin crawled with goose bumps as he took one look at the ultrasound monitor and said, "We need to get you to the hospital now!"

Luckily, the hospital was right across the parking lot, and I was able to walk there. But the thirty-foot walk across the parking lot was unlike any other. My heart was pounding so loudly in my ears that I could no longer hear the traffic zooming by. My legs truly felt like they were made of lead as I struggled to put one foot in front of the other. I noticed a pay phone to my right. Looking for any reason to stall, I said I needed to call my parents to tell them what was going on. As I stood there listening to the dial tone, I noticed a city bus pull up, and I wondered what would happen if I ran over and hopped on. But I knew I had to go into that hospital whether I liked it or not. As I stood in silence in the elevator, I knew my days of partying were over. I couldn't keep a goldfish alive. How was I going to keep a baby alive?

A few hours after my son was born, I was wheeled into the NICU to see him for the first time. As I stared at him through the glass of the incubator, I was numb. There were so many tubes and wires hooked up to him. I was suddenly filled with sadness, with empathy. No human being, especially one so young, should have to have tubes in his nose and needles in his head. As I stared down at his tiny body, the words my father had said to me the night he learned I was pregnant forcefully flashed through my mind, "What if he has problems? You can't take care of a special needs baby." I couldn't help but wonder if my father was right. Was my baby being punished for the mistakes I had made?

The first time I held my son, I suppose it should have been a joyous moment. I knew I was supposed to love him, but when I looked at him I saw and felt nothing. Would I ever love him? Was it something that could be acquired over time? How could you love a stranger?

When it came time for my hospital stay to be over, I learned that my son wouldn't be able to come home with me. I remember thinking, "Well, I can get some sleep." As they brought my son into my room so I could say goodbye, I held him and continued to stare in shock. What was I going to do with a baby?

As the minutes ticked on, the nurse told me it was time to take him back to the NICU. I looked at her and could not bring myself to hand my son over. My arms would not budge. Instantly, my heart became too heavy to bear, and a rush of warm tears exploded from the bottle that had been containing them for so long. I knew in that split second that I had suddenly found something I had been searching for my whole life. Through the tears I knew, this was love — pure, raw, and unconditional — and it hurt more than I could bear. I held onto his tiny body as tightly as I could. The nurse told me again and again, "It's time to take him back." But I couldn't bring myself to hand him over.

I looked to my mother for some guidance and saw something I had rarely seen before: She was crying, too. I didn't know if she was crying because her own child was in pain or because she knew what I was experiencing since she had had to leave a baby behind, too. Maybe it was a little bit of both, but at that moment some of the tension that had consumed our relationship over the past few months lifted, and it was a new start.

The nurse finally pried my son from my arms and took him back to the NICU. I struggled to pull myself together and find the strength to walk to my mother's truck. On the ride home, a light seemed to turn on in my head. I knew with 100 percent certainty why this baby had come into my life. He was there to save me from my own destruction, to save my life. I knew right then I was meant to be a mother. I was meant to be his mother. I was forever changed that day. He was no longer just a baby to me. He was Micheal. And he was my son.

~Alyssa Ast

# Motherhood: Not Quite a Stroll in the Park

*Mothers and daughters are closest, when daughters become mothers.*
~Author Unknown

As a young woman, I used to work at a pharmacy right in the middle of London's affluent neighbourhood of Holland Park. At the same time every morning, I would look out of the shop to see a particular mother out on a stroll with her pretty baby propped up cosily in what must have been the latest state-of-the-art pram. Sometimes, she would grace the pharmacy with her presence. On some days, she would glide in dressed in a very feminine, floaty dress. Other days, she would be smartly attired in a casual designer suit. Her hair was always immaculately coiffured. Invariably, she looked elegant, like a woman in full possession of her mental and emotional faculties. She would look around the shop and peruse the shelves for the latest beauty products. She looked like she did not have a care in the world. Most impressively, she manoeuvred the baby and the pram around effortlessly, as though they were merely fashion accessories.

Fast forward four years later, in a different continent altogether. In that reality, I have become a mother myself. I could not have been a more stark contrast to that calm and collected Holland Park mom who I imagined must have had a whole army of nannies and other support staff to manage her baby, household and wardrobe for her. For a start, I would never be dressed in anything other than a crease-proof T-shirt and the most comfortable pair of jeans. I dressed for the sole purpose of ensuring that the main source of nourishment for my baby — my breasts — could be easily accessed. The accompanying accessories to my outfits were often some stain or lingering smell of something the baby had regurgitated. My hair would always be carelessly pinned back in no particular fashion, strictly to keep loose strands from getting into my baby's face as I bent down to kiss him for the thousandth time.

I could not have loved my precious newborn more, and I wanted to spend all my waking and sleeping hours with him by my side. In those early days when I walked around bleary-eyed and dishevelled from surviving on perhaps three or four hours of sleep each night, I cared about nothing but the wellbeing of my baby. When I wasn't cradling, changing, feeding or burping him, I would be poring over parenting books and magazines in a frenzied search for the answers to questions that were crowding my already addled head. Why did my baby constantly need to be breastfed with hardly any respite between each feed? Was it natural for every single feed to shoot straight out of the other end? What if his cognitive or physical development did not quite meet the milestone markers clearly laid out in parenting books? I had also become a constant fixture in the paediatrician's office, furnishing soiled diapers with faeces of questionable colour or consistency for him to examine and tirelessly besieging him with one query after another about all manner of things related to the baby and parenting. Bless that lovely man, for he never once judged me or let on that he felt I was making a beeline for the funny farm.

Yet whilst I was completely immersed in the world of motherhood, I could feel a rift widening between my husband and me. Soon after the birth of our baby, he started being given greater responsibilities at work. This required him to travel out of the country quite frequently. If he were to come home at night, I would already be deep in slumberland, quite often with the baby still in my arms. At times,

I would just pretend to be asleep. I had begun to develop a slight resentment for how his life had not changed in the least after the baby. The increasingly fewer conversations we had would inevitably end up with me launching into a tirade about how exhausted I was and how yet another one of his relatives had visited. The trouble with those visitors is they could never resist dishing out unsolicited advice about parenting, which predictably questioned the way I was caring for my baby. They were also fond of making comparisons between my little angel and so-and-so's child of a similar age. In any case, their visits were never something I looked forward to.

Then one day whilst on the phone with my mother, I broke down in hysterics and told her how I often felt frustrated about not coping as a mother. My mother listened very attentively throughout and then spoke, "It's only natural to be experiencing all these feelings that you are having right now. I'm still discovering new things about motherhood at my age. I now have to learn to be a mother to someone who has become a mother herself." I just had to chuckle at that. She then added, "I know how busy the baby keeps you, but you must make the time to enjoy the things that you did before the baby came along. And you must make the effort to keep the spark in your marriage alive."

I kept thinking about what my mother had said. A couple of days later, my old boss rang me and asked if I would be interested in helping out with some mini projects that she was working on. I did not hesitate to call my mom straightaway and ask if she could babysit for a couple of days a week. In the end, it was not just those couple of days that I would turn up at my mom's.

My mom had insisted that I keep a set of baby clothes, a pack of diapers, toiletries, feeding bowls and a sterilizer at her house. That way, I could just strap my baby in the car seat straight after breakfast and literally deposit him at her doorstep whenever I was running late for the classes I had agreed to teach. My mom was truly a godsend. When my baby showed little interest in eating his pureed vegetables, my mom taught me that by sweetening them with a little fruit puree, we could make him eat every last drop. When my baby started babbling, my mom sang songs and read wonderful books to him to boost his speech development. My mom bought him his very first Thomas the Tank Engine toy, which grew into a large collection of trains, tracks and books. It was so apparent that Grandma and baby delighted and flourished in the company of one another. Although the travelling to and fro my mom's was a little tiring, we were all infinitely happier.

With Mom ever willing to volunteer her babysitting services, I managed to find the time for the occasional hair treatment, pampering massages and, most importantly, the romantic nights out my husband and I had missed and sorely needed. I never quite got my act together enough to dress and carry myself with the admirable composure of the Holland Park mom I had encountered in my youth. But there were actually days when I caught myself in the mirror and smiled at what I saw. I realized that motherhood is seldom a stroll in the park. It is not something you gain mastery of overnight. However, if you can accept that and reach out to ask a trusted person for help along the way, it makes motherhood so much more manageable and enjoyable. Getting my mother involved in the caring of my firstborn was the best thing I ever did for myself, my baby and my marriage.

By the way, my husband has become an incredibly supportive and amazing father since those early days of parenthood. We now have two kids, and they both put him on a pedestal where he rightly belongs. My mother continues to be the best grandmother any child could ever ask for.

~Maizura Abas

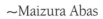

# An Unexpected Blessing

*Babies are always more trouble than you thought—and more wonderful.*
*~Charles Osgood*

The lump in my throat almost choked me as I watched a faint plus sign appear on the home pregnancy test. In nearly fourteen years of marriage, my husband Gil and I had never planned to have children. And after losing my job just a couple of weeks earlier, I felt less prepared than ever.

As a little girl, I had dreamed of one day getting married. But I had never dreamed of having children. The truth was I didn't enjoy children all that much. They were fun to play with for a little while, but I much preferred giving them back to their parents! I had seen how much my parents sacrificed for me, and as selfish as it sounds, I had no interest in that kind of sacrifice. I liked my life just the way it was.

But I was pregnant, and as the months progressed, I realized why women are pregnant for nine months. I was sure it would take that long to get used to the idea of becoming a parent! Still, though I felt more prepared, I feared that I wouldn't be a good mom.

Gil continually encouraged me. Once we realized we were the oldest couple in our birthing class, we felt our life experience might give us a parenting advantage. As the midwife described the process of labor and delivery, she mentioned that all the pain and hard work would be worth it when I held my little one for the first time. I wasn't so sure.

At the pregnancy's halfway point, we had an ultrasound and discovered we were expecting a boy. A whole new set of fears rushed in. I didn't know anything about boys! How would I relate to a son? How would I meet his needs?

When Jedidiah was born, we began our parenting journey in earnest. I had seen red and wrinkly newborns who were not as cute as their parents claimed. But within the first week, I saw that Jed was incredibly handsome. I asked Gil if he agreed that our son was cute, and he said, "Of course. All babies are. It's their defense mechanism." Indeed, Jed's tiny features, downy hair, and adorable cooing quickly melted my heart in spite of new-parent exhaustion and a huge learning curve.

Almost as soon as I gave birth, the baby blues engulfed me. My concerns about my ability to be a good parent, coupled with fatigue, often overwhelmed me emotionally. And this frequently happened without warning. One night when Gil innocently asked how many diapers we had left, I crumpled into sobs. When the midwife called to check up on me, she assured me that my emotional roller coaster was entirely normal and would even out soon.

It did. And within days, Jed developed colic. My heart broke as I watched my tiny, helpless son wail and writhe in pain, even after I had done everything I knew to help him. Well-meaning friends and family bombarded us with advice, everything from old wives' tales to proven medical help. Some of the advice seemed to put our parenting skills into question. Maybe my diet was affecting my milk and giving Jed gas. Or maybe we were simply spoiling our son by holding him too much.

As we learned what worked—and what didn't—and got to know Jed better, we became more confident as parents. With the help of a homeopathic colic elixir, frequent swaddling, and other remedies, Jed's colic eventually subsided, and he continued to develop normally.

Then one day as Jed was nursing and looking into my eyes, I

realized that I was a good mom. I know this realization will be followed by many opportunities to question myself in the years to come. But I also know that I love my son. And I strive to do what is best for him by researching expert opinions, asking those who have been through it before, and following my intuition.

I also realize that I am a better person because of Jed. The self-sacrifice I had wanted to avoid now comes naturally. And joyfully. And every time I change a particularly messy diaper, am kept awake throughout the night, or eat a cold meal because I need to feed Jed first, I love him more. His smiles and giggles and baby burbles continually encourage me.

Just the other evening as I prepared for bed, I thought back over all I had accomplished that day. The hours had been spent entirely at home and were full of dirty diapers, feedings, spit-up, laundry, and frequently interrupted housework. I cannot remember another time in my life when I have completed a day feeling so fulfilled.

I was meant to be a mom.

~Aimee J. Lenger

# I'm Pregnant

*The guys who fear becoming fathers don't understand that fathering is not something perfect men do, but something that perfects the man. The end product of child raising is not the child but the parent.*
~Frank Pittman, Man Enough

Those words, first uttered to me in November 2008, were ones I thought I'd never hear in this lifetime.

On the verge of turning forty, I was what's called a "late bloomer," that is, waiting until I almost reached middle age to get married and settle down. I had just turned thirty-seven and my wife was going on thirty-four when we tied the knot. Neither of us had ever married before or had children.

Margie was enthusiastic about becoming a mother while I, on the other hand, was more than a little trepidatious about the whole business. One reason I had shied away from the whole marriage concept was because I valued my freedom and the ability to take off and do whatever I wanted, whenever I wanted. It was one reason why I chose to become a radio announcer, with its often vagabond-esque lifestyle.

As I got older, I came to realize that I wasn't getting any younger, and that spending my sunset years alone and in old-age-related failing health was not the way I saw my future, I decided that the time was right for me to marry. I didn't think too much about bringing children into the mix.

After a couple of years of marriage, Margie finally pressed the issue and wanted to know why I wouldn't talk about it. I hadn't ignored the issue, but more or less tap-danced around it. I liked the glamour of being a "power couple," into our careers and still enjoying our freedom. But I knew that in most marriages, family is part of the deal, and I'd never deny my wife what she wanted more than anything in this world.

I wanted it, too. What I didn't want to go through was the ritual of middle-of-the-night feedings, frequent diaper changes, toilet training, things like that. I don't do well with little ones as a rule; I do better with teens. They can take care of themselves and don't need as much supervision.

Finally, Margie took matters into her own hands and announced that she wanted us to start trying to have a child. She knew I was scared, but assured me that she had no doubts whatsoever that I would be a good father. A friend of mine from high school, who had raised two daughters of her own, knew my fears and put it in perspective for me very well: "It's a world you never knew you wanted."

One month after we officially "started" trying, Margie became pregnant. The night she made the announcement, I had noticed that she was a little emotionally distant. Being a sensitive husband, I asked her if she was all right. Then came those words.

"I'm pregnant," Margie said. I asked if she was sure. She had taken two home pregnancy tests that came back positive. But she said that she had made an appointment with her OB-GYN to make sure, and that she wanted me to come with her. I assured her I would.

Fear was replaced with relief. Me? A dad? Who'd have thunk it?

The doctor visits became more frequent, and when we had the first ultrasound done, they told us they were going to do a chromosome test to make sure that the child didn't have Down syndrome. It was due to something they called AMA — Advanced Maternal Age. Having just turned thirty-six, Margie fell into this category. They explained all the risks involved with having a baby at this age.

We went out to the car, and I watched Margie slowly dissolve into tears once we got inside her Jeep. "I'm scared," she said. I immediately took her into my arms and assured her that we were going to be fine. I would be by her side no matter what, and God wouldn't give us more than we could handle. It was in His hands. We prayed for Him to give us a healthy child, but we would accept whatever He gave us.

I attended Lamaze classes with Margie and did the breathing exercises with her. I rubbed her back and her feet, and did what I could to make her pregnancy as trouble-free as possible. She was fortunate not to have morning sickness, and as the summer months came, it was one of the mildest that western Pennsylvania had seen in years, so she wasn't totally uncomfortable. The only real craving she had was orange soda, which I was more than happy to supply.

Then came the name. We both had wanted a daughter, and the second ultrasound confirmed what the first one said: We would have a little girl. I had my own ideas for names after we both decided that our child would not be named after any relatives or friends. Margie came to me with one suggestion: Savannah. Savannah, Georgia was a city that Margie had taken me to shortly after I proposed to her on the beaches of Hilton Head Island, South Carolina. I fell in love with the place, and every trip we had taken to Hilton Head since then has included a trip to Savannah, about a half-hour away. When Margie offered up her suggestion, it was settled. No other name would do.

Our little daughter, Savannah Rose, weighed in at nine pounds, fourteen ounces, and she was an impressive twenty-three inches long. It was a difficult delivery. At one point, Margie was bleeding profusely and on the verge of losing consciousness, but everyone pulled through just fine in the end. Self included.

The first week we had Savannah home was especially brutal, but the first three months that my best friend had told me were the most difficult seemed to fly by faster than I ever imagined. We were blessed with a very healthy and happy little girl, with a full head of jet-black hair who continues to grow like a weed. It is a big relief for both of us.

Margie's dad told me "they'll teach you" once we learned Margie was pregnant. Now I know what he meant. I give Margie and Savannah all the credit for making me who I am today. I couldn't be a good dad without the support of a great mom like Margie.

My friend was right. It is a world I never knew I wanted—but I can't imagine how I ever lived without it.

~Ken Hoculock

## Chapter 6

# New Moms

## Words of Wisdom

*Nobody can give you wiser advice than yourself.*

*~Cicero*

# Gestation Citations

*The best advice is this: Don't take advice and don't give advice.*
~Author Unknown

Most pregnant women have met them, perhaps even been stopped by them. And a ticket? Well, that's not out of the question either. Anything is possible when you encounter the pregnancy police.

I first met these constables of conception when I announced my pregnancy to co-workers. People who had barely muttered "good morning" in the past were suddenly concerned about whether I had signed up for a short-term disability policy or if I had a flexible spending account for the baby's medical care. I assured them that I had everything under control. In reality, I had just gotten used to the idea that a baby was actually inside me. Though they were well-meaning, the pregnancy police managed to make me feel more inadequate than I ever imagined.

As my baby grew, so did the list of suggestions from the pregnancy patrol. I was issued a warning for coffee drinking in the break room at work. "You really should switch to decaf," a concerned citizen offered. "Caffeine is not good for the baby. And remember, that brownie contains caffeine, too." I thanked her for the reminder and went on with my business.

A few weeks later, I came down with a terrible sinus infection and stayed out of work for two days. When I returned, I was swiftly subpoenaed to my department's meeting area. A panel of investigators wanted to know what was wrong. "Have you had a fever?" they asked. "How high was it? You know you can only take Tylenol, don't you?" I did know. But I thanked them for their concern anyway and returned to my desk.

Tired, nauseous, and congested, I did my best to fly beneath the radar of the pregnancy police. I walked quickly in the hallways, hid behind the piles of work on my desk, and avoided the break room. But they always discovered me, even if to simply point out that I was "starting to show" and would soon need to shop for maternity clothes. I really appreciated their observations, especially the ones about my increasing chest size.

My co-workers weren't the only undercover officers I ran into. Oh, no, the pregnancy police often were plain-clothed neighbors, churchgoers, and friends. They could spot a pregnancy "glow" from across town, and they were eager to pat a protruding belly in the cereal aisle of the grocery store.

I sometimes met up with them at 7-Eleven's Slurpee counter. "Don't have too many of these now. You don't want to end up with gestational diabetes." No, I sure didn't. I quickly reached for a smaller cup and went to the cashier to pay.

The pregnancy police weren't trying to scare me; they were merely providing a public service. After all, it was their duty to warn me about the harmful effects of caffeine, the risks of gestational diabetes, and off-limits medications.

They didn't mean to annoy me when they rattled off their lists of "you shoulds." ("You should consider breastfeeding." "You should start looking for a pediatrician." "You should sign up for a birthing class.")

"How far along are you? Twenty weeks? You should be feeling some movement by now." But I hadn't, and their suppositions were making me even more nervous.

Recently, I met two girlfriends for lunch. We hadn't seen each other in ages. "You're really five months?" Lucy questioned. "Good grief! You hardly even look pregnant!" I knew she meant well, but her remark made me wonder if my baby was developing properly. Suddenly, I couldn't wait for my next obstetric appointment.

For the majority of our meal, my friends' badges remained hidden. We caught up on the statuses of high school classmates, gossiped about people in town, and laughed over stories from our teenage years.

But every once in a while, I would catch a knowing look in response to something I said about my pregnancy or plans for motherhood. Then, I stopped talking and smiled, realizing I was under surveillance. They asked me how many children I planned to have. "Three," I responded, confidently. I saw Lucy wink at Gretchen across the table. It was a gesture that said, "Let's wait and see how she feels after this first one."

Although sometimes annoying and occasionally intrusive, these comments come from people who truly care. My co-workers, friends, and neighbors just wish to share their experiences and impart their wisdom.

These women have knowledge that comes only from having conceived, delivered, and raised their own babies. I am a child-rearing novice and thus grateful for their advice, warnings, and suggestions. After all, it takes a village to raise a child, perhaps even to bring one to full term. And every village needs a police force.

~Melissa Face

# A Pot of Soup

*Soup puts the heart at ease, calms down the violence of hunger, eliminates the tension of the day, and awakens and refines the appetite.*
*~Auguste Escoffier*

There I was, sitting in a shabby chair in a shabby apartment on a shabby street in a shabby part of town. The apartment was the upstairs of a shabby... all right, rundown house located across the street from an extremely odorous dairy. "Shabby" is the most accurate word that comes to mind when I think back to that time and place, and it also describes my state of mind.

The year was 1963. I was a brand new mother, having given birth to my first precious child only a few days earlier. The birth was difficult, including forty hours of labor and the use of forceps. Cesareans were rare back then, and paternity leaves were nonexistent. Thank goodness changes have been made in that regard, and fathers now share equally (well, almost) in the joys and terrors of this grand adventure.

On this particular day, my husband was at work and would leave for one of his frequent business trips the next day. I had no family nearby, and since we were new to the area, we'd had little chance to make friends. As I sat there holding my very cranky baby, I felt so sad and exhausted. The stirrings of hopelessness began to creep into my soul. Postpartum depression was not a household word then. I looked around the tiny room, then at my beautiful little daughter, and wondered how on earth I would be able to care for her, be a good mother and wife or even cook dinner later that evening.

When a knock sounded at my door a few minutes later, I was just preparing for a good cry, but managed to stifle the tears in order to answer the door. There stood a smiling young woman close to my own age, carrying a gigantic kettle. She stepped inside, placed the kettle on my kitchen table, and then introduced herself. She lived in another shabby apartment in another shabby house nearby, and somehow had heard that a new mom lived here. She, too, had a new baby, just a few weeks ago, and knew that I would undoubtedly be too tired to cook. So, she brought me a big pot of homemade soup.

I am convinced that her kindness saved my sanity that day. The soup lasted for many days, and it tasted like caviar, steak and crème brûlée to me. Our friendship lasted for years until we both moved away and, sadly, lost track of each other.

My baby girl grew up to be a brilliant and fabulous young woman, earning two master's degrees, an MBA, and a PhD, and then to marry and have four beautiful children of her own. She accomplished all of this with a severe hearing loss, and eventually had two successful cochlear implants.

Despite all of that, I haven't forgotten my early distress, and the wonderful gift of the heart given to me at my lowest time, by my caring neighbor. I have continued the tradition and have given a pot of soup to many new mothers among my acquaintance along the way.

Wherever you are, my lovely friend of long ago, thank you!

~Catherine Ring Saliba

# Expert Advice

*Seek advice but use your own common sense.*
*~Yiddish Proverb*

Shortly after my wedding, and long before my first child was even a twinkle in my eye, well-meaning friends and relatives began doling out parenting advice: "You don't want to wait too long before getting started on your family. You never know how long it will take," I heard from the relatives. From my younger friends, "Don't be in a rush to have kids" was the constant refrain. No wonder I was confused!

My husband and I, reasonably enough, took the middle ground, delaying our decision to have children for a few years. But three years into our marriage, even though we were still in grad school, I knew I was ready to start our family. Mom's not-so-subtle hints that she was ready for grandchildren didn't hurt either. So we were filled with great joy when, later that year, my physician confirmed my first pregnancy.

But if I thought that was the end of the unsolicited advice, I couldn't have been more wrong.

"What are you going to name the baby?" everyone wanted to know.

"Jeffrey if it's a boy, and Emily if it's a girl," was my stock answer. At first, anyway.

"Jeffrey?" a friend asked dubiously. "That name's so common.

Why not Brandon or Justin? And Emily?" she forged on. "Too old-fashioned!"

"But I like the names," I floundered, "and, believe me, it was no mean feat to find two names my husband and I actually agreed on."

"What about Michaela?" she continued, as if I hadn't spoken. I sighed. Everyone it seemed, from my neighbors to my mother, had their own opinions on what the baby should be called.

I finally resorted to smiling mysteriously when people asked. "We haven't decided yet," I'd say, "but we'll let you know when we do." After that, we kept our names strictly under wraps.

Finally, the early October day came when, bending to tie up the irises, I felt the unmistakable twinges of... well, of what I wasn't quite sure. Were these true labor pains or more Braxton-Hicks contractions? I called Mom.

"What did you say contractions felt like again?" I asked her.

Her voice rose an octave. "Are you in labor, honey?"

"I don't know, Dr. Mom," I joked. "I'm asking you."

Within three minutes, Mom ascertained that I was in labor. Never mind that she was 600 miles away at the time. It never occurred to me to doubt her. After all, wasn't my mom, the mother of five children, the expert on all things child-related? It was time to call my midwife.

"Call me again when the contractions are just a few minutes apart," Rhonda counseled. "Remember, if this is real labor, contractions should get longer, stronger, and closer together."

"Longer, stronger, and closer together. Longer, stronger and closer together," I mumbled to myself like a mantra. It was 4:00 a.m. when we finally headed to the hospital. Hours later, a perfectly formed and very vocal Jeffrey Daniel was placed in my arms. To say that he was not a happy camper is an understatement. Before the morning had passed, there wasn't a single nurse on the ward who hadn't commented on the capacity of his lungs.

But, finally, after a few awkward attempts at nursing, he settled down and nursed as if he had been doing it all his life. I had a bit more difficulty with the process. Nobody had warned me that a toothless, seven-pound baby could latch on with all the ferocity of a baby barracuda. In fact, nobody had warned me about a lot of things, and I found there was no substitute for learning on the job. And learn I did. With a copy of Dr. Spock's *Baby and Child Care* on my nightstand, and my pediatrician's and mother's phone numbers in my speed dial, help was always at my fingertips.

The next three months were a whirlwind of activity, with long days and even longer nights. "Sleep when he sleeps," my mom advised. This turned out to be some of the best advice I ever got. Jeffrey apparently hadn't heard the news that the average newborn sleeps upwards of twelve hours a day.

There were many other little tidbits of advice handed down from friends, wise aunts and, yes, especially Mom. "Don't get started with a binkie; he'll become dependent on it to sleep" (didn't follow); "Let him cry it out at night; you need your sleep" (didn't have the heart to); "Keep the house noisy so he doesn't need it quiet to sleep" (I tried, but really, how noisy can two sleep-deprived adults be?); "Put him on a nursing schedule, or he'll run you ragged" (didn't); and, "Let him nurse on demand" (oh, boy, did I!).

Yes, there was always helpful and not so helpful advice to sort out, but life was lively, our little one was thriving, and I felt a glow of pride every time the pediatrician weighed our son and the ounces and pounds crept up. As I sat half-asleep in the wee hours of the morning, rocking and nursing my baby, all the tension would go out of me, and I felt consumed with love for this tiny being who gazed at me so trustingly.

As we all got more sleep, our lives settled down, but my biggest decision still loomed—one I had been putting off for a long time. In order to finish up my dissertation, I would have to arrange for some kind of part-time childcare for Jeffrey. At the rate I was going, I figured he'd be about twenty-one or so before I finished unless I spent more hours a day on my research. And here the expert advice flew fast and furious.

There was no consensus. "Finish up school and establish your career first. He'll be fine in childcare," those who had done so themselves told me. And from the stay-at-home moms: "There's time enough to go back to work later. Stay home with him now. You won't be sorry."

I went back and forth, trying to reason things out. If the experts couldn't agree on what was best for me and my son, what hope had I, a relatively new mom, of figuring it out? I continued to collect opinions and tried my best to put off the day I would have to make a definite decision.

One day when Jeffrey was about ten months old, we were out in the yard when something caught his eye, and he took one… two… three faltering steps, his very first, before collapsing into my arms with a smile of triumph on his face. As I held him, I knew in that instant that my decision had been made—my career would have to wait. I would be a stay-at-home mom for now. And suddenly I realized something else, too. After countless feedings, nighttime wakings, and long days together with my baby, it was no longer necessary to consult the experts every time I needed to make a parenting decision—I had become the expert!

~Cara Holman

# The New Silence

*There are times when silence has the loudest voice.*
~Leroy Browlow

Before my sons were born, the most common piece of advice I received was to enjoy the quiet time I had. Once the baby was born, I was never going to get that time again. Unlike many of the other things that I was told, these words were right.

My first son was the quiet baby. He rarely cried, but that may have been from being constantly held by either me or my husband. When my second son was born, though, he was proud to declare to the entire world when he was in need of something. From morning until night, which was quickly becoming a blur to me, he would cry. It got to the point where I could no longer hear myself think, and sometimes I would wake from sleep believing that I was hearing him cry. I was running on automatic. My friends would laugh when I told them that if someone drew my blood, they would find it mysteriously replaced by coffee.

The worst part was that when he would cry, it would make his older brother cry, too. This would make me fuss with my husband to help me, but I had to raise my voice to an almost shouting level for him to be able to hear me over the crying. I am surprised the neighbors did not think we were fighting with each other every day.

Just when I thought I couldn't handle any more, my sons and my husband came down with a cold, which caused them to take some medicine that put them to sleep. I placed the baby down in his crib and slowly backed out of the room. Finally, I had the alone time I deserved. I drew myself a warm bath, which I had not had since he was born, and relaxed. After thirty minutes, I got up and went into the living room to read the book I had wanted to read for the past few months. But even though no one else was awake, I wasn't able to concentrate on my book for some reason.

I placed the book down on the couch and walked over to my baby's crib. He was sleeping with his mouth slightly open. I smiled and walked out of the room, hoping not to wake him, and returned to my book. The words were not making sense to me. I was too distracted to read. I flipped through a few of the remaining pages and closed the book. I looked around the room. There were toys on the ground, plates in the sink, and clothes to be put into the washing machine. There were plenty of things I could do. It just didn't seem right. There was something wrong.

I turned on the television. Maybe some noise would help me to get back on track. I found the television show to be annoying. I didn't want to watch it. I turned it off and continued to sit on the couch and think. Something was out of place. Then it hit me. There was no noise in my house. There was no crying, laughing or yelling at each other. There was just silence.

I went to every room and checked on the patients. They were all asleep. I peered down at my younger son asleep in his crib. Then I did the one thing I knew I should not do — I poked him. Not a hard poke — just enough to wake him up. He stirred for a moment before returning to his slumber state. I ran my finger along his soft cheek, trying to nudge him awake. The same response. So I poked him again. It wasn't until the fourth or fifth poke that he started to really move around and open his eyes. Then I heard the most wonderful sound in the world — his cry.

"There, there. It's okay. Mommy's here," I told him as I picked him up. He immediately stopped crying and returned to sleep. This time, I walked with him back into the living room and sat with him against me. Even though I could barely hear it, his breathing was enough noise for me.

People were right when they said that the time I had alone when I was pregnant was never going to happen again. But what they didn't realize is that I wouldn't want it any other way.

~Danielle Kazemi

# 43

# The Motherhood Marathon

*Birth is not only about making babies. Birth is about making mothers...
strong, competent, capable mothers who trust themselves
and know their inner strength.*
~Barbara Katz Rothman

My first child arrived ten months and three days after my wedding—not what I had expected.

I was thirty-one when I married; my husband was thirty-six. We'd talked about having a child in the second year of our marriage. However, we took no measures to prevent conception, so I shouldn't have been surprised when the doctor confirmed my pregnancy just two months after I said, "I do." And I wasn't surprised. I was numb.

I believe that God orchestrates all aspects of our lives. Therefore I embraced my unplanned pregnancy with trembling confidence that God knew what He was doing. But as my belly grew, my apprehension about becoming a mother also grew.

I wasn't unfamiliar with babies. I'd cared for all six of my nieces and nephews at various times during their infancy. I was also a teacher by profession, but I had never taught children below the sixth grade. Entertaining and educating children who could talk and reason with me was enjoyable. But what, I wondered, do you do with a baby all day every day? How will I know what my baby wants? How will I communicate with him?

Well-meaning friends assured me that caring for a baby was simple.

"You're the mother," one said. "You'll know. It's instinctive."

"Feed it, change it, love it," advised another. "That's all there is to it."

I read books about motherhood. I prayed about motherhood. I still dreaded motherhood. And then, fifteen days before the due date, my water broke. Within a few short hours, I was holding a seven-pound baby boy in my arms. We hadn't even bought a car seat yet because I had assumed first babies were always late. I thought I had plenty of time to get ready—my first motherhood mistake.

Nothing prepares a woman for the 24/7 motherhood marathon. No book. No well-meaning advice. No online chat room. Nothing. My mother came to help out for the first two weeks; after that, my husband and I were on our own. My sister, the nearest relative on either side, lived an hour away, worked full-time, and had three teenagers. Therefore, we jogged out onto the parenthood track alone.

So how did we survive? First, my husband took our son from my hands every afternoon when he arrived home from his teaching job. They relaxed on the couch or rode around on the tractor in the backyard while I prepared dinner. Chopping vegetables and washing dishes became a refuge of silence and sanity in my day.

My son didn't sleep through the night until he was thirteen months old, but he was a good napper. During his morning nap, I sweated to the oldies with a Richard Simmons exercise video. During his afternoon nap, I lay on the couch reading my Bible and then a book. Me time. Not one moment of his naptime was ever invested in cleaning or other chores.

On Friday mornings, I met with four other mothers from my church at alternating houses. Those laughter-laced play dates pushed us through our children's infancy and toddlerhood. Eventually, I discovered that a new neighbor had a son seven months younger than my son. We swapped stories and sipped coffee every Monday morning. Forging friendships with other mothers of young children provided encouragement and camaraderie. Their support prevented me from thinking that I was the only one who thought she was a terrible mother.

By nature, I'm a self-motivated and solitary worker. But I learned quickly that motherhood is not a game of Solitaire. Every mother needs a break; therefore, every mother needs both a flesh-and-blood support system and a spiritual support system. I had both.

I'll be the first to admit that Jeff's infancy and toddler years made me feel like I'd been shoved into a psychological washing machine—soaked, spun, and drained. Because I nursed him for ten months, I stumbled through nights of interrupted sleep and days of no caffeine with what seemed like perpetual jetlag. I also missed the intellectual stimulation of being in a classroom and interacting with students who communicated with words instead of smiles and tears. Sometimes I laid my wailing son in his crib, staring at him in a sleep-deprived daze and wondering how I would ever make it to 4:00 when my husband came home.

But, by God's grace, I did make it around the first lap of the motherhood track during Jeff's infancy. I trudged on through his toddler years and his sister's infancy. The laps became less strenuous for me as the elementary and middle school years passed. The high school laps have had some staggering inclines and torturous descents, but neither my husband nor I have dropped out of the parenthood race, even when taking the next breath seemed impossible.

I'm a grateful mom—thankful for my husband, my friends, and my God. These faithful companions have picked me up when I have fallen, laughed and cried with me, and shoved me back onto the track when I wanted to sit on the sidelines and call it quits.

Releasing my children into adulthood isn't the end of the motherhood marathon. It's just different terrain that requires different equipment. Sometimes I still want to drop out of the race. But my running buddies urge me to continue. Daily, I grab a bottle of perspective (prayer) and take a few bites of my spiritual energy bar (my Bible). Often, I reach for the hand of a supportive companion. And we all keep running.

~Denise K. Loock

# The Great Name Debate

*What's in a name? That which we call a rose*
*By any other name would smell as sweet.*
~William Shakespeare, Romeo and Juliet

"You're depriving me of my right," my mom whined.

"Since when is a grandmother entitled to name her grandchild?" I shot back in a tense whisper, hoping my bathroom stall mates wouldn't overhear. I'd waddled into the office restroom with my cell phone since I was making my tenth trip before noon, and because my mother was determined to continue the conversation.

We'd been volleying the topic of baby appellations back and forth for two trimesters of the pregnancy—my first—and I was growing tired of her flood of suggestions and persistent questions.

"Did Grandma name me?" I needled, knowing there's no way my strong-willed mother would've allowed it. Rather than concede the point, she grunted, then continued her campaign.

Not long after conceiving, my husband, Jay, and I talked to several more experienced friends about the moniker minefield. The universal advice was to keep secret the running list of contenders, so we made a pact to do just that. When people inquired, we'd simply smile and say, "We're working on it."

Before we learned the baby's sex, when my mother was convinced it was a girl, she'd heap her favorites on us. "How about Patricia?" (Her name—this one came up repeatedly.) "Or Elizabeth? Katherine?" Once she learned a grandson was on the way, she reluctantly shifted gears. "An old boyfriend used to call me Patrick... What about James? Seth? That's my friend's husband's brother." She was maniacal, but not alone.

Jay's mother, who'd always relied on more subtle methods of persuasion, called one day to report she'd had a vision. A red fox had run across her yard, and she regarded the incident as extraordinary because, for some forgotten reason, such animals reminded her of her father. "I interpret it as Granville giving the baby his blessing," she said with great emphasis.

My Mona Lisa act only lasted a few months. When Jay's mom asked about candidates over brunch one Sunday, I got caught up in the good cheer of the moment and couldn't deny her. "Maybe Roman? We felt his first kick in Rome," I explained gleefully. She made a sound resembling air escaping from a tire and said, "That sounds like a celebrity's baby." At the meal's end, I left deflated.

Next, I proceeded to make the same mistake with my mother. In a weak moment, after surviving what felt like my fourth or fifth round of the Inquisition, I buckled, rattling off some of the less-loved appellations. "Maybe Foster or Sawyer? I like Campbell, too." Her response: first silence, then a critical and suspicious, "Those are family names." I pointed out that they weren't, since no one in either family had them, but realized we were getting more to the issue. Translation: "Who wins—us or them?"

The tricky part is that Jay and I represent a mixed cultural bag. Between the two of us we've melded Pakistani, WASP, Irish and Italian heritages. We love the idea of honoring our family with a selection that echoes previous generations, but which family to honor? With patriarchs Mahmud (his father) and Ashby (mine), there's really no middle-of-the-road compromise.

I'm also cognizant of the impression that names make. I like mine, but there is a bit of a disconnect between me and it. My freshman year roommate in college, upon meeting me for the first time, breathed an audible sigh of relief and exclaimed, "Victoria Ashby Grantham! I was sure you'd be a blonde in head-to-toe Laura Ashley, lobbying for high tea." Instead, she got a mouthy half-Italian, sporting ripped jeans, curly hair and olive skin. Reflecting on that, I told both mothers, "Maybe we have to meet him first." For once, they rendered identical verdicts: "Totally unnecessary."

I think about how my parents named me. I'm my Uncle Victor's namesake. He was a much-loved relative who acted as a surrogate father to my mother. Taking a very different approach, Jay's parents dreamt up Jaiman. They liked the sound, and it struck them as a cultural compromise. Though the two methods are dramatically different, I see how they both have merit.

When my son threatened to arrive ten weeks early, we scrambled to get the essentials (diapers, a car seat, a going-home outfit) in case he successfully escaped my womb. (Thankfully, he did not.) At that moment we were forced to put things in perspective. He would come into the world on his own terms, and his name, no matter how other people felt about it, would be right because it would be something he made his mark on — not the other way around.

After much discussion, we named our baby Graham Wyatt Bangash. Graham is a nod to Grantham (my last name) and to Granville (Jay's grandfather), and Wyatt, one of the hundreds of names my mother suggested, because we love the strong, all-American sound of it.

~Victoria Grantham

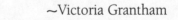

# In Like a Lion, Out Like a Lamb

*No animal is so inexhaustible as an excited infant.*
*~Amy Leslie*

I tried to comfort my two-week-old babe, but he wouldn't be comforted. I held him over my shoulder. He cried. I stretched him over my lap and rubbed his belly. No comfort. I sang softly into his tiny pink ears. He cried louder.

"I don't know what to do," I said.

"Let me try," Aunt Jane said. She'd arrived the day before from out of town. She swooped in and intercepted Logan. She bounced him and rubbed his back and moved her body in the mama-sway, but Logan still cried. "Well, I don't know what to do either," she eventually said. Aunt Jane continued to jostle and jiggle my babe, and I perched on the edge of the sofa.

"Maybe he wants to be rocked," I said.

Aunt Jane plopped into the rocker and turbo-rocked. Logan's fists curled into tiny red balls.

I could tell that the crying was unnerving Aunt Jane. She was older than me. She had raised her own children. And though she possessed a wealth of experience, she was accustomed to a quiet, still household.

Truth was, I was unnerved, too. Logan seemed to have his days and nights reversed, and I hadn't slept for fourteen moons. Aunt

Jane's visit added pressure. As much as she desired to help, I needed to figure out how this new baby thing worked.

"He needs to nurse," my aunt said. "That's a hunger cry."

I'd tried to nurse him ten minutes before. He was too mad. But Aunt Jane was older and wiser. "Okay, I'll try," I said.

Aunt Jane slipped Logan into my arms. I tried to fashion a drape from his receiving blanket, but it was hard to do with seven pounds of wriggling baby on my lap.

When I thought I'd created a sufficient tent, I lifted Logan and fumbled under the Mickey Mouse flannel. Aunt Jane poked her head under the blanket.

"You have to get him latched right," she said.

Logan's rosy, tiny mouth stretched and contorted and produced louder, faster screams. He beat against the blanket. He had grown sweaty, and so had I. I could feel my own heart pounding in my head. Could I take Tylenol? I didn't know. I couldn't think.

Just then my husband, Lonny, whisked through the back door. He'd been helping the neighbor. "I heard the baby screaming all the way down the block," he said. "I came right home. Let me help."

Lonny reached under the collapsing flannel and extracted Logan. "Daddy's here," he said. More bouncing. More jostling. More singing.

"Try this," Aunt Jane said. Suddenly, Logan was in her arms again. She held him in one arm and did something that looked like it should involve a hula hoop.

"No," Lonny said. "I read that babies like the washing machine. Let's go start the washer." Lonny and Aunt Jane started down the stairs. Jane was wringing her hands, and Lonny was on a mission.

I caught a glimpse of Logan's dear, sweet, purple face as they rounded the corner.

I ran my fingers through my hair and bit my lip. I didn't want to cry. I was too tired to cry. I tried to listen to the muffled conversation in the laundry room, but Logan's shrieks drowned out the words.

Then my body kicked into action. Milk. Running hard and fast and making deep red stains of color on my red T-shirt. I could hear the washer chugging and Logan screaming. Aunt Jane and Lonny were coming back up the stairs, devising the next plan. The noise and the tension mounted.

I didn't hear the back door open. Suddenly, my neighbor friend, Barb, stood in the center of the chaos. Her hands were on her hips, and she wore that take-charge-mama face that I'd seen her wear with her teenagers.

"What is going on here?" she asked. "That poor baby's cries are traveling clear across town."

No one answered, except for Logan, whose cries had grown raspy and jagged.

Barb looked at Lonny and Aunt Jane, still flipping Logan back and forth. She noticed my T-shirt, growing more deep red by the minute.

"This baby is over-stimulated. You're moving him back and forth like a Hacky Sack. Mama is tired and uptight." Then she walked over to Lonny. "Now put that baby down."

Lonny was surprised. But he listened. He walked to the cradle and set the tiny bundle inside.

Logan drew a few deep gulps of air. His arms and legs relaxed. His eyes closed, and his color returned to a healthy pink.

Barb turned to me. "Now you go shower while your baby is sleeping. Then you curl up on this sofa and take a rest, too."

Then she turned to Lonny and Aunt Jane. "Lonny, you go back to your work outside. Jane, it would be a good time to make dinner."

Lonny and Aunt Jane looked at one another. Then their eyes refocused on Barb. They knew she wasn't finished.

"Now when Logan wakes up, you keep busy. Let Shawnelle and Logan have some time. The baby will need to eat, and that only takes two. They have everything they need."

The room had grown quiet. Very, very quiet.

"Now I'm going home," Barb said. She turned and left, leaving the three of us bewildered. There was no sound except for the swoosh and click of the back door.

After a moment, Lonny broke the silence. "What just happened?" he asked.

"I don't know," I said. I peered into the cradle. Logan's breath had fallen into a sweet, peaceful rhythm. "But it worked."

Lonny shrugged. "Guess I'll go mow the lawn," he said.

"I'll peel some potatoes," Aunt Jane said. "And start the pot roast."

"I'm heading for the shower," I said.

We dispersed.

I climbed the stairs for the shower and shook my head. The house was so quiet, I could hear the creak of the steps.

I was grateful for Lonny and Aunt Jane's well-intended help. But mostly I was grateful for Barb, who walked into a household that roared like a lion and walked out of a household that was quiet as a lamb.

~Shawnelle Eliasen

# What a New Mom Needs to Hear

*To accept good advice is but to increase one's own ability.*
*~Johann Wolfgang von Goethe*

I'd just had my first baby—the one who was supposed to eat, sleep, and poop on schedule. Oh, and cry only when really necessary and only for a moment until I swooped in and figured out his needs with ease. The one for whom I went to birthing classes and read too many books.

The fantasy of having a newborn is so different from the reality. In my dreams, my baby would be easygoing, easy to figure out, and fit neatly into the package I called my life. In real life, that wasn't the case. My son cried all the time, and was rarely consoled by my constant shushing, rocking, and walking. He didn't want to sleep or eat and certainly didn't respond to anything I had read in a book.

By the tenth day of having my baby at home, I was completely overwhelmed, exhausted, and desperate for help. Rocking my baby in my arms at 3:00 a.m., I picked up the phone and dialed my mom.

She answered with a sleepy "Hello?"

I screamed into the phone: "Help! I'm going crazy here. I'm tired, I'm hungry, I'm sore, I'm confused. I don't know what to do!!! What did I get myself into?"

I continued on, sobbing, wondering what I had done to deserve a baby who didn't follow the "rules" and why I couldn't figure out how to meet his newborn needs.

She listened to me patiently, letting me get all my fears and emotions out. Then she calmly spoke the most important words I have ever heard: "You are doing a great job! You will get through this, I promise! The mere fact that you care about your child's needs so much is a clear indication that you are a good mother. You love your baby and, right now, that is enough!"

Through my sobs, I told her how much her encouragement meant to me. I was genuinely tired, sore, frustrated and confused. I was completely unprepared for the changes that would occur in my life when I had my baby. Everyone had an opinion about what I should do with my ten-day-old, but with each piece of helpful advice or correction, I felt a little less capable, a little less confident, a lot less sure of what I had gotten myself into.

The truth is, when I called my mom, overwhelmed by having a brand new baby in my arms, I didn't need advice. I needed reassurance that I was good at being a new mom and would get better with time. I needed to know that some parts of motherhood aren't instinctual and take time to get the hang of. I needed to know that I was an awesome mom just because I loved my baby enough to be worried about him.

I hung up the phone, shaking and crying. As I rocked my baby in my arms, touching his ten-day-old fingers and kissing his ten-day-old nose, I knew that my mom was right. I was a good mom. I loved my baby, and that was absolutely enough!

~Sarah Sweet Newcomb

# A Little Hard-Earned Advice

*The trouble with learning to parent on the job is that your child is the teacher.*
~Robert Brault, www.robertbrault.com

We had it all figured out. My husband and I dated and married when we were nearly thirty — after single years in our twenties and a couple of heartaches. We were smug with confidence in our decision and one another. Boy, were we in for a wake-up call!

The call came via a seven-pound bundle named Abby, fourteen months after the wedding. Before she arrived, we enjoyed our two-career lives and an active social life. After her arrival, we spent our days and nights "redefining normal," as my husband succinctly described it. During the pregnancy, we heard new parents complain that they'd lost all track of time. We'd shake our heads in private — "They're just not managing their time well," we sniffed. When we became parents, our time got managed all right — around her schedule. If she missed a nap or meal, we knew immediately, and paid for it with a cranky child... the kind you see in restaurants that you vow will never be yours.

Humbled and sleep-deprived, we learned a few lessons. If I met an expectant couple today, and they were open to advice (unlike one overly confident, judgmental pair years ago), I'd offer some suggestions for their success—and, some days, survival—during the newborn stage of bringing up baby:

1) Rest when the baby rests. When the baby's quiet, it's so tempting to clean the house a little, throw in a load of laundry or make a few phone calls. When my baby napped, I felt emancipated, and raced around the house tending to what I thought were important, urgent and essential tasks. Inevitably, the fatigue caught up with me. Just as I'd settle in for a nap, restless noises would drift from the nursery, followed by coos and, eventually, cries. My precious window of quiet time gone, I'd drag myself from my bed and start the cycle again.

Believe me, the chores can wait. The most important, urgent and essential task is to take care of yourself so you can care for the baby. Which brings me to my next suggestion…

2) Call on others and ask for help. Ask for what you need and receive it with gratitude. As point one illustrates, don't try to be Supermom. Not only do you have a demanding, impatient little one to take care of, but your body is healing physically, hormonally, emotionally, spiritually, and mentally.

I suffered through a bout of mastitis while nursing. I was completely exhausted. With no immediate family available, a friend suggested I call our local church for help. I was connected to the head of the seniors' group, who was absolutely tickled at the notion of caring for a newborn. He scheduled shifts of volunteers for later in the week. My pride couldn't accept the help. After a day on antibiotics, I declared myself capable and called him to say, "Thanks, but no thanks." I can still hear the disappointment in his voice as he said, "Well, okay," and hung up the phone. To this day, I deeply regret not letting those dear folks come to our home and love my baby and me with a few hours of TLC.

People want to help, so let them and accept it with gratitude. With their assistance, you'll get the rest you need, which is key to the next two suggestions…

3) Be in the moment with your child. One of the most profound lessons of parenting is to be in the moment. You cannot negotiate

with a hungry or tired infant. They need to be fed now, or changed now, or comforted now. Plus, even the tiniest infant is learning and growing by interacting with you. Don't deny the baby or yourself these irreplaceable moments. Learning to set aside what we have planned is one challenge of parenting. Roll with it, rather than fight it, and see what surprises are in store.

4) Pray every day. Take time with your Creator—the one who gave life to you and this little bundle of needs. Your relationship with God is the primary one in your life, so make it a priority. The peace you'll find in these quiet moments will set the tone for your day and help you be more present to your child. I'm famous for jumping out of bed and crossing off the to-do list. When I start with prayer before the tasks, I'm in a better frame of mind and can handle whatever situations arise during the day with grace and humor.

5) Trust your instincts. There will be times when you're so sleep-deprived and dizzy that you won't know what to do. Stop worrying about what the experts might say and call on your intuition. Dr. Spock's work is laced with the idea that "No one knows your child better than you do, and you should trust your instincts." Look for guidance and listen to your heart to make the best decisions you can.

6) Forgive yourself. Motherhood is truly on-the-job training, and some shifts will go more smoothly than others. Don't hold on to regrets—the "If I'd known then what I know now" kind. Everyone knows you're doing the best you can. Imagine a friend confiding her self-judgment to you. How would you treat her? Comfort yourself with the same love and compassion you would give to your friend.

7) What bothers you most about being a parent is probably the very change you need to make. Part of the gift this little one brings is what he or she will teach you. I mentioned earlier being "in the moment" with your child. This is my big issue—regretting the past, or worrying about the future and missing what's right in front of me. My daughter's care, her need for my attention, and her new smile and shining eyes drew me into that present moment with her. When I released those distractions, I was at peace and surrounded by love.

For my husband, he's learned greater patience. So, rather than focusing on the inconvenience of caring for a child, look for the ways this little one is helping you to grow. Those tiny hands are holding up a mirror to you. Gaze lovingly at what you see, take it to prayer, and keep your heart open.

My husband and I thought we knew it all, but we were like children again—learning our new roles as parents. Our daughter's arrival changed everything, permanently, and created a "new normal" in our home. For all the changes she's instigated, my abiding sense has been of how well it all just seems to fit.

"We have an Abby!" the doctor announced the moment she made her entrance. He placed her in my arms, and my heart rejoiced with a simple, "Of course." Of course, this was Abby. And, of course, she was ours. She would be the one to transform this self-centered couple into a family. Yet, as I held her tiny body in my arms, it was as if she'd been there all along.

~Maria Rodgers O'Rourke

# Those Trying First Weeks

*Motherhood is like Albania—you can't trust the descriptions in the books, you have to go there.*
~Marni Jackson

I've learned more about life in the past six months than I did in four years of college and eighteen months (and counting) of graduate school. Namely, I've learned that parenthood is hard. And not just hard, but positively hellish in those first few weeks. This is something they don't tell you in the hospital.

Of course, now that my son Tyler is a delicious six-month-old, I can recall everything in a rather fond way, instead of sobbing maniacally along with a baby who won't eat or can't poop or seems to sleep only in seven-minute increments. This is what I've learned from my induction into motherhood:

- A good meal in those early weeks is defined as one that is actually fully consumed, usually in about ninety seconds, while standing over the sink. Also, there's nothing wrong with everyone eating three times a day the loaf of banana bread your neighbor brought over. If anyone complains, you have the right to kick him where it counts.

- People with young infants frequently drive at excessive speeds.

Now I know why. Simply put, driving around with a screaming newborn is a lot like having a lit cigarette shoved up your nostril—you want to get it out as soon as possible.

- I can sleep when I'm dead. This heartening piece of advice was gleefully given to me on Day 5 by my good friend with two boys under the age of three. Apparently, sleep is a luxury item, a lot like a massage or a three-day cruise.

- In all likelihood, I won't go to hell for hating the lying women who claim they wore their pre-pregnancy jeans home from the hospital, not to mention anyone who says they weigh less than they did before they got pregnant. For the record, those are disgusting statements, and we normal women do not want to hear them, thank you very much.

- Motherhood is a crash course in bodily functions, including, but not limited to, using a bulb-like thingy to suction snot from the baby's nose, and describing to the doctor, in amazingly creative detail, the color, texture and consistency of a daily poop—if you are, in fact, lucky enough to get a daily poop.

- The word "sex" is simply that—a word to denote whether a person is male or female. Any other considerations for the term are incomprehensible. In addition, both parties are generally terrified of the act that has now resulted in so much chaos.

On a more serious note, I've learned that I'm not the worst mother in the world, and I'm certainly not the best either, but that's okay. I've learned to let go of the guilt I often have about not doing something "right" or maybe being able to do something better. As my mother put it, Tyler's stuck with me, and I'm stuck with him. Someone put us together for a reason, and we're just going to have to do the best we know how.

And, nowadays, we all sleep pretty well. I even wear make-up and wash my hair again. Dinners aren't banana bread anymore, although I have to admit they're not much better. (I never was much of a cook.)

Most of all, I've learned that Tyler is the most miraculous gift we've ever received. I am changed forever. And I'm really glad we're stuck with each other. I only hope I don't mess it up.

~Christa Gala

# Chapter 7

# New Moms

## Born of My Heart

*Adoption is when a child grew in its mommy's heart instead of her tummy.*

*~Author Unknown*

# A Free Fall with a Soft Landing

*However motherhood comes to you it's a miracle.*
*~Valerie Harper*

She never believed. Not in her core. Not the way she believes that morning follows night. Or that ice melts in the heat. Or that if you throw something into the air, it will fall back to earth. This kind of certainty eluded her.

Tara's faith was tenuous. Some days she hoped. Some days she despaired. Most days she wondered if she would ever be a mother.

Her mother, Jill, tried to help. "It will happen, Tara," she said. "I promise you. And when it does, you will look back at this time and think it was worth the wait."

But the drumbeat in Tara's head was "When? When? When?" And it never stopped. It was like a radio left on in an adjoining room.

It takes love and faith and courage to raise a child, any child. It takes closing your eyes and leaping into the unknown, then free-falling to the ground below.

But how far below? When you adopt, you don't know. So it takes patience, too, the wait harder because it's uncertain, waiting always a strain even when you can draw a circle on a date and point to it and make plans.

But when you can't point? When the pages of the calendar turn again and again and there is no circle?

Tara and Rob made plans anyway. They decorated a room, bought a crib, books, blankets, and stuffed animals, and dared to imagine at every child-centered celebration that went on in their lives — their families big, their world full of other people's children — that soon they would have a child, too.

Maybe next Christmas. Maybe next spring. Definitely next year.

Days drag when you're counting minutes, but somehow seasons fly. Summer came again, and there was still no baby. Babies were everywhere, the beach full of them.

Summer was Tara's season of discontent.

"It will happen, Tara. I promise," Jill continued to say. But it was getting harder and harder for Tara to believe.

And then the call came, and a picture of a baby boy. And there was relief and joy and hope and thanksgiving. But still no circle on the calendar. He could arrive in two months. Or it could be four or six or eight months.

His picture sustained her. This was her son. But then came the "what ifs." What if something went wrong? What if he didn't come? What if now, after falling in love with him, memorizing the shape of his lips, his eyes, the tussle of his hair, she lost him?

She didn't. Chase Henry Matthews arrived at Logan Airport, eight months old and beautiful, so wanted and already beloved.

A woman half a world away loved him enough that she gave birth to him. Another woman, his foster mother, loved him as her own for eight months. Another brought him here, to the United States, to Tara and Rob, who loved him even before they knew him.

It doesn't seem so long now, the long, long wait. This is what happens when you land on soft ground. You forget the time spent sad and afraid and crying. You forget everything except the baby in your arms.

Tara's mother had told her this. But children never believe their mothers, not even grown children, not even when their mothers have walked where they've walked, not even when they've wept the same tears.

For Jill's promise was never based on faith alone. She knows firsthand not just that morning follows night and that ice melts in the heat. But that the heart melts, too, and forgets its sadness in the presence of joy. For many years ago, when she herself was a young woman yearning for motherhood, the clock was a drumbeat for her, too, years of days spent playing with my children while waiting for a child of her own.

And then a social worker put Tara, just three days old, in Jill's arms. It was February, not October, in an apartment, not an airport. And it was thirty-two years ago.

But the moment of absolute love was the same.

Back then, I watched Jill cradle Tara, breathe in her smell, stroke her cheek, look into her eyes and adore her.

And now I have watched Tara, too, cradle Chase and do all the same things.

Sometimes, a woman gives birth and becomes a mother.

But sometimes more is required. Sometimes a woman has to leap off a cliff with her eyes closed and her arms open and wait and trust that her mother is right.

"It will happen," Jill said.

And miraculously—for every child is a miracle—it has.

~Beverly Beckham

# 50

# A Promise

> *We look at adoption as a very sacred exchange. It was not done lightly on either side. I would dedicate my life to this child.*
> *~Jamie Lee Curtis*

The judge fixed his gaze on me from his lofty perch. "Do you promise to love, care for, provide for, and parent your daughter to the best of your ability?"

My almost two-year-old daughter squirmed in my lap and let out something akin to a giggle. I wanted to join her. In spite of the solemnity of the moment, I was tempted to answer, "What do you think I've been doing for the past twelve months?"

This court date was the final step in a long journey laden with paperwork, background checks, medical appointments, and months of waiting to adopt our daughter. Twelve months ago, my husband and I sat in a sunlit room of a governmental building in southern China, waiting to meet and adopt our almost eleven-month-old daughter. Surrounded by families all waiting for children of their own, I felt lightheaded and giddy, not to mention slightly nauseous. What were we doing adopting a baby halfway around the world and rocking our stable family of three?

Steadying myself on faith and my husband next to me, I rose to my feet as the Chinese nannies brought the babies into the room, one at a time. It was another interval of waiting in what seemed to be a lifetime of waiting.

My husband spotted her first. "There she is."

And there she was, our daughter, in the arms of a caregiver, next in line to enter the room of anxiously waiting parents. She had big, beautiful doe eyes, soft full cheeks, and a tuft of hair shooting up from her little round head. Our translator asked us for the necessary documents, and we handed them over with trembling hands. She reviewed them, and checked the homemade identification tag on my daughter, and the next thing I knew the most beautiful baby girl in the world was placed in my arms. She melted into my embrace, soft and tender as a marshmallow. She didn't join in the chorus of infants crying, but I sure did. Only silent tears slipped down her beautiful cheeks as her wide eyes took in her surroundings, the chaos around her, and us—her new and rather bumbling parents. I wanted to communicate to her that it would be perfectly fine to cry, healthy in fact, that she didn't need to hold it all together. After all, she had been handed off to virtual strangers who looked, smelled, and sounded like nothing she had ever experienced before.

With the other spellbound parents, we took our daughter back on the bus and to the hotel where she promptly found her vocal cords. Like the other parents, we had been given little information about how to care for her; we only had a schedule that the orphanage had adhered to as they strove to simultaneously care for dozens of babies. With our six-year-old waiting for us at home, we weren't brand new parents. But in all the ways that mattered, we were. Through the blare of my daughter's ear-piercing shrieks, I scrambled to make up a bottle, only to have her reject it. I had made it "Western style," not the thick, piping-hot sludge she was accustomed to. I tried again, and she slurped it down in what appeared to be relief.

The next few days were nothing short of an emotional roller coaster, a precarious dance as we got to know each other. We cuddled and played, sang and snuggled, and she slowly emerged from her shell. At first, when we were out and about and random Chinese women reached out to hold our daughter (perfectly acceptable in their culture), our daughter would readily go to them, most likely relieved to see a familiar-looking face. But then one evening, when our Chinese waitress reached out to hold her, my daughter turned into my chest as if to say, "No, thanks. I'm with my mom." My heart soared because even though I realized she might need time, I had completely and irrevocably fallen in love with my daughter.

A week later, with our governmental paperwork and appointments complete, we landed back on home soil to reunite with our waiting son and introduce our new daughter to a slew of family and friends, just in time for Christmas. We showed her how to unwrap presents and let her feel snow. She ate her first Cheerio and learned to say Papa. We celebrated her first birthday, and she took her first steps. She caught pneumonia, and I rocked her as she coughed throughout the night. She discovered the kitchen cabinets and emptied them daily. She learned to dance and played hide-and-seek with her brother. She asserted her will and threw a tantrum. She splashed in the water at the beach and squealed in delight while swinging in the park. In short, we became a family.

And a year after she took her place in our arms and hearts forever, we sat before the judge as he dutifully and solemnly asked us to reaffirm our commitment as parents.

Did we promise to love, care for, provide for and parent our daughter to the best of our abilities?

Yes, yes. A million times yes.

~Rachel Allord

# The Right Choices

*My basic principle is that you don't make decisions because they are easy; you don't make them because they are cheap; you don't make them because they're popular; you make them because they're right.*
~Theodore Hesburgh

When I was seventeen years old, I gave birth to a vigorous baby girl whose vibrancy of spirit glowed in her green eyes. Those eyes lit up the dark, deserted garage, which I had chosen for its thick, blood pink cotton insulation that solemnly kept all secrets behind broken bits of plaster. As the heavy, dizzy droning subsided from my ears, I looked down to see a limp baby doll covered in slippery mucous. I pushed stringy, loose strands of my hair away from my face and reached down to lightly graze a finger down the back of the baby doll. The skin was wet and cool. Fingers and toes were curled, gripping the air in desperation. Miniscule fingernails, so rectangular and perfect, were blue. I picked up the baby doll; it stirred. The doll suddenly animated into life, and a shrill, breathy cry bounced off of the garage's ash gray walls. Thin eyelids fluttered open, and I looked into the baby's eyes. I felt nothing.

I clasped the baby tighter to my chest, praying for our hearts to match in rhythm. Pa-dum, pa-dum. The baby's long eyelashes flickered up against her face, and her deep green eyes read into the secrets and fears of my brown ones. I still felt nothing.

It wasn't until later, when I placed her into the arms of a beaming young woman whose cheeks were damp with joyful tears and I saw how her husband gazed at their new baby in boundless happiness that I felt my heart stir. I'm doing the right thing, I thought.

It wasn't until I stood at the edge of the park and watched how the green-eyed doll laughed in glee and pleaded for her mother to "push me higher" on the swings that I felt tears threatening to betray my apathy. I chose to focus on the grass. But even the green of the manicured lawn paled in comparison to the jade green of my baby. Their baby. Did I do the right thing?

It wasn't until I held her little hand in my own and listened to her parents tell her that I was her "birth mommy" that I felt a blush escape to my cheeks, matching the pink that had already overpowered her cream complexion. Is this the right thing?

It wasn't until I watched her throw her hard-earned cap into the air that I felt a sense of pride that had not accompanied my bachelor's, master's or doctorate. I hoped she'd do the right things.

It wasn't until I gripped her tightly curled fingers, nails tinged blue with pressure, and heard the strong, shrill cry of her brown-eyed baby girl mixed in with the happy exclamations and sobs of her husband that I knew. I did the right thing.

~Pearl Lee

# The Match

*Somehow destiny comes into play. These children end up with you and you end up with them. It's something quite magical.*
~Nicole Kidman

In the months before becoming a mom for the first time, most women worry. We worry about the health of the baby. We worry that we won't know what to do when the baby cries and cries. We worry about how the baby will change our marriages, our careers, our lives. We worry about what kind of mother we will be, and if it will be enough.

But when your first child is not growing inside you, but inside another woman — a young girl who will be your baby's birth mother — your list of worries changes and grows.

Along with all of the normal concerns, you worry about whether or not there has been sufficient prenatal care, or whether drugs and alcohol are being used. And sometimes you worry about whether you'll be able to love an adopted child the same way you would love a child you had conceived... the same way you would love one who shares your DNA, your pale skin, and your husband's long eyelashes.

We received the phone call from our adoption agency in late summer that a birth mother and birth father had chosen us to parent their unborn child. The baby was due in just six weeks.

We'd heard stories of these life-changing "match" calls. I always envisioned that when the call came for us, I would shed happy tears, maybe jump up and down, and dance a little "our dreams are coming true" dance. I assumed that my elation would be something uncontainable, spreading over us like wildfire.

Instead, I was startled by my reaction. There was a small bit of cautious joy, yes. But it was fleeting, and then far outweighed by another, more overwhelming non-emotion that I hadn't been prepared for: numbness.

It was like I had stepped into a cold, rushing creek in the middle of a hot day, and I knew I should be feeling the relief, or the movement of the cool water around my ankles, the tickle of creek bed mud loosening beneath me, the warm, inviting sun on my face. But I didn't. I couldn't.

Psychologically, I knew I was protecting myself, keeping my heart safe behind a wall of control. After all, adoptions can be risky. People change their minds. A birth parent can have a change of heart just before the baby is born, or right afterward.

You can prepare a nursery, buy a crib, tell your close friends—and still end up without a baby. I understood this. And I couldn't set that knowledge aside.

We met the young birth parents soon after our match call. Jill and John (names have been changed) seemed to be resolutely aware they weren't in a position to provide for another child.

Also at that first meeting, Jill asked if I wanted to accompany her to a sonogram appointment the next week. I was touched that she would share such a private moment with me. When I told her that, she said, "Well, I'm thinking of this as your child now." The statement seemed to swirl around me. I didn't know how to respond. Was this my child?

At the sonogram, I sat beside Jill and watched the images on the computer screen. This baby, the one that Jill believed would be my child, was a boy. It was the first confirmation of the baby's gender we'd had. I waited for emotion to come barreling toward me. It didn't. My feelings seemed frozen, iced over.

The technician printed out sonogram pictures for both of us.

Jill smiled at me. I swallowed another lump of anxiety and took the photograph with shaking hands.

I wanted to believe this was my baby, the soul I would love unconditionally and raise into adulthood, the toddler I would read *Goodnight Moon* to every night, the child I would hold and comfort when he scraped his knee, the son we would take camping every summer and plan birthday parties for every fall.

I wanted to believe my hope of having a family would be realized in this black-and-white image of bone and tissue. I wanted to believe the long little toes I could so clearly make out would soon be the ones I would count and tickle in the evenings as I rocked him in front of a warm fire.

But nothing inside of me told me this was true.

The remaining weeks of Jill's pregnancy went by quickly. Just after midnight on October first, she called us. She asked if we were ready for our son to be born.

Jill and John allowed us to be in the room during the delivery, another touching gesture. We stood nearby, but not too close, waiting in those final minutes as Jill pushed. We watched as the baby came into the world, red-pink and slippery and a little mad about the whole ordeal.

Looking back, I remember those moments as if I were outside my own body, watching a scene unfold before me. I remember the room seemed too bright. I remember my husband held my hand. I remember tears running down his cheeks, something I had rarely seen. I remember biting my lip so hard it bled.

And I remember thinking: This is Jill's baby. But is he mine, too?

While the doctor and nurse attended to Jill, another nurse took the baby aside for all those rush of things necessary right after birth. Then she motioned for us to come over.

I was hesitant at first, almost like a child waiting to sit on Santa's lap. I had looked forward to this for so long. But now, I felt uneasy, unsure.

I gingerly placed my pointer finger in one palm of this perfect, beautiful creature with eyes the color of the sea and a full head of brown hair. With more force than I could have imagined, he curled his full hand around my finger and held it. He didn't let go, and neither did I.

It was in that all-consuming moment that I knew. Absolutely and without doubt. With that simple, reflex motion of an infant's hand responding to mine, it was as if every cell in my own structure underwent a transformation. I couldn't have stopped it if I had wanted to. This was my child.

The months following our son's birth certainly contained no more assurance than the weeks prior to his birth. In our state and many others, adoptive parents are merely foster parents for several months, until the birth parents can officially relinquish their parental rights. And then there is additional time between that event and when the adoption can be finalized.

But unlike those weeks after our match call, the months we spent as "foster parents" were full of unprecedented and unmarred joyfulness and excitement. We loved as if there were no tomorrow—or as if there were a million tomorrows.

It's been three years now. Our son is happy and healthy, and continues to amaze us every day. When he hurts, I hurt. When he laughs, I laugh. Some days I wonder just where I end and he begins.

And when I look at him, he may not be a reflection of my hair color, or the shape of my nose, or the exact color of my eyes, but he is, undeniably, a reflection of me—my love for him and my husband, my values, my sense of humor, my way of seeing the world.

I still worry, of course. But now, it's about a high fever, or preschool, or cavities in his light-up-a-room smile. It is never, ever about whether or not he was meant to be mine. Or whether I was meant to be his.

~Kathy Lynn Harris

# The Labor of Two Moms

*Not flesh of my flesh, Nor bone of my bone, But still miraculously my own. Never forget for a single minute, You didn't grow under my heart—but in it.*
~Fleur Conkling Heyliger

"I was in labor for eight years." That is how almost all new moms begin the story of their child's arrival. So, to fit in with all the other new moms, I decided to begin my story that way, too.

But I wasn't really "in labor" all that time. I was waiting. It was a cycle of home studies and social workers, adoption agencies and lawyers... endless paperwork and parenting classes that spoke of the days to come. Eight years of preparation for the child we hoped would be ours one day.

And then, just as an expectant woman gives birth, we became parents overnight. The most wonderful gift I was ever given came to me from a perfect stranger who had enough faith to believe that this was the right thing to do. This stranger's face is as familiar to me as my own. I can count her freckles, and see my reflection in the piercing blue eyes that grace the peaches-and-cream complexion. I know her well, though we haven't met. Wrapped in a pink blanket, she came—the most precious of gifts, my daughter.

When I heard the words, "We have a baby girl for you," I knew my life was about to change. And it did. I became a mom, with all the same experiences of any new mom. There were diapers and formula, toys and nap times. There have been moments of pride and joy unlike any other experience in life. She is almost grown now, and it has been a wonderful journey. These are my experiences because a young woman had a difficult choice to make, and she chose wisely. She chose with the wisdom of a mother.

Her act of love created the best part of my life. Because of her gift, I am able to hear the sound of my daughter's voice when she says "Mom." I am a mother forever because of the choices made by one young woman. Someday, I hope to be able to thank her and tell her about the miracle who is my daughter. She is the child of my heart.

One day, I will share this with her other mom. I will tell her of the most beautiful baby, of the dark hair and blue eyes that swept me away when I first held her, and of the love I felt at that precise moment. I will tell her of the toddler with the bouncing pigtails who delighted everyone with her smile. I will tell her of the kindergartner who worried about a little boy in her class who was teased by the other children, and how she shared her first kiss with a boy when she was only five.

I will share my Halloween costume design for the rainbow unicorn pony that she just had to be when she was six, and for the Dalmatian costume that was a black dog with white spots. I will describe the butterfly outfit she wore in second grade, and share the memories of her first Christmas when the families spoiled her so thoroughly that she had to take a nap just to have enough energy to open all her presents. I will share the photos that tell the story of our daughter growing up.

I will tell her of all the Mother's Days that have passed, when I thanked her silently for each and every day of being a mother to my daughter. I will tell her of the wonderful young woman she has become, one who loves music and sign language, works hard at school, and loves to read and write poetry and stories.

I don't know if she has become a mother again, but I know the time will soon come to share my daughter. A part of me feels this is only fair, as I have had the privilege of being her mother for more than seventeen years. But another part of me wants to hold onto her for myself, to prevent any possible hurt. Someone as wonderful as my daughter deserves to be shared with the woman who gave her life. I will always be the mom who was there when she had an ear infection or the chickenpox. But there is another who also deserves to know her.

So, when the time comes to meet my daughter's other mother, here's what I'll say to her: Please be careful when you meet her. Remember that she loves you unconditionally. She does not know the specific reasons for your choices, but she wants to know, and she wants to know you. You hold her heart in your hands in a way I will never be able to do for her, no matter how intense the love I have for her. As you once treated her gently in your womb, treat her gently now. She is most vulnerable to being hurt by you, but also hoping for your love. She wants to know if she is like you, and I believe that she is. But she is also a part of me and my husband, her father, so please understand how torn her feelings may be.

She is an only child, and though I wished for her to have a sibling, that was not in God's plan for my family. I am hoping that you may be able to give this to her. I only want the best for my daughter—our daughter. You gave her life, and I gave her the mother's love that she needed to grow up a happy and healthy young woman. She has been the best part of my life, and your choice made this possible for me.

I have a choice now, too. With faith and hope, you once gave her to me. Now I can share her with you with that same faith and hope. We both have had to make some difficult choices. You made the right choice then, and I am asking you to do so again. Treat her gently and love her. That is what I ask now—just as you once asked of me.

~Kathleen E. Jones

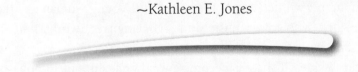

# Just Like Any Other

*It has been said that adoption is more like a marriage than a birth: two (or more) individuals, each with their own unique mix of needs, patterns, and genetic history, coming together with love, hope, and commitment for a joint future. You become a family not because you share the same genes, but because you share love for each other.*
~Joan McNamara

Bringing my daughter home on that cold November day was like many other new parents bringing their baby home. I sat in the back seat with her as she slept while my husband drove. My mind was racing, as was my heart. I looked at her and wondered how we could ever live up to such a tremendous responsibility. She seemed so fragile and innocent. I felt paralyzed by the fear that this was too great of an undertaking. The past nine months of anticipation for this very moment, where I had been consumed with nothing but how to get to this exact place, and now I was panic-stricken.

The difference in my story of bringing my daughter home was that she was eight years old on her first day with us. What seemed to be the end of a long road was really the beginning. We were finally at the end of a long home study process, her at the end of a nearly five-year foster care stay. In reality, it was the beginning of a long journey to building our lives together as a family.

I slept very little the first month she was home. I spent the first year with her hardly ever out of my sight. We did everything that we were told to do to facilitate bonding and attachment. At first, the all-consuming schedule was more than I could take. I had to choose what she wore, what she ate, who she talked to... every move she made was supervised by me. It was surreal to have a new person just appear in our lives and our family. Again, it was very similar to having a newborn in the house.

I'm not quite sure when it happened. We went from almost strangers, to family, to a very close mother/daughter team. Our family didn't begin in a very typical fashion, but we are a family just like any other. We've overcome obstacles and rejoiced together. My story of being a new mom, my fears, and my delights are like most others. So is my love for my daughter. I look back now, and the memory of all of the hard times, waiting for her to come home, and the fears I had those first few months are all just a blur.

~Dena May

# Three Mothers, One Heart

*Mother's love grows by giving.*
*~Charles Lamb*

Recently, our family celebrated our daughter's sixteenth Forever Day, the day we stood in court and promised a judge that we would love and take care of our daughter forever. It didn't matter that we told the judge or anyone in the courtroom; it was true without the legalities of it.

Seventeen years ago, we began this journey of parenthood, but not in the way I had imagined so long ago when I stood at the wedding altar beside Richard and thought about our future together. And yet, the result of reams of paperwork, hours of parenting classes, home visits, interviews, and nerve-racking times of waiting was glorious.

Once Michelle came into our lives, nothing was ever the same. For twelve years, we'd prayed for the child of our heart. Richard and I knew we wanted children from the moment we decided to marry. Our plan was to have two children and adopt a third. The second part of our dream came true and overshadowed the loss of the first part.

Within a couple of weeks of the phone call telling us of the nine-month-old girl waiting for us, we were sitting in the living room of her foster parents. Nothing had prepared me for the way I felt when my daughter crawled into my lap. Gayla Michelle, our caseworker

Three Mothers, One Heart : Born of My Heart 201

had said. How perfect. Richard and I had long ago chosen the name Michael or Michelle for our first child. I hoped she could get used to the name switch for we intended to call her Michelle.

"She's beautiful," I said.

Tina, her foster mother, smiled—the way I'd seen my own mother's smile of pride. She told me how smart and friendly my daughter was, which I could see.

"She's wonderful. I can't wait for her to come home," I said quickly.

This woman who had raised my daughter for her first eight months of life stared at me. Her smile disappeared, and she stood suddenly and let me know she had a box of clothes and toys we could have.

I realized how hard it must be to let go. And I realized how scared I was. Would Michelle like her new nursery? Would she love us or be afraid? I wanted to cry. I turned toward Tina and saw that she was crying.

"She's like my own daughter," she whispered.

We stood at the nursery door, sizing one another up. I was surprised at the carousels decorating the nursery and explained that our nursery was decorated similarly.

"Michelle will feel at home," Tina said.

It was then that I learned how they'd always called her Michelle. When I told Tina that was the name we had chosen, she smiled and grabbed my hand. "You'll really love her, won't you?"

"More than my life," I promised.

That was what she needed to hear. Tension slipped away, and we were quickly giggling over photos and videos.

My daughter's first days had been traumatic. She'd been taken from her birth mother, drugs in her tiny body. But in reality, Michelle's first nine months had been blessed. She had the love of three mothers. One who gave her life. Another who gave her a loving home to wait in. And the third—me—who would give her a mother's lifelong love and commitment.

For so many years, I had cried out in pain, asking why we were denied the child we desperately wanted. And twelve years later, I was amazed at how the lives of three women had been lined up to bring us together through the love of one little girl.

This tiny girl united three women's hearts in a special bond of motherhood, not limited by pregnancy and childbirth, but bonded instead through our dreams for Michelle's future. It was a bond with endless boundaries and many years to celebrate her Forever Day.

~Kathryn Lay

# When You Least Expect It

*Every perfect gift is from above...*
*~James 1:17*

While sitting across the table from my friend, Nancy, tears rolled down my face and splashed onto my plate. "I don't think we're ever going to receive a baby," I wept.

"You will," Nancy comforted me. "When you least expect it, the call will come, and you'll be a mommy."

"It's been several years since we applied for adoption, and still... no baby. The wait seems endless."

"The waiting seemed endless for us, too. But then one day, when we least expected it, the adoption agency called and told us that our baby had just been born. Don't lose hope, Debbie. The Lord will provide at just the right time."

I hoped she was right.

After we finished eating, Nancy drove me home. Before I got out of the car, she reached over and put her hand on my shoulder. "Remember," she smiled, "when you least expect it, your baby will arrive."

"Thanks for the encouragement. I really needed your support today. It's been a painful and difficult journey." I got out of the car and waved goodbye as she drove away.

While walking up to our front door, I spotted a colorful package on the porch. I picked it up and carried it into the house where I eagerly tore open the wrappings. Inside the box was a beautiful pastel mug that read, "No mom is half as good as you!" Puzzled by this strange gift, I read the attached card from my husband, Tom. "Congratulations on your new arrival! Call me!"

I rushed to the phone and fumbled to dial the number. It was April Fool's Day, and I was hoping this wasn't a prank. "Tom, this isn't a joke, is it?" I asked nervously.

"No, Debbie. I'd never do something like that to you. I have great news!"

I could tell by the tone in his voice that he was excited. "The social worker at the adoption agency called while you were out to breakfast with Nancy. Our baby is here!"

"Our baby is here?" I paused, absorbing the shock. "I can't believe it. I sure wasn't expecting this today. Is it a boy or a girl?"

"I'm coming home for lunch. I'll give you all the details then."

I couldn't believe that Tom wanted me to wait until lunchtime to learn more about our baby, but I sensed that he wanted to share the news in person. To honor his wishes, I accepted his proposition. After I hung up the phone, I climbed the stairs and went into the smallest bedroom reserved for a nursery. When I opened the door and stepped inside, I wept. My lifelong dream to be a mommy was about to be realized, and I was overwhelmed with emotion.

For a while I stood thinking to myself. I wondered what our baby would look like. I hoped that our child would be healthy and strong. I thought about different personalities, hobbies, and talents, and I pondered those possibilities in my heart. I was so excited to meet our precious little one, but I had no idea what to expect.

When Tom came home over his lunch hour, he told me all about our blessing. We hugged each other excitedly, and then called our friends and family members to share the wonderful news. There was so much to be done before our baby's homecoming. From decorating the nursery to shopping, packing, and making travel arrangements, our days were going to be busy as we prepared for our baby's arrival.

A few days later, in the midst of our joy, unexpected trouble came. We had already decorated and stocked the nursery, packed our bags, and made flight reservations when we learned that our home study had expired by one week. As a result, governing officials gave us strict orders not to leave the state until these important papers were brought up to date and reapproved. That could take weeks!

By this point, physical and mental exhaustion had taken its toll, and I crumbled under the weight of stress. But the Lord was watching over us and saw our tears. When we called our local agency, it happened to be after closing. Even so, to our surprise, a very kind man answered the phone. He informed us that the social worker we had been working with was no longer employed there, but after he heard our dilemma he encouraged us. "If you can leave right away, I'll wait for you and see what I can do to help." After our interview with him, he assured us that he would move things along as quickly as possible.

We flew out of town as originally scheduled; however, we were warned not to go to the out-of-state agency or anywhere near the baby until all the paperwork was cleared. If we did, we would lose all rights to ever adopting a child. Once we got to our destination, there was more waiting and uncertainty. By this time, Tom and I had resigned ourselves to the fact that if this was indeed the child the Lord had selected for us, things would come together before our flight home. If it wasn't meant to be, we would return empty-handed. While waiting and hoping, we made special time to pray and do some sightseeing in the area.

One week later, we returned home, and signs of spring were everywhere we looked. When we drove into the driveway, we noticed that not only were the trees in bud, but the branches were also covered with bright pink balloons. A large sign hung above the garage door and read, "Welcome Home, Mommy, Daddy, and Kylea!" Our hearts danced with joy as we carried our precious little girl up the stairs and into her nursery.

The moment I sat down in the rocker, Kylea snuggled against me, cooed, and closed her sleepy eyes. What a blessing! The Lord had answered our prayers. We had waited so long for a child, and now all those intense feelings of pain and discouragement suddenly melted away. The paperwork had gone through without any further glitches, and the adoption ceremony was beautiful. Happiness blossomed within our hearts and the reality of parenting hit hard the first time we heard her cry. She was indeed a beautiful little girl created by God especially for us.

The next day, I thought about our adoption experience and realized that God's timing was perfect! Easter Sunday represents Christ's resurrection and new life, and we had just experienced those principles in our current situation. I thought it was extra special that Easter was going to be our first Sunday together as a family. God's ways are always right and wonderful, and it's good to be a part of His plan.

~Debbie Schmid

# Your Son Looks Just Like You

*I did not make you in my own image;*
*I created you from the imagery of my heart.*
*~Nancy McGuire Roche*

"Your son looks just like you!" a lady at church exclaims to me one Sunday morning after mass. I simply smile at her and say, "Thank you." We make our way to our car in the parking lot; I am walking on a cloud, certain my feet are not touching the ground. This woman cannot possibly imagine how fulfilling those words are to me, for so many different reasons.

We discovered after about a year of trying to get pregnant that we were part of the "advanced fertility issues" category. We attempted in-vitro fertilization one time, unsuccessfully. We went on to attempt two frozen embryo transfers; again, our attempts were met by failure.

Adoption was our next step in this process. As an adopted child myself, I have a special understanding of what a beautiful gift adoption really is. My dear friend, who knew of our struggles, called one day to tell me of someone she worked with whose daughter had just learned she was pregnant and had decided to place her child for adoption. My friend put us in contact with this woman, but at the time we had no idea how this simple gesture from a friend would impact our lives.

I began communicating with the woman, and eventually we

met in person to discuss the situation. Then I began speaking to her daughter about choosing us as her adoptive family and formulating an adoption plan. My husband and I could simply not believe that by telling our friend of our struggles and our desire for children, she had been placed in the exact right place, at the exact right time, with the exact right person who could ultimately lead to us to becoming parents. If we had not previously believed in miracles, we certainly do now.

The waiting at times felt unbearable. We were so close to becoming a family of three. The months seemed to drag by, our minds constantly racing with "what ifs." If we called our son's birth mother and the call went unreturned, or she seemed distant on the phone, our minds would wander and we'd begin to think she was changing her mind. We were hesitant to purchase any baby items or decorate a nursery. The thought of coming home with no baby and seeing these things was too much to bear.

But one day I was thinking of our son and how he deserved to come home to the very best nursery we could provide him, and my husband and I agreed to just go for it! We deserved to enjoy the fact that we were parents-to-be just like any other parents, so we decorated the nursery. We picked out our son's "coming-home outfit," and purchased a car seat and stroller. We threw caution to the wind—in a very cautious manner. We tucked the receipts for all of our purchases away and instructed both of our mothers where they were, so they could remove all of the items and turn the nursery back into a guest room if all did not go as planned. The thought of coming home to a nursery that wasn't needed was heartbreaking in theory; it had to be unimaginable in reality.

The months passed, and finally it was baby time! Though we lived in Ohio, our son's birth mother resided in Florida. We packed up and hit the road, hoping to come back to Ohio as a newly established family of three. We arrived the day before my son was to be born and checked in to a local hotel. Those hours in the hotel waiting on any news about his arrival were so difficult. We were having labor pains with no epidural! Our minds raced with thoughts of what he would look like, how much he'd weigh, whether he would have a lot of hair. I had a picture in my mind of what I thought he would look like.

Finally, we got the call telling us our son had arrived. We were overjoyed to hear he was here and healthy, and the birth had gone as planned. We could not wait to get to the hospital to see our son, but had to wait until the evening after his birth when we would only be allowed one hour with him. I was heartbroken knowing he had arrived and yet he didn't know we were out there longing to hold him, kiss him, and love him. I wanted to rush to the hospital and kiss his downy soft hair, count his fingers and toes, stare at him and memorize his face, every crinkle of his nose. The time between knowing he had arrived and being able to hold him was physically painful; my arms literally ached to hold my son.

We arrived at the hospital the following evening to meet our son for the first time, and my whole body was trembling with anticipation. We walked into the room, and he was in the bassinet. My heart exploded in my chest. There was my son! My husband and I took turns holding him. It was the fastest hour I have ever spent in my life. I was certain my heart had already been broken by the entire infertility process, but it broke a little more that evening as I walked out of the doors of that hospital without my son.

The following day was when the papers would be signed, relinquishing the rights of the birth family to our son. I spent the day in a hotel room waiting for the phone to ring. Again, the waiting was endless. I cried and cried that day, certain that this dream was about to end for us. It was going to be impossible for our son's birth mother to do this. She had held him in her arms and knew him now. She had an impossible decision to make.

Finally, the phone rang. I was told to come to the hospital to get my son. My broken heart mended with those words. We arrived at the hospital, and he was waiting for us. I held him so tight and close; I know he felt our love pouring out over him. He cuddled into me like he belonged there.

We whispered "I love you" a million times, kissed him a billion times, and left the hospital with our son. We love him endlessly, and always will. And when someone tells me he looks like me, I can't help but get a huge smile on my face and simply say, "Thank you."

~Sharon Pheifer

# Letter to the Birth Mother

*Biology is the least of what makes someone a mother.*
*~Oprah Winfrey*

I've never seen your actual face, only evidence of it in your daughter, my daughter, our child. I can't tell you my thoughts. I don't know your name or address—only the child you carried in your belly, who you passed through your uterus and into this world. Sometimes, I think we are like the two chambers of her heart. You made the blood and the muscle of her heart, but I keep the blood flowing and feed her 24/7 love.

If I could take the blue of the sky, the green of the trees and the yellow in the petal of a sunflower, I would make a palette for you and use the beauty of nature to try to reach you. I would send secret messages in Morse code through shooting stars and tell you, "Today, we went to the museum. She, now five, was exuberant. She stood inside the bubble-making machine, trying to create a see-through film around her. She placed particles of rug under magnifying glasses and used her hands to pedal a bike, which powered an electric bulb."

If I could, I would tell you how she was cradled in my arms on the subway ride home like a baby in the fetal position, and said, "Mama, Mama, I'm tired." Fifteen minutes later as the train emptied, she hung from the silver handles overhead like an Olympian. She lifted both legs waist high as I spotted her.

If I could, I would tell you how your daughter, my girl, has missed you. I have held her while she is deep in a keening cry, a thundering primal scream that makes me ache every time. I scratch and rub her sleepy back, and say, "It's okay. There. There. I love you. You're safe," until she returns to sleep, sometimes on me, "the mommy mattress." When she screams "Mama" in that guttural way, I know she's not crying for me. Do you know how she calls out for you?

How many times did she cry, unanswered in the orphanage, for your arms, your touch, your body? And how did she feel when you did not come? Didn't you hear her? What could have kept you from running to her side? I can't know. But I wish I could tell you she's okay. She's happy, curious, radiant, and playful. She's deep and thoughtful and silly.

She cried for weeks when she started pre-school. The first day she didn't cry, another girl did. She went over to her and said, "It's okay. Your mama will be back." They are still friends.

I realize how much you mean to me, and how distinct and private her journey to you will be. I hesitate to say too much about her now as she will speak for herself someday. And I don't know what she will feel about you. I can tell you my feelings, though. I am grateful you carried her to full term. I am sorry you live in a country with a one child policy, poverty, and overpopulation. I try not to judge you.

Once, when she said she loved you as much as she loves me, I kissed her head and said, "I love her, too, honey. She made you." I felt a grace I didn't know I possessed, and a tenderness I never predicted.

I don't always know the right thing to say to her, but at least we can talk. I don't know what thoughts or feelings you try to send to her. I wish you knew how wonderful she is, how I could fill a letter a day detailing our lives, but I know it would never reach you.

You share her blood. I share her home. You share her ethnicity. I share her days. If I could turn air into an aroma that would bring you a moment of my time, I would take you to her, to watch and see her for yourself as she is in the act of becoming. Now, at seven, she says things like, "I'm only 60 percent full on my hug-o-meter," or,

"Did you notice how I'm getting less shy?" She doesn't remember you, but sometimes she tries to imagine what you look like. Sometimes, I wonder which of her features is most like yours. Did she get her dimples or her thickening black hair from you?

In one photo of her crossing the monkey bars, her father said, "Look at that fierce determination on your face. I love it."

"I don't," she said as she rubbed her hands. "My hands hurt looking at the picture. I can feel it."

She feels you that deeply. Sometimes you are a gaping hole that makes her weep. Other times, you are a space she inhabits with pride. I'm trying to tell you what I can't say to your face, on a letter or over the phone. Your daughter, my daughter, our daughter loves and misses you.

~Christine White

# Chapter 8

# New Moms

## Tough Stuff

*If you can find a path with no obstacles,
it probably doesn't lead anywhere.*

~Frank A. Clark

# The Power of Two

*A daughter is a gift of love.*
~Author Unknown

Two words can change everything. "Wait a minute," I interrupted the doctor standing beside us in the recovery room. "What do you mean 'chromosomal abnormality'? You mean, like Down's?"

The rest of his words disappeared into a silent scream that went something like "I can't! I can't! I can't!" The next moment, my husband crumpled on top of me, and I realized that I didn't have the luxury of grief. I had a newborn who needed a mother, and a husband who needed a wife. And so I shoved the scream into a box and slammed the lid shut.

At times like this, the soul goes into shock. Just as the body under extreme duress has its priorities—heart and lungs at the expense of fingers and toes—so does the mind.

For the next thirty-six hours, I felt nothing but dull exhaustion as I tried to process a whole new reality. I was numb, as if my emotions had severed from their source. I held the baby... a baby who seemed foreign, somehow. Alien. A baby whose name we had chosen, but to whom I didn't feel connected. I went through the motions. Nursed. Kissed her cheeks. But only because I knew I had to. Dispassionately, I reminded myself that love is a choice, not an emotion.

But in the solitude of the hospital night, after my husband had gone home with our two-year-old son, the darkest corners of my mind writhed with the thought that I really didn't want this baby and all the difficulties her life would inevitably bring.

On Sunday morning, I woke to darkness, long before the nurses' morning check of vitals, long before the baby was due to nurse. Turmoil rumbled uneasily at the edges of my consciousness. To keep it at bay, I turned on the light and reached for the laptop to check e-mail.

And then, as clear as if the voice was speaking aloud instead of inside my head, I heard: "Put it away. You need this time to grieve."

My scattered thoughts ground to a halt. I turned the light back off and leaned back, my stomach pirouetting as I carefully pulled the lid off the box where I had stuffed my emotions.

"God, I can't do this," I said. "I don't want to do this. Take it away!" And the tears spilled over, searing my eyelids as they fell.

At first, the pain seemed to expand. For the first time in my life, I understood how limited and self-absorbed my concept of love was. For the first time, I understood the subtle bigotry that lay beneath my desire for a "healthy" child. I was standing face to face with myself, and I didn't like what I saw.

And yet as I wept—as I choked out the words to express my fear and shame—the pressure began to ease. And when it was over, everything was different. My limbs quivered as if I had been through some great exertion, yet the silence inside me hummed with the serenity of acceptance—and potential.

*It doesn't matter. She is yours now. This wasn't what you wanted, but this is what you have been given, and it is good.*

I heard the clacking of a hospital crib approaching my room. The door opened, the metal wheels bumped over the threshold, and my heart squeezed tight as I saw a silky-skinned, dark-haired newborn named Julianna lying inside it.

Two words really can change everything. My daughter.

~Kathleen M. Basi

# A Rough Start

*The best advice from my mother was a reminder to tell my children every day: "Remember you are loved."*
~Evelyn McCormick

Our son, Quin, was born on a beautiful May day. On another beautiful day, exactly one month later, he was admitted to Seattle Children's Hospital. It's amazing how quickly life can change.

I was a new mom, and though I hadn't had much experience with babies, my intuition was telling me something was not right. That first month, he cried a lot, and he squirmed in what seemed like discomfort quite often. His sleep was only in short spurts but everyone assured us this was normal.

That particular day, though, he had been lethargic, hadn't really eaten, and was sleeping almost constantly. Rather than stay home alone while my husband went to play soccer, my instincts told me not to be alone, so I went to my brother and sister-in-law's house. They had a three-year-old, so I figured Quin and I were in good hands.

Thinking his crying might be due to gas, my sister-in-law started gently pushing Quin's legs in a cycling motion that she thought might help get things moving along. That was the last moment that we still thought this was normal newborn stuff. Moments later, when his diaper started seeping blood, we wasted no time getting him to the hospital.

At first, they didn't know what was wrong with him. The doctors ran test after test, but could not figure out the source of his bleeding. He spent a few nights in the ICU and then, after one procedure, he seemed to stabilize. They explained to us what they thought had happened, and we all assumed he was okay. They were actually going to release him after one more night of observation. And what a night that turned out to be.

I sent our family and my husband home to get some rest, and I stayed to sleep in Quin's hospital room. I woke to find him surrounded by doctors and nurses with all sorts of questions for me. Was this moaning sound he was making normal for him? Had he vomited bile before? Was he always this pale? No, no, and no!

They asked the nurse who had watched over him in the ICU the previous days to come down and let them know if he had been like this on her watch. She took one look at him, literally scooped him up in her arms, and hurried him to the ICU.

The next words I heard from doctors and nurses are blurred together. They go something like this: emergency exploratory surgery, very sick baby, colostomy bag, we don't know... I'm sure their words were much more eloquent, but I heard only the worst.

The surgery seemed to last for hours. By this time, there were about ten of us holed up in the private family waiting area. I know now that the doors are there to create privacy, but also to contain the worry and grief that permeate the room. Finally, the surgeon came with good news. They had found a cyst in his bowels, a large one, but they had successfully removed it and been able to leave most of the bowel intact. It's funny that I considered that good news, but at the time it really was. We all left the hospital for a celebratory lunch so we could be back to see our little baby boy once he was back in his room recovering.

Once we returned to the hospital, though, the rug was once again pulled out from under us. Quin had survived the surgery, but we were told he was septic and not at all out of the woods. You could almost hear time stop. I think it was in that very moment I realized I was the grown-up. I was the mom. I was at risk of having my son die. Was this really happening?

In times of severe stress, something else takes over. That's my theory anyway. How else could I sleep at night? How else could I continue to pump breast milk every four hours for six weeks? How else could I go on with my life knowing that I might end up a mother without a son?

The next few weeks were grueling. Blood counts, blood pressure, heart rate, fluid output. "Do you have a blood-clotting disorder in your family?" "Do you have any autoimmune diseases in your family?" "We aren't sure why he isn't getting better." "We're so sorry to say that he'll need another surgery." "He's come down with rotavirus from exposure in the hospital." "We can't find any more veins in his arms and legs, so we'll have to put IVs in his head."

There were times when I didn't think the nightmare would end. There were times when I couldn't fathom why he wasn't healing. But there wasn't one time that I was willing to give up on him. There wasn't one time when I let myself think about life without him. It just wasn't possible for him to die. He was my little baby, and I wasn't willing to lose him.

It's funny how life goes on even when time has stopped being kind. My husband had to return to work, I resigned from my job, and our visitors gradually diminished as people waited for this part of our story to reveal its ending. Fourth of July in a hospital is less than you'd hope for. Sunny summer days spent lunching at the hospital cafeteria leave much to be desired. But my innocent and somewhat selfish existence was over, and if being at the hospital meant my son was alive, then that is where I would spend my time.

This journey has a happy ending. Six weeks to the day after Quin was admitted to the hospital, we were able to take him home. He is now a happy, smart, funny and feisty eight-year-old boy. From time to time, I catch him showing off his scar to his buddies. He knows he was sick as a baby, and he also knows that he's perfectly fine now. And so am I.

~Erin Cloherty Baebler

# Will's Whole World

*Motherhood: All love begins and ends there.*
~Robert Browning

Within one hour of Will's arrival, his seven-pound, three-ounce body shook my world to its core and sent it spiraling in a direction I never knew I could handle, much less embrace. The moments following his birth appear to me only as flashes of time, blurred memories I can't quite piece together. I remember his tiny, quivering, slimy body lying on my chest, soaking my hospital gown. I remember my husband Jeff, giddy that we'd had a boy, with tears running down his face screaming, "He's got nuts! I can see his nuts!" I remember after the commotion had settled and Will was comfortable under the warmer, the midwife and nurse standing over Will's little body and whispering. That's when my memory returns. Crystal clear. That's also when I lose track of my emotions and my world.

I'm not sure if I knew something was wrong when I saw the two women whispering, but I knew it was significant. At first, I thought they were ogling him. But when the nurse quietly slipped out of the room, and Kerry, the midwife, picked up our new son, swaddled tightly in his blankets, and sat down on my bed, I knew she wasn't about to rave about his good looks.

"Hey, guys," she started, "so I'm looking at William, and he's perfect, but I think—and I don't know for certain—but I think he might have Down syndrome."

She went on to list the features that made her reach this decision: his flat-bridged nose, somewhat almond-shaped eyes, straight, flat line on the palms of his hands, and a wide space between his first and second toes. That's when I lost track of my world. An instant disconnect occurred between me and my emotions, and me and my new son. Kerry told us a pediatrician was coming in to check on Will and validate her suspicions. Until then, she was taking Will into the nursery, and Jeff and I were to get some sleep.

Once she left, Jeff and I cried. We apologized to each other and yet swore we still loved him, no matter what. We agreed we wouldn't say anything to our families until we got a definitive answer from the pediatrician. Jeff made his way over to the daybed for daddies, and I rolled onto my side, wishing I was still pregnant and none of this was happening.

As promised, the pediatrician came. Without hesitation, but with utter professionalism, he said, "Well, yeah. Kerry was right. He's got Down syndrome."

This time, as much as it hurt to hear, it wasn't such a shock. Though Jeff and I found hope in Kerry's reluctance to make the assessment, I think we all knew the doctor would agree. We asked the pediatrician some questions about what this meant for Will, and he rambled off some complications that might occur in a newborn with this diagnosis. Then he said something that provided us an infinite amount of comfort.

"I know this was unexpected, and it might take a while to get used to," he acknowledged, "but before you know it, he'll be your number-one guy. He'll be your whole world." We took that with us as we told our family about our son.

Throughout Will's first night, long after our family helped us mull over the what-ifs and the how-comes, and wiped the tears from their eyes, Will was placed in a warming bed, given a steady stream of oxygen, and had a feeding tube inserted into his tender body. When we woke up the next morning, Jeff and I immediately went to the nursery. Jeff began to cry as we looked at our son, lying in a spread eagle with a fan of wires and tubes suctioned on him and stuck into him. Because Will's body temperature was low, I couldn't pick him up out of the warmer, but I was secretly relieved. I looked at this slight creature and felt at a loss. As an expectant mother, I had anticipated an instant connection with the life I'd carried for nine months. Now, I couldn't quite grasp that connection. I felt withdrawn and hesitant. I had gone into this pregnancy with one picture in my mind, and had been given something completely different.

I think my sister-in-law said it best the previous night. She affirmed, "You have to mourn the child you didn't have, but embrace the child you do."

Looking at my son less than twenty-four hours into his life, I decided I would not mourn anything about this precious baby, but celebrate him completely. As the day went on, I had to constantly remind myself to accept this decision.

Our second morning in the hospital was my last as a patient. We walked into the nursery and asked how our boy was.

"Good," a nurse chimed. "You can hold him if you want. Maybe feed him through the tube?"

I was surprised to find I was elated to hold my son. The nurse placed the sweet sleeping bundle in my arms, and I could feel the tears punching at my eyes. She said his umbilical cord had fallen off because the warmer had dried it out. My eyes started to well. I swallowed hard and smiled. Next, she told us he finished passing meconium. The tears rained down. I started crying so hard that Jeff thought I might drop the baby. The nurse asked if I was okay. Did I need to put the baby down? Did I want a tissue? I just sat there and wept, and wouldn't let anyone take Will from my arms.

I cried for about ten minutes before Jeff convinced me to leave the nursery and guided me through the corridor. When we got back to our room, I collapsed in his arms. But I wasn't crying for the reasons he thought. It wasn't because of the almond-shaped eyes or the possible life Will faced. I was crying because I was Will's mother, and I couldn't take care of him. I wasn't there when his umbilical stump fell off, the final attachment to the life I had once supported. I didn't get to change his diaper for the first time. I couldn't make him better, make him happy. I didn't begrudge the nurses their job—I was grateful for the care they gave my son—but it was supposed to be my job. I felt helpless and invalid. Expendable.

At that moment, I forgot about making peace with this new being and what he brought into my world. I didn't worry about accepting my decision to celebrate him; I did so without thought or notion. I sifted through my emotions from the previous two days, released any hesitation I felt, and embraced what I was left with—fear and love. But it wasn't fear of having a baby with Down syndrome and what that meant. It wasn't about a genetic code or a facial feature to tell the world he might be a little different. The fear came from not being able to care for my son. Will having Down syndrome wasn't something that happened to us; it just was. It wasn't predetermined because Jeff and I "could handle it"; it's how we made him. It's not a test, or a punishment, or a meant-to-be. Will is Will, forty-seven chromosomes and all. And all I wanted to do was love him.

•••

Two months later, I sang and danced a tired two-month-old around his bedroom, trying to put him to sleep. His little face peered up at me as I sang, mesmerized, focused. Our eyes met, and he smiled—a happy, content, pure loving smile. I knew at that moment he was right where he wanted to be, always. He loved me and knew that I loved him. I tripped over the words I was singing and started to cry. I cried for my reaction during his tumultuous first days. I cried for doubting the place he had in my world. I cried for how simple and complete this little being's world was, only because I was in it. I cried because I knew: I was Will's whole world.

~Amy Bourque

# Surviving Postpartum Anxiety

*Panic is a sudden desertion of us,
and a going over to the enemy of our imagination.*
~Christian Nevell Bovee

Two weeks after my daughter was born, I knew something was wrong, but I couldn't put my finger on it. I felt fine most of the time. It was just those moments when my mind turned on me. Three distinct and very fearful scenarios regularly invaded my thoughts, terrifying me each time they occurred.

The first was a fear of holding my newborn on our upper deck. Images of me accidentally losing my grip and dropping her, and her falling to the ground below flashed before my eyes. It bothered me to the point that I wouldn't go out on the upper deck with her. If I had to go out, it was only to quickly descend the stairs to the safety of the lower deck, resting one foot above solid ground. I developed a phobia of being on that upper deck.

The fear of kitchen knives also plagued my thoughts. I could not prepare meals using a knife if my daughter was in the room. My brain tortured me with vivid images of the knife slipping out of my hand and cutting my precious child's skull open. Oddly, no other sharp objects were of concern. I confidently handled scissors and utility knives around her. The nightmare was in the kitchen. Being so frightfully concerned for her, I refused to touch the soft fontanel at the top of her head for any reason.

The last devil invading my thoughts pertained to my husband's wellbeing as he drove home from work each day. If he wasn't home by 6:00 every evening, my mind entered into a *CSI*-style conversation with two non-existent male police officers standing at my door. The conversation was always the same.

"Mrs. George, we regret to inform you that your husband has been killed in a horrific car accident. We need you to accompany us to the hospital to identify his remains."

Widowed with two young children under the age of four—the emotions, so real and powerful, the event, completely fictional. And yet my heart would race uncontrollably to the point that I could barely breathe through the tears.

In an attempt to control this particular fear, I finally had the sense of mind to ask my husband to call if he was going to be late. His calls effectively prevented this insane scene from invading my mind any longer. I could only tell him that I needed to know he was safe. I couldn't verbalize the depth of my need-to-know status.

In fact, for months I told no one what I was feeling. I was afraid that if I tried to explain the situation, someone would think I was crazy and call Child Protective Services. The thought of my children being taken away from me was unbearable. Besides, I knew I wasn't crazy. These "episodes" were unique in that they related to specific events. I wasn't depressed; I really felt fine most of the time. It was just in those moments that my usually calm mind betrayed me.

Then one day, about a year and a half after my daughter was born, I was reading through an issue of a parenting magazine while she napped. It featured an article on postpartum anxiety and related the story of a woman in San Francisco who suffered from acute postpartum anxiety attacks. The article stated that her attacks became so severe that she quit taking her newborn child onto her deck for fear that her thoughts would manifest themselves, and she would drop her baby over the edge.

I sat dumbfounded as I realized that I identified completely with this woman. I now had a name for this beast that had so viciously tormented me.

I called my doctor and made an appointment. It may seem ridiculous that I didn't seek medical help for a year and a half, but in my mind's eye, I honestly thought my children would be taken away from me. I didn't dare take the risk. I'd rather live with those hellish, numbing thoughts interrupting my days.

I took the article with me to my appointment. The written word, the identification of evidence, gave me confidence. He confirmed that I was most likely suffering from postpartum anxiety attacks. A combination of hormone-balancing creams and serotonin boosters eliminated the daytime nightmares in less than two weeks.

The relief was indescribable. I walked onto the deck without fear. I chopped veggies in the kitchen while my daughter played at my feet. I quit watching the clock strike 6:00 p.m., wondering if my husband was pulling into the driveway. I finally had the peace of mind to share the depth of my struggle with my husband and mom.

Still disturbing, though, is the fact that I suffered so long before being able to identify the problem. Why hasn't more been written about postpartum anxiety? While depression is commonly understood and discussed, especially in motherhood circles, I had never heard of its cousin. Maybe, as the article suggested, it's difficult for healthcare professionals to identify and diagnose, even though the effects can be just as damaging.

If I could thank that woman in San Francisco for her bravery in telling her story, I would do so in an instant. If I could thank the editors of that magazine (no longer published) for believing the subject matter important enough to write about, there's no question I would. Because of their conviction to bring postpartum anxiety to light, I finally sought help. As a result, I now have the courage to put my own experiences on paper, in hopes that other new moms won't feel compelled to wait to get help for lack of a name for an entirely treatable, and very real, medical condition.

~Jenny R. George

# Delivered Not by the Stork

*Where did you come from, baby dear?*
*Out of the everywhere into here.*
~George MacDonald

Many of my friends have children, and I have heard all the stories about their water breaking, labor pains, and the mad dash to the hospital. They go on to tell me in full detail how dilated they were and how they weren't supposed to push. Then through their emotional tears they tell me about the final push and how this little miracle of life came into the world. It is always a moving story, and I am very happy for them as I hold their little bundle of joy.

But my story is different. I have never been pregnant. I've never experienced morning sickness, stretch marks or the cravings for pickles and ice cream. Due to circumstances beyond my control, mainly a bout with breast cancer, I could not have my own children. But pregnancy and stretch marks are not the only way to have a family. The route I chose was international adoption.

I didn't need to make a trip to the hospital in order to have my little bundle of joy delivered. All I had to do was answer the front door.

I adopted my daughter from Russia. I was in the process of adopting a baby girl from Moscow when my first husband was killed in a plane crash. Understandably, the adoption agency was concerned that with all of the difficulties of dealing with his death that perhaps adoption wasn't right for me at that time. Nope, I wanted my baby. I had lost my husband, and I had no intention of losing my daughter. The agency must have been convinced that I meant business because they agreed to proceed with the adoption, but only after a six-month waiting period. If I could prove to them I could handle an adoption so soon after my husband's death, then they would let me complete the process.

I patiently waited the six months. During this time, I quit my job, temporarily moved in with my parents, bought a house, and moved halfway across the country. And I tried to figure out how I was going to raise a baby all by myself.

Then the day finally came when I received a call from my adoption social worker. A picture of my daughter had been sent by FedEx the day before, and I should receive it by 10:30 a.m. Needless to say, I freaked out! I called my parents and friends to announce that Elle's delivery was imminent. I ran out and bought a scanner so I could scan her picture and e-mail it to everyone I knew.

I was trying to figure out how to set up the scanner when the doorbell rang. My heart momentarily stopped as I dashed downstairs to open the door. Unfortunately, it was the DHL deliveryman with a package containing some of my late husband's personal effects. That threw me for a loop and opened up a whole other can of emotions. I cried and laughed at the irony that on the very same morning I was to receive a picture of our daughter, I would receive his wallet that was recovered from the crash site.

Then the doorbell rang again. My heart momentarily stopped again as I dashed back down the stairs. This time it was the FedEx deliveryman with a package from my adoption agency. I had been on the phone with my father when the doorbell rang the second time, so he waited while I ran down to get my FedEx package. I was so nervous I almost couldn't open the package, all while Daddy asked me questions about what she looked like.

Finally, the package was open, and I pulled out three pictures of my daughter. Zoya Alexandrovna. Through my tears, I told my father, "She is so beautiful." This was closely followed by, "She looks like a frog." She was so lovely and so little and so bald. I spent the rest of the day trying to set up the scanner so I could e-mail her picture.

A few months later, I was ready to fly to Russia to bring her home. I flew Delta Air Lines from Kansas City to Moscow and back—a fourteen-plus-hour flight both ways. I wasn't the only person on the plane who was bringing back an adopted child. There were five families on the flight from Moscow to JFK Airport. The flight attendants were used to parents carrying crying infants up and down the aisles. They told me this was referred to as the "baby flight." Eventually, we made it home from our marathon trip halfway around the world... safely delivered by Delta Air Lines.

So, I was never rushed to the hospital in a curtain of labor pains, but every time I see a FedEx truck or a Delta Air Lines plane, I always think about the "delivery" of my child.

Thanks to Delta and FedEx for making my family complete!

~Lanita Moss

# He's the Same Baby

*Attitude is a little thing that makes a big difference.*
*~Winston Churchill*

"He's the same baby he was this morning," our pediatrician told me as I held you tighter than tight. "Your son was born with Smith-Magenis syndrome," he continued as he looked over the lab results. His voice sounded far away as I heard the words "mental retardation" and "autistic behaviors."

No! I wanted to scream. That's not my baby. This morning, he was so smart. He was going to wave at me from the kindergarten bus and ignore me from the middle school bus stop. He was going to be the high school valedictorian. He was going to graduate from medical school some day.

"He's the same baby he was last Sunday," our preacher told me as I rocked you in the pew. "You are just learning about your son, but God has known him all along."

You're wrong! I wanted to shout. That's not my baby. Last Sunday, he was so pleasant. He was going to be an altar boy and light the candles. He was going to lead the youth group on mission trips. He was going to graduate from the seminary some day.

"He's the same baby he was last year," our family told me as I blew out your two candles. "He still has your eyes and Daddy's smile."

That's not true! I wanted to cry. That's not my baby. Last year, he was so strong and beautiful. He was going to be a star athlete and the most popular boy. He was going to marry a girl just like me some day.

"He's the same baby we brought home from the hospital," your daddy told me as I lay you down in your crib. But this is not what I had dreamed for you.

You are my baby boy, but I will never lose my voice from cheering at your Little League games. Instead, I will shout when you learn how to walk without your leg braces. You are my child, but you will never be the class president. Instead, you will have fewer friends, but they will all be true friends. You are my firstborn, but I will never drive away from your dorm room with tears in my eyes. Instead, I will be sobbing when it takes you an hour to leave Children's Hospital because you must hug every child in a wheelchair. You are my son, but you will never be the father of my grandchildren. Instead, you will be their favorite uncle who still believes in Santa Claus and the Tooth Fairy.

It seems everyone was right. You are the same baby. But I am not the same mother.

~Tina Marie McGrevy

# Jefferson's Journey

*Life is God's novel. Let him write it.*
~Isaac Bashevis Singer

From the earliest I can remember, I knew I would be a mother. Even at a young age, I was realistic about it — if, when I grew up and got married, I couldn't have my own, we would adopt. The plan was to have several, evenly spaced. But, of course, I'd be satisfied with what God gave me.

It was always natural to surround myself with children of all ages. I finished high school, found myself majoring in special education in college, started teaching middle school, married a godly man, volunteered in high school and college age groups, had our first child, and then became Children's Ministry Director under my husband as a bi-vocational Family Pastor, nurturing and caring for children and their families from birth through elementary school.

After several years of trying to have another child, my husband and I grew to appreciate that God must have other plans. We had one bright, healthy daughter in our home and plenty of others to guide outside of it! Life was complete, and we had come to terms with having one child of our own unless He deemed it otherwise, in whatever manner He desired.

Right before our daughter turned eight, we discovered that we were expecting. It was somewhat of a shock. I had gone back to teaching, and as a family, we maintained our normal fast pace of juggling work, ministry, home, and school life. Before too long, our newest addition was making it clear that he would not go unnoticed. I was told to "slow down, take it easy."

Very soon afterward, that turned into "modified bed rest" and all manner of monitoring. We had found out the baby was a boy and nicknamed him "Rowdy" for all the ruckus he was causing.

At thirty weeks and within days of closing on a new home, our baby boy decided he could no longer wait to see the world. We rushed to the hospital where we learned my placenta was more than 50 percent abrupted.

There was no choice. We would have a son that night. To say it was a defining moment in our lives is an understatement. My husband kept asking the doctor if everything was going to be okay, only to hear him respond over and over, "Your wife will be fine." I wish I could say that my spirit rose to the challenge and I was full of strength and valor. Instead, I was blank. You see, I'm not very good in situations beyond my control.

After what seemed an eternity, I was in a cold, crowded operating room, surrounded by my husband, my doctor, and a handful of strangers. There were two teams—one for me, and one for the baby, who would be immediately rushed to the local children's hospital. The doctor worked swiftly.

Silence… Way too much silence…

They handed him over to the neonatologist and his team. More silence. Finally, a scream! My three-pound, seventeen-inch son had been born. I was not able to hold him. Less than a minute later, he was being rushed to the NICU miles away, so deep red he was almost purple. He was encased in a plastic bubble and covered in wires and monitors.

When a doctor says to your face that God must have something very special planned for your child, you know you're in for a ride! Our journey had officially begun… learning more medical terms than we cared to, spending countless hours in the NICU (sometimes with an eight-year-old who wanted so badly to help but just wore herself and others out on the swivel chairs), watching our baby sleep, watching the monitors, watching his heart rate and oxygen levels go up and down... All the while, we were coming home to boxes that weren't going to be unpacked anytime soon, relying on friends and family to accomplish daily tasks I was not able to complete.

Then, just like that, it was time to go home. After months of not being able to hold him at will, not being the one to change every diaper, give every feeding, spend every moment with him, we were supposed to do this on our own? Just take him home with us? Alone?

I wish I could say the fear of being alone, the sense that no one understood, that everyone else was going on with their wonderful lives after struggling greatly to feed my own child, and worrying about his lagging behind on just about every developmental chart went away immediately. I wish it hadn't bothered me that just when one hurdle was over, another seemed to arise—torticollis, and then plagiocephaly. A cranial orthotic device (corrective helmet) and physical therapy.

The red-faced, angry screaming that comes with pushing your child beyond his limits can certainly get to me. Still, God reminds me of His provision. Recently, I found an entry I wrote at the end of a journal given to me before he came home, which was filled with love and words of wisdom from others:

"This is what a family of God looks like: caring for each other, lifting one another through prayer, and being the hands and feet of God. Among the people you'll read about in this book are individuals who were meeting challenges of their own: surgeries, deaths of loved ones, financial strife, marital conflicts, job loss and other personal issues... Yet these people—these amazing men and women... families—stopped long enough to look up and recognize our joys and our needs. You are blessed, son. I am grateful to our Father for the gift of them!"

Almost a year later, reminders linger. Weekly physical therapy ensues. Jefferson remains behind on some milestones. I still struggle with not comparing him to the charts.

But the truth is this: Most of this struggle was my struggle. My child is the same as every child. With every small step forward (figuratively speaking), I learn something new. About him. About myself.

About my marriage and family and friends. And about what God is trying to do in all of our lives.

~Brandy Kleinhans as told to Mary Z. Smith

# Chapter 9

# New Moms

## Giggles & Mischief

*Humor is the great thing, the saving thing.*
*The minute it crops up, all our irritation and resentments slip away,*
*and a sunny spirit takes their place.*

~Mark Twain

# The Perfect Accessory

*It is the unseen, unforgettable, ultimate accessory of fashion that heralds your arrival and prolongs your departure.*
~Coco Chanel

There's a point in everyone's life when change whacks you upside the head, forcing you to move on. Pregnancy and birth are the ultimate whammy. You've got a Greek chorus of hormones telling you to change your ways. So you give up cocktails and cigarettes, and you develop some sort of sense. You don the red cape of "mommy" with all the superpowers that entails.

Okay, I'd seen the fashion costs of motherhood. I didn't want to give up any of my spunky style, and I figured any gal with good fashion sense and bright red hair could make this transition from glam to ma'am. I didn't imagine the ultimate sacrifice.

Yes, ladies, it's true. The survivors sleep deep in the back of my closet, protected from the elements and my dormant yearnings. No, I'm not talking shoes. I am mourning the loss of the best handbags this world has ever known. A moment of silence if you would...

For any event or occasion, I could go through my collection to find just the right bag. Sure, my obsession might have been a tad unhealthy, but isn't it always something? I had quite a collection: a few vintage pieces for those classy evenings, patent leather with embroidered cherries for rock-a-billy sass, Chinese brocade for elegance, the perfect jewel-encrusted clutch to spark up that little black dress. I even made a few from cigar boxes with a chic nod to my crafty side. Yes, ladies, it was a collection to drool for. And it was mine. All mine.

Until the guest room turned into the nursery. That closet could no longer serve as my repository for irresponsible spending. No, it had to make way for onesies and toys he can't play with for years. (Thanks, Uncle Joe.)

I decided I would keep ten. A nice round number, and enough to fulfill any fashion issues that might arise in the next year or so. Who knows? There could be a wedding or some cocktail party that we might be able to get a sitter for and might have the energy to actually attend. Ten. Tucked in until needed. Secreted away.

I cried. I physically shed tears over the choices I had to make. I wasn't crying for a knock-off Louis Vuitton bag. No, I knew this was it. No more spunky gal out on the town for a night. No more spending hours deciding which bag was just right. Those days were coming to an end, and it was time to buck up and start the cycle of sacrifices every mommy has to make. My life was no longer about me. Sure, the *Today* show has all sorts of segments about women holding on to their identity and being a mom. And, gee, aren't they something? But even they had to have had this moment. Bringing home a baby changes everything.

I wanted to be an example to my child. I didn't want him to grow up with irrational attachments. How could I raise a responsible human being when I had an entire closet full of irresponsibility? It's the one thing the books don't tell you while you're eating bon-bons and dreaming about soft cheeks and gurgly smiles. You have nine months to get yourself together. Nine months to recognize you are not #1. Nine months to (gulp) grow up.

They weren't just handbags. They were my freedom, my youth. They were carefree days full of promise. They were little girl memories in a grown-up world. Giving up these bags meant real growth — however necessary and painful. If I wanted to be a good parent, I needed to "put childish ways behind me" (1 Corinthians 13:11 NIV).

So I culled and had a garage sale — and, yes, I made a killing feeding the obsessions of young ladies free to buy frippery. I used those funds to buy the diaper bag I now carry—an Eddie Bauer backpack with tons of pockets, and room for anything and everything under the sun. I wear it casually on my back so that my hands are free. I have something much more precious to carry now, and he has proven to be the perfect accessory for every occasion.

~Dawn Hentrich

# Noah to the Rescue

*Now, as always, the most automated appliance in a household is the mother.*
*~Beverly Jones*

Everyone, at one time or another, gets locked out. You get locked out of the car, out of the house, out of the office. Generally, people don't get locked in. But, as a new mom, I did just that. I got locked in the nursery.

Before we were parents to a human baby, we were pet-parents to two cantankerous cats and a spoiled dog. In preparing for the birth of our first child, I read all the books, listened to all the advice, and followed all the expert recommendations so our baby would have the best start. In an attempt to keep the cats (and their hair) out of the crib, we took the advice of a couple further down the road of childrearing and installed a screen door on the nursery. It solved the problem of keeping the cats out and the baby in, and still allowed air and sound to escape.

One bright spring morning, I rocked and nursed my four-month-old baby for his first feeding of the day. My husband stirred in the next room, dressed, and stopped by the nursery on his way to work. Pushing open the screen door, he leaned in for a kiss from me.

"I probably won't be home for lunch today. Are you two going to be alright on your own?"

I grinned and cocked an eyebrow at him. "Oh, I think we'll manage. Especially since only one of us eats solid food."

"I'll see you at dinner." He planted a kiss on the top of our son's head, earning himself a toothless, sloppy grin.

Without his audience, my baby returned to nursing as I slowly rocked. I heard my husband's truck pull out of the driveway and closed my eyes, leaning my head against the back of the rocker, enjoying the warm sunlight pouring in through the windows. A few moments later, my eyes flew open as I registered the metallic sound I'd heard just after my husband left the room. It was the unmistakable sound of a little metal hook sliding into a little round circle on the outside of the door.

I finished nursing the baby, quickly made my way to the door, and gave it a tug. Locked. Trying not to panic, I assessed the situation. My four-month-old baby and I were locked in a second-story bedroom with no chance of escape until at least ten hours later when my husband returned for dinner. No phone, no food, and no bathroom. Our closest neighbors lived too far to hear my yell even if they could pick the dead-bolted doors. Thankfully, at least my son's food, entertainment, and diapers were within reach.

I changed his diaper, wound up the mobile hanging from his crib, and placed him underneath. As he cooed and kicked, I tried to figure out what to do. Lord, help me think of something!

Minutes passed. I shook the door thinking maybe I could dislodge the hook. Nothing. I examined the hinges, wondering if I could take the door apart. Nope. I pulled the door toward me and tried to wedge my finger in the gap. Not gonna do it. But if I could find something longer and thinner, it just might work.

I looked in the closets hoping to find a wire hanger, but cute plastic baby hangers mocked me. I tried the end of the bulb syringe, but it buckled under the pressure. Finally, my eyes fell on a small, stuffed patchwork figure of Noah, surrounded by plush animals, two by two, sitting on the dresser. In his little hand, he held a black wire staff. Yes! I slid the staff from his grip, pulled the door toward me once again to create a gap, and pushed the wire toward the hook closure. I pushed up, but the hook didn't budge. Loosening my hold on the door a little, I tried again. This time that little bit of slack allowed me to shove the hook up and out of the hole, springing me from my pint-sized prison.

That day, as a new mom, I learned that there were going to be times when I'd have to rely solely on myself and my wits. I learned that over the next eighteen years or more, I would need to be resourceful. I also learned that, when faced with adversity, I would need to be creative and use things and situations to my (and my child's) advantage.

I also learned to prop the door open when I entered the nursery. And I made sure that as long as the screen door stayed on the nursery, Noah never left the room while I was still inside.

~Nikki Studebaker Barcus

# Drew and the Pacifier Blues

*Habit is habit, and not to be flung out of the window by any man, but coaxed downstairs a step at a time.*
~Mark Twain

Between eighteen and twenty months of age, my firstborn son, Drew, lost his pacifier before naptime at Mother's Day Out. I was concerned about this until the day care provider told me, "He fussed for about ten minutes, and then he went to sleep." I became excited at the thought of not enduring another middle-of-the-night search for the elusive pacifier. (I have since learned, with number-two son, to dump every pacifier we own into the crib while he sleeps.)

That night, Drew fussed about ten minutes without his passy, and then went to sleep. I had forgotten just how wonderful a night of uninterrupted sleep could be. I thought to myself, "This is going to be a cinch." Certain friends had told me it took two weeks to break the pacifier habit. Other friends, like myself, were still trying to find the magic key to unlock the hidden mysteries to de-pacifierization.

The morning after my first full night's rest, I was busy whistling a happy little tune when I walked into the kitchen to prepare breakfast. There to my utter disbelief was my toddler son digging in a drawer that he was not even tall enough to see into.

"Paapaa!" he called. "Paapaa!"

In my excitement the night before, I had failed to rid the household of any lingering pacifiers.

I held my breath, whispering a prayer. "Please, oh please, oh please." But I could tell Drew had nabbed one when his face lit up as if it were Christmas morning.

"Paapaa, oh, paapaa!" It was the sweetest, most heart-wrenching cry I had ever heard come out of his pre-terrible-twos mouth. Drew had rediscovered a long-lost friend, the only friend he had or cared to have at the moment.

That morning, upon arriving at the Mother's Day Out program, I casually instructed the personnel to lose the pacifier again, which they kindly did. After that, Drew would occasionally ask for his paapaa, but the major battle had been won, or so I thought.

In February 1995, my second son, Dallas, was born. After he was about three weeks old, Drew realized Dallas was now a permanent fixture, and no amount of slapping the baby on the top of his head was going to send him back to where he came from. For Drew, the upside of Dallas's arrival was that Dallas took a pacifier. Drew began to like Dallas a little more. After all, any pacifier friend of Dallas's must be a friend of Drew's. There we went again!

I was instructed, throughout all the self-help baby books I could get my hands on, about sibling rivalry, to let the older child participate as much as possible in caring for the new baby. Before I knew it, my twenty-five-month-old thirty-four-pounder wanted his diaper changed on the changing table. Drew also wanted to nurse, or "eat like Daddas." You can guess that now the pacifier was on the endangered species list in our home. The first month or so, I felt this phase would pass, but as time marched on… I wasn't so sure.

Dallas took the pacifier only while he slept, but before I knew it, Drew had the pacifier in his mouth during Dallas's awake hours. I began to tell Drew only babies took pacifiers. He told me, "I a baby." I told him he was my baby, but only itty-bitty babies needed a pacifier. Drew then told me, "I itty-bitty baby." I finally told Drew that babies needed lots of sleep, and if he wanted to take the pacifier he needed to take a lot of naps. That worked! He gave it up in a heartbeat. Drew loves to sleep, but he didn't want to sleep nearly as much as Dallas.

This little solution seemed to be working fine until one day when I couldn't find a single pacifier—or Drew. As I was running throughout the house with a screaming baby on my hip, I came across my now two-and-a-half-year-old son crouched behind the living room rocking chair with his small hands cupped over his mouth.

"Drew," I said. "What's that in your mouth?"

"Uhhh, don't know."

"Drew, if that's Dallas's passy, he needs it!" I yelled over my screaming five-month-old. After what seemed a five-minute standoff, Drew reluctantly handed me the pacifier.

As I looked into Drew's little face, I realized my son had a problem... a pacifier problem. I likened him to an ex-smoker having nicotine fits. He had gone cold turkey from his addiction, and now—his first relapse.

I put down Dallas and his passy and picked up Drew.

"Together, we can fight this," I told him. "I'll get you professional help. There must be a twelve-step program we can get you into." Poor Drew, I had no idea he had come so far as to hide to steal a drag from the pacifier.

Well, a few months passed, and I truly believed the pacifier attraction was just a phase, so I didn't seek counseling. Drew's cravings came and went, and we would still find him hiding behind a piece of furniture, enjoying an occasional drag.

I finally came to terms with this, though. If the only addiction Drew had in his life was a pacifier, then let him surround himself with them! I mean, there are no proven facts that they stunt your growth, cause any fatal diseases, or give you bad breath. Even so, there will be no pacifiers when he graduates from high school, goes to college, and eventually walks down the aisle. But why am I carrying on so? He is, after all, only two-and-a-half years old!

~Leslie Boulden Marable

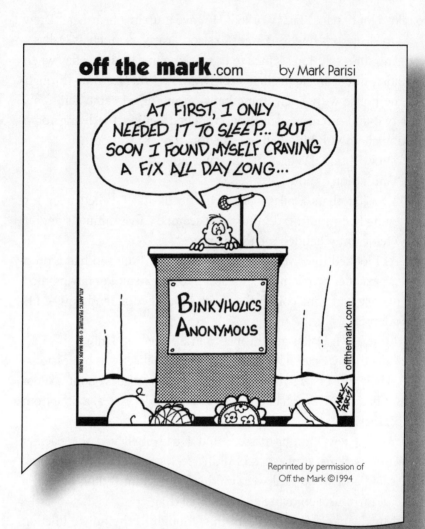

Reprinted by permission of
Off the Mark ©1994

# Confessions of an Earth Mama Wannabe

*Diaper backward spells repaid. Think about it.*
~Marshall McLuhan

I was pregnant in Seattle, where I shopped at Trader Joe's, grew herbs on my condo lanai, and reused the protective sleeves on my piping hot lattes. I tried to be an Earth Mama, I really did. Before my son was born, I was determined to attempt cloth diapers. Yes, attempt. Not exactly committed to the cause, but taking credit for the effort. I might have been stronger in my conviction for green diapering had I not been privy to the memory of my mother hunched over a putrid white bucket, rinsing a thick septic mess of my brother's nappies. However, we'd come a long way since the stinking seventies. In my 1998 urban existence, I had access to something my mother never could have imagined or afforded from the secluded farmhouse of my childhood: diaper service. With support, I could be a Good Mother, an Earth Mama even.

I could try, anyway.

It might have gone down differently if not for the circumcision. Like most of my contemporaries, I had my baby boy snipped shortly after his birth. On the West Coast, this — along with not eating the placenta, or at least planting it in the yard under a Very Special

Tree—put a serious pall on my potential for environmentally friendly mothering. I would have to pick a lot of blackberries in the park, do hours of yoga, and eat buckets full of granola to make up for this crime.

At the nurses' suggestion—to avoid diaper rash on his extra sensitive parts—we used disposable diapers for the first week at home. Throwaway sticky tabs were my friends, as was the space age mock-cotton that held about a gallon of "liquid." Eager to prove my nature-loving worthiness, I circled the two-week mark on the calendar and called the service to schedule my initial delivery. On the big day, I received a ten-foot stack of new diapers and a contraption for storing the soiled ones. The next week, they would swap out the used for fresh.

I quickly got to work trying out the new diapers. My son humored me, lying calmly through my struggles with the intricate diaper origami. Ten years ago, you needed an engineering degree to maneuver a cloth diaper. My son and I blew through four outfits that afternoon, in part because of the gaping diaper-to-skin issues, and partially because my dear progeny refused to pace himself.

Still, I was determined. Right up until it came time to pack for a weekend trip away. I calculated the number of diapers I'd need for the two-day trip and piled them on the bed. Turns out you go through a lot more cloth diapers than disposable because, in contrast to their Earth-ravaging counterparts, reusable diapers hold approximately a quarter teaspoon of pee. I filled an entire suitcase with the mountain of diapers. I sighed, crossed my arms, squinted, and huffed. Then I took the diapers out of the suitcase, loaded them back into the sack in which they had arrived, and called the service.

"This just isn't working out."

"Ma'am, don't you at least want to give it until the end of the day?"

"It's been six hours. I get it." It was not the first time in my brief tenure as Mother that I realized things would not always proceed as planned. But the pacifier incident is another story.

One-fourth of a day. Not bad for an herb-growing, latte-sipping, ozone-destroying Earth Mama Wannabe.

~Lela Davidson

# The Baby Olympics

*Child rearing myth #1: Labor ends when the baby is born.*
*~Anonymous*

Forget the Olympics. I have a real challenge for you: The Baby Olympics. Instead of the decathlon—ten events merely requiring speed, strength, and endurance—I propose a contest which also requires superhuman patience, bottomless goodwill, and the ability to function on chronic lack of sleep.

I give you the ten events of the Parent-athlon:

1. **Getting Out the Door.** You must get yourself and your baby up, dressed, and out the door before dark. Any contestant in danger of succeeding will no doubt be spit up on (or worse) by her baby, and have to return to the starting block.

2. **The Car Seat Toss.** In this event, contestants stand outside the open rear passenger door of their vehicle and hurl a ten-pound car seat—complete with strapped-in infant—into place on the seat. Points will be awarded for both accuracy and speed. Contestants missing the car altogether will be disqualified.

3. **Grocery Shopping.** In place of the 110-meter hurdles, we have the infinitely harder attempt to get through a grocery store with your baby in the cart. You are scored on the

number of items making it to checkout that haven't been mauled beyond recognition by a drooling infant. Extra points for actually securing the items you went in to purchase. Points off if your baby pulls down the wall of soup cans because you foolishly wheeled your cart close enough to read the labels.

4. **Diaper Changing.** A cross between the hog-tie and wrestling, this event will separate the parents from the wannabes. To fully test their skills in this area, contestants are given a baby who insists on rolling over on the changing table, clutching the side, and standing up—when not reaching down into his or her own dirty diaper. Contestants are graded on cleanliness and speed. Points off for letting the baby roll onto the floor.

5. **Finding a Place to Change the Baby in Public Buildings.** Female contestants will have an unfair advantage in this event, as men's rooms with baby-changing stations are still almost nonexistent. This does not bother the judges, however, due to the lifelong injustice of there never being enough stalls in the ladies' room.

6. **Stroller Derby.** The winner of this event will have memorized the locations of curb cuts, flights of steps, tree roots, uneven pavements, and revolving doors on her local course, and will be the first to get back to the starting place without catapulting the sleeping baby out of the stroller.

7. **Fifty-Two Hundred Pickup.** Lasting most of the competition day, this event consists of following your baby around the gaming area and picking up whatever he or she has strewn about the course—generally the pieces of a toy you have just painstakingly put together. Bonus points are

awarded for the retrieval of car keys, cooking utensils, and food items less than a week old.

8. **Feeding Time.** Defined as the depositing of food in the general vicinity of the baby, this event is scored similarly to horseshoes: three points for every spoonful in the baby's mouth; one point for food landing elsewhere on the baby. A finite number of spoons will be provided.

9. **Bath Time.** The main objective of this event is to tire the baby enough for the finale. The amount of water on the floor at the bath's conclusion will be weighed and subtracted from your score. Swimwear is advised for serious contestants.

10. **The Bedtime Marathon.** An endurance test, this event can last anywhere from fifteen minutes (in your dreams!) to several hours of rocking, singing, storytelling, pacing the floor, and rocking again. Strict drug tests will be conducted on the contents of that bedtime bottle. The winner of this event will be allowed to collapse, fully clothed, on her bed until awakened by crying once again.

The winner of all ten events is truly entitled to call her- or himself the "World's Strongest Parent." However, there is one more difference between this and that other competition. There, the winner can rest on her laurels for four years, until the next Olympiad. Here, even the winner must get up and do it all over again in the morning.

Let the games begin!

~Judy Epstein

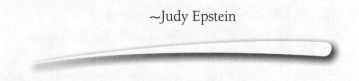

# Mom on the Run

*It is a bad plan that admits of no modification.*
*~Publilius Syrus*

"Are we there yet?" As a new mom, I knew that someday those four words would be directed at me, just as I had directed them toward the front seat of a Chevy Impala in the late seventies. My dad had predicted they'd make their first appearance about fifteen minutes south of Paybacksville, a not-so-lovely suburb where our misdeeds of youth settle accounts with our adult selves.

It was just too early for those words. And the person issuing those words wasn't my firstborn son. At seven months, Collin was clearly the most intellectually gifted child I'd encountered. But he was too busy wailing at the top of his lungs to attempt complex sentence structure.

Instead, it was his forty-year-old dad, Kipp. And his look of desperation matched my own. And neither was a match against the fact that we were six miles, a jogging stroller, and a rainstorm away from home. And it was my fault.

A little background.

I'm a TV reporter and morning news anchor. My workday ends at lunchtime, and for years that left me with hours of free time while my friends were nine-to-fiving. For a while, I swam with a seniors' swimming group. Who else has time to hang out with you in the middle of the day? But eventually hanging out with octogenarians in the hot tub after laps started wearing on me, and presumably them. So, I decided to take my energy on the road and take my running more seriously.

I ran marathon after marathon, getting faster and more efficient. I loved the discipline and the buzz of crossing finish lines. It was an addiction.

How addictive? I ran throughout my pregnancy and put in six miles the day Collin was born. No wonder the kid's birth was so lightning fast. He wanted out so he could relax.

I loved my baby. I really loved our shiny new jogging stroller, and within four months our family was on the road training for the San Diego Rock-N-Roll Marathon.

"You're sure this is a good idea?" asked Kipp.

"It's going to be great," I assured him. "Collin is so much easier than other babies."

And for a while, I was right.

Kipp and I ran while Collin napped in the jogger. I formulated routes around his formula needs, all the while thinking it was only a matter of time before *Runner's World* profiled me as some kind of "Super Mom on the Run."

Then came that day.

Marathon training requires "the long run." It's at least a twenty-mile training run that makes sure the body is ready to handle the rigors of 26.2 miles on race day.

At seven months, Collin was easily sleeping three hours during his afternoon naps. We needed three hours to do the run. On paper, it was the perfect plan.

I loaded the stroller with a bottle, diapers, blankets, etc., just to be safe and headed out with the newbie parental confidence that if you pack a stroller to the seams, you'll need none of its contents.

We were feeling good and not too shy about patting ourselves on the back for not being those kind of parents who stop doing things because they have a kid.

Six miles in.

Feeling great. Collin is snoring. Life is good.

Ten miles in.

Feeling a little less great. Collin is snoring. Life is still good.

It's the halfway point. The turnaround. I suggest to Kipp that we go one more mile. A twenty-two-mile roundtrip is better preparation than a twenty-miler. He agrees based on what, in retrospect, he blames on runner's high, and we extend the run two more miles. Fourteen miles in.

The wind picks up. We slow down. My internal running clock confers with my mom clock and both agree we may have a problem.

Sixteen miles. It's raining. Collin is awake. And Daddy-o has that "what now Mommy" look on his face.

"I'll bet he's hungry," I say, forcing a smile on my face.

"I'll feed him a bottle on that bench while you're stretching, and then he'll go back to sleep while we finish up."

By this point, other runners and cyclists on the bike trail are starting to look at this bizarre and very loud scene unfolding on a park bench. A baby is screaming, while a woman clearly in the middle of a workout is trying to jam a bottle in his mouth.

"Where is his mother?" asks one woman.

I resist the urge to say Mexico and fess up that I am the guilty, Nike-clad party trying to calm her baby down in the middle of a rain shower while on a twenty-, make that twenty-two-mile run.

Like I said, it looked good on paper.

But it clearly didn't look good in the middle of the bike trail. And it didn't feel good, either. I packed up our stuff, shielded Collin from the rain, and reflected on the drops now coming from my eyes.

We were six miles out from home.

"Are we there yet?" asked Kipp.

He was trying to infuse a little comedy into what felt and certainly sounded like a desperate situation. Our kid was screaming at the top of his lungs, and we couldn't really do much about it other than keep on moving.

We stopped every mile or so to try to calm down Collin and deter other bike trail users from calling CPS.

Am I there yet? I thought. Am I ready to look ahead to what my child needs rather than what I want? Clearly, the answer was a soggy no on this day.

As a mom, we teach our kids the value of putting one foot in front of the other. You have to crawl before you can walk. You have to walk before you can run.

Sometimes, a parent has to parent before she can run, read or do anything else that gives her an outlet to still be who she was before everyone, including her husband, started calling her "Mommy."

And so it was that day I learned the lesson of being prepared. And it had nothing to do with stuffing the stroller with stuff. It had everything to do with not putting my baby in a situation where the exit door is a six-mile run away.

Two miles from home. The rain is lightening up. I wish Collin's screams and the preachy people on the bike trail would lighten up. Each of their looks coupled with my now cramping calves is a preach penance.

One mile from home. The rain is gone. Collin's screams are reduced to infrequent reminders that I'm under new management. I've promised Kipp that I'll never suggest something so stupid again. I've learned a lesson, a twenty-two-mile-long lesson.

One block from home. Collin is quiet. I peek in the stroller, and he's asleep.

I look at Kipp and suggest with a smile on my face, "You know, if we go down to the next intersection and back, we'd get one more mile."

We're home.

~Deirdre Fitzpatrick

# Yoga Night

*Blessed are the flexible, for they shall not be bent out of shape.*
*~Author Unknown*

Almost a year after the birth of my first child, it's high time for some fitness. Relaxing one evening with my husband and ten-month-old son, I push the channel button on our television remote and discover, to my delight, the prelude to a yoga program. I quickly fetch the required mat, dutifully put on my most yoga-like workout clothes, and prepare to engage in a few moments of peaceful meditation and physical exertion.

Curiously watching the scene, my boy crawls over with eyebrows lifted and mouth agape, while my husband assures me he will help if our little man gets in the way. Closing my eyes, I listen to the calming flute music, take a deep breath, and attempt to block out distractions.

A sultry, breathy voice guides me through each position: cat pose, warrior, mountain. During a standing pose, I become aware of a sensation making its way up my leg.

"Mamamama."

Opening one eye, I peer down to see the grinning face of my son looking up at me as he grasps my pants and pulls on my leg.

"Ignore it—continue moving—get through this workout," I say quietly.

As I lower to a sitting position, he circles around twice and plants himself beside me. I resume deep breathing and, in the middle of a stretch, throw my head back in a pleading attempt to catch my husband's attention—the husband whose eyes are fixed on his computer screen. He glances over. Without speaking, so as not to interrupt my focused state of relaxation, I put on my most serious but sweet can-you-just-watch-him-for-the-next-twenty-minutes-so-I-can-do-something-for-myself look. It works. Daddy saves me as I change positions.

"I've got him," he says.

One minute passes. Stretch out slowly, breathe evenly. Looking up at the ceiling with my back suspended, I sense a presence under me and get the feeling I'd better hold that pose longer than Ms. Sexy Voice instructs.

"Oops," says my husband, trying to coax the baby to come toward him.

My son does, crawling right over my stomach on the way. Each time a new position requires me to create a space between myself and the floor, he comes whizzing by, looking at me while smiling and trying to slide underneath my torso or clamber over my legs. Hold your pose. Push up with your arms. Relax. The sounds of the flute soften. As I move into the downward facing dog, he rolls over onto his back and lies face up, staring at me as I attempt to look back at my ankles as instructed. Irritated, I check to see if my husband is still around. He is—and grinning broadly at both of us while fumbling with the camera.

I smile in an attempt to remain relaxed and try one more time to block out distractions. It does not work. My boy still looks up at me in innocent, but desperate bids for acknowledgement. Losing my concentration, I start laughing and collapse to the floor. At this stage in motherhood, there is no point in getting frustrated. Who am I kidding? Do I really think I can complete a routine of this sort without interference? I look over at my son just in time to watch him perfectly imitate a yoga position, and I realize this is one great photo op.

Though the benefits of yoga are numerous, I really don't need to spend much time finding my center; an extra ten pounds of it is wrapped around what used to be my waist. Meditation? I am regularly in meditation for this child, the kind that always involves prayer and occasionally involves rocking back and forth.

Making time to exercise without the presence of my little workout partner will be a challenge. But heeding the advice of those who have gone before me, I decide not to sweat the small stuff.

There's enough sweating during the yoga.

~Rhonda Bocock Franz

# A Dime Worth of Hope

*So where did these cravings come from?
I concluded it's the baby ordering in. Prenatal takeout.*
~Paul Reiser, Babyhood

I was eight months pregnant and very round. My office was located right across from a fast-food place with golden arches that I longed for that early morning. I was craving a fish sandwich and a glass of milk. I counted the hours until lunchtime. I worked absentmindedly as I felt my baby move around and kick me, almost yelling out, "I want fish! I want milk! Now!" My swollen feet rested on a stool I had placed under my desk. They would carry me over there, and my hunger would be sated.

Slowly, time clicked away until the minute I was free to cure my craving.

As I stood in the long line, I relished the thought of that crunchy yet soft fish meal, with cool, refreshing milk washing it all down. My baby made a flip inside my big belly. All was about to be well.

Or so I thought.

As I placed my order, the young boy behind the counter announced I owed him four dollars and thirty-five cents.

A small price to pay for paradise in one's mouth.

Problem was, I only had four dollars and twenty-five cents — a dime short.

Could he let me have the food, and I would pay him later when I walked back to my office and borrowed a dime from a co-worker?

No. No way, he said. He needed it all right then.

Credit cards were not accepted either; cash only.

Listen, I urged, begging with a plea only an eight-months-pregnant woman understands, I HAVE TO HAVE THAT FOOD! Here, take my watch, rub my belly, anything for a dime. DO YOU UNDERSTAND?? My feet are bigger than your teenaged head. AND I WANT THAT FOOD!

I debated whether or not I could lunge over the counter and grab that bag of delight he was withholding from me. Could I?

Would I give birth to my firstborn behind bars?

Would I hear "jailbird" as I pushed out my daughter?

The people behind me began to grumble. They, too, had cravings. And I was preventing them from fulfilling theirs.

All I needed was a dime. Ten cents. A mere 1/10th of a dollar. I threw my purse open on the counter, hoping a dime would appear.

It did not.

I began to cry. I was so hungry and so tired. And so broke.

A man behind me tapped me on the shoulder and handed me a dime. I hugged him. I told him I would name my child after him, only to see his shirt had the name "Herman" on it, and I questioned my sanity.

A dime. Thank you, sir, thank you. You have saved my life.

Others in line clapped. The young boy who was now fearing for his life thanked Herman, too.

I had paradise in my hand, and I ate it quickly as I walked back to my office.

As I sat at my desk, my baby kicked softly, as if to say she appreciated Herman, too.

And slowly, one by one, my officemates came and each put a dime in my hand, laughing and telling me my daughter would be a fisherman.

You never know where hope might come from, even a dime's worth in time of great expectancy.

~Malinda Dunlap Fillingim

# Not So Small Packages

*Let your dreams outgrow the shoes of your expectations.*
~Ryunosuke Satoro

"Are all of those babies preemies?" I asked as I passed the nursery window on my recovery laps around the postpartum ward.

"No, dear, those are regular babies," was the nurse's gently amused reply.

At ten pounds, four ounces, our daughter was over the 95th percentile for weight at birth. The operating room staff took bets on her size during my Cesarean, and all simultaneously cried "Wow!" when she emerged. We never used any of the cute newborn clothes our friends had given us, except for stuffing our daughter into her going-home outfit like a little sausage-baby in ducky-covered casing.

Parents of a large baby learn quickly that it's very possible for an infant to outgrow items before she or he is developmentally ready, or before Mama has managed to find a workaround. We ditched the "infant" car seat when our baby's five-month-old feet dangled over the edge; at one year she was both young enough to need a rear-facing car seat and big enough for a toddler headrest at the same time. When I was the frazzled stay-at-home mother of a four-month-old, I was delighted to discover I could take her into the shower with me in her sitting-pod. Finally, a guaranteed shower every day! This was a moment of pure Mommy genius. Until, of course, she outgrew said pod a month later, long before learning to sit on her own. No amount of soapy lather could squeeze those thighs into that molded rubber seat, and my carefree days of certain cleanliness were short-lived.

She's tall, too, this baby. Before she was born, I researched wraps, slings and other baby carriers, excited to "wear" her as much as possible to maximize bonding and free up my hands. At less than a year, however, the top of her head blocked my view so completely that we had to give up on a front-carry and wait for Daddy to come home to help us into rear-facing mode. Add a fluffy cloth-diaper-covered bottom to the mix, and it's easy to understand the comment a fellow new mother made at her birthday party: "I never understood why they made Happy First Birthday clothes in 18-24-month sizes... until I met your daughter!"

At Mommy-and-Me exercise class, our teacher—an ex-Marine who in no way looked like she'd just given birth—encouraged us to use our babies to do chest presses. I watched the other mothers easily lifting their tiny babies and tried not to grunt too loudly as I struggled to hold my twenty-pounder above me, afraid I might drop her in my pursuit of postpartum fitness.

Although she's currently eighteen months, she's reached the 97th percentile for height and weight and looks somewhat older than she is. I sometimes imagine our tall and stocky baby as a spy, masquerading as an older child and infiltrating their circles at day care. She must report back to the other toddlers about such three-year-olds' secrets as potty-training and fork usage. She loves to climb and wrestle with the "big kids," and they don't seem to notice the difference... perhaps until they try to hold a conversation with her? I remember my friend's four-year-old complaining to his mother, "Why won't that kid play with me?" She was ten months old at the time, but so dwarfed his own seven-month-old sister that he refused to believe she, too, was just a baby.

Life with a big baby does have its advantages: My arms are getting toned in ways I never thought possible, and because she could eat more, she slept through the night earlier than most infants. Her chubby leg rolls and full, round cheeks are heartbreakingly adorable, and she's strong and ready to play without fear or hesitation.

She's everything we ever dreamed our daughter could be, but we will admit that when we wished for a baby who was far above average, this wasn't exactly what we had in mind!

~Jess Holland

# The Gold Dust Twins

*There are two things in life for which we are never truly prepared: twins.*
*~Josh Billings*

"So, did you get any work done today?" my husband asked, home from a long hard day of work and spying my not-so-clean clothes.

Shaking my head, I suppressed a laugh. "Not exactly. You wouldn't believe the day I had." In the six months since giving birth to twins, we'd stumbled our way through endless sleepless nights, feedings, and diaper changes. Asking about work had become our little joke. How naïve I'd been to think I could keep working on my furniture refinishing in a tiny apartment overflowing with twins.

Now that we'd finally managed to get into a routine that included sleeping at night, the days were more exhausting than ever: The boys were crawling.

"Help me move the books," I asked my husband one evening. "Your sons managed to pull out those heavy textbooks."

Before they could tear them to shreds, we reorganized, doubling rows of books on the upper shelves and bolting the case into the wall so it wouldn't topple over.

Then it was the knickknacks on the coffee table. In a matter of days, our crawling babies had managed to find every unsafe object two feet from the ground. Surveying the place every morning, I was certain it was finally safe.

And so, on this particular morning, the boys were sitting,

contentedly playing with blocks. How silly it seemed to disrupt them and stick them in their cribs, while I dashed into the bathroom.

It couldn't have been more than a minute later when I charged out to find them sitting happily where I'd left them on the rug in the living room.

They smiled at me, blue eyes and pink lips popping out against their golden skin.

"Golden?" I did a double take. "Oh, no. Boys, what have you done?"

What they'd done was find the one cabinet we had missed. It held a container of gold dust that I used for gold-leafing furniture. At least they hadn't eaten it… yet. I was panicked; this stuff was toxic. It was time for damage control.

Quickly, I picked up one baby and put him in a crib. Then I put his brother in the same crib; why mess up two? They giggled like two Cupids come to life.

By this time, the front of my shirt was gilded. Like Midas, everything I touched became marred with fine gold powder. I put the jar that had caused all this trouble in the top cabinet. The rug was hopelessly sparkling with ground-in gold dust.

It was more important to get that stuff off my precious babies. One at a time, I declothed a baby and cleaned him in the sink. That stuff did not want to come off. And this was not the time for my sons to discover the joy of splashing. Finally, I put one clean baby in the clean crib. It was time for baby number two. My gilded sink and counter were regilded. Thank goodness I hadn't had triplets!

Carefully holding him away from me so I wouldn't get more gold on him, I put him next to his brother. They smiled sleepily, like cherubic pink angels.

By the time I'd attempted to clean the rug and the bathroom again, bundled all the sheets from the crib and all of my clothes for washing, and bathed myself, the boys were up and ready for another round.

I hallucinated gold dust everywhere while I carefully spoon-fed them. As my hair dried, I could see gold sparkling amongst the red. Close inspection of my face showed still more. Would this ever end?

When my husband came home, it was no wonder he thought I'd been working on furniture.

"Well," he said after inspecting and hugging the boys, "they don't look any worse for wear."

Before I could stop him, he held me tight and kissed me. And when I looked down, I saw that the Midas Touch still lingered, and I'd soon have a gold-dusted husband.

~Rosalind Zane as told to D. B. Zane

# New Moms

## The Long Road

*A bend in the road is not the end of the road...
unless you fail to make the turn.*

~Author Unknown

# Elliott Comes to Play

*A new baby is like the beginning of all things—
wonder, hope, a dream of possibilities.*
~Eda J. Le Shan

"Today's the day," Sarah announced when I dashed into our office juggling a cell phone, coffee cup, and over-priced, fat-laden muffin. Her enthusiasm exhausted me. I'd had another late night coupled with too much work on the train. Papers spilled from my bulging tote.

Sarah was settled at her desk, computer on, research in a tidy stack. Even her bulletin board was neat. A lopsided arc of Post-it Notes dotted the wall around my computer screen. The desk was strewn with reports, unsorted mail, and the budget I still needed to review. Someone had dumped a listing pile of papers on my chair. I sighed and bit deeply into the muffin. As I dropped my things, I noticed a half-empty cup on the bookcase filled with—my God, is that mold?—and thought, "Some supervisor you make. You can't even get to work on time."

I sipped my coffee and struggled to remember today's importance. It had been chaos since Amy went on maternity leave three months earlier.

"Don't worry, it's not another meeting," Sarah said. "Amy's visiting."

Yes, now I remembered. Today, we were to meet the baby.

It was almost 11:00 when Amy and baby Elliott arrived. Sarah rushed out the door of our shared office, but I lingered to finish an e-mail. Just down the hall, a chorus of co-workers exclaimed over Elliott's impressive cuteness.

"Amy, what are you feeding this kid? He's almost big enough to paddle a canoe."

I did four more e-mails, and the laughter grew louder. I was archiving old messages when my internal etiquette monitor kicked in. She worked for you, it said, and she's your friend. Get out there, you coward, and say hello. It's just a baby.

I hate etiquette.

I swung my chair around and stared at Amy's vacant desk. It was no secret I was struggling with infertility. Thanks to me, all fifteen co-workers understood the ins and outs of in vitro fertilization. They also knew it had failed me twice. If I were a no-show, they'd whisper how horrible it was I had to share an office with Amy. They'd be wrong. I liked my vicarious pregnancy. While most people awkwardly avoided the subject, Amy joked about food cravings and shared her birth plan. She let me touch her stomach when the baby kicked. She treated me like I was normal, even when I wasn't.

I dragged myself to the lobby where Amy and Elliott were holding court. I loitered on the fringe, studying the child I once felt somersaulting beneath the palm of my hand. Everyone was taking turns carrying Elliott, a plump two-month-old with a shock of blond hair. Eugenia, who has a multitude of grandchildren, held Elliott with an ease that demonstrated years of practice. I'd expected that. It was my single co-workers who shocked me. They handled Elliott with a nonchalance I didn't possess. Did they teach that stuff in school?

I stared at my hands so I didn't have to look at Elliott and his new best friends, my self-esteem leaking onto the pale blue carpet. Lately it seemed I couldn't succeed at anything. My failure to get pregnant had spilled over into the rest of my life. I was terrified someone would thrust Elliott at me and he would dangle from my arms, his neck cracked like a chicken bone, and they'd think, "Perhaps it was a good thing she hadn't gotten pregnant. Who would have guessed?"

I picked at my cuticles and wondered if I had new e-mail.

Thankfully, no one offered me Elliott. I stood there stiff and awkward, my confidence evaporating like summer morning fog. It felt like a junior high school dance, my stomach in knots, my face plastered with a fake smile. No one was asking me to disco to the Bee Gees. Suddenly, I was conscious I was born a decade earlier than my twenty-something co-workers. I was old, damn it. They were the ones who were having kids. Someone up there must know about my lack of skill, my poor judgment, my self-absorption, my procrastination, my tardiness, my cuticle picking. I couldn't even keep my desk clean. How could I possibly parent a child? My gray roots felt like a neon sign flashing, "Too old."

"Cynthia, what are you waiting for?" Amy said. "Elliott practically knows you already."

Instantly, I remembered all the reasons I missed Amy. How she made me laugh when I was trapped in a black hormonal mood. How she made grant reports fun and could draw anyone into conversation, even crusty old farmers who eyed her stomach like she was a mare or a ewe. I don't know if it was her smile or her disposition or something mysterious and indefinable, but she made everything seem easy, including pregnancy. She was good with details and calm under pressure. She's the kind of woman you knew would make a great mother.

My throat caught, so instead of speaking, I held out my arms. Please, God, don't let me look stupid. I hadn't counted on the neck issue.

Traci passed Elliott over, and I was surprised he didn't flop like a fish on the line. I could feel his heat. We stared at each other for a long moment, and when it occurred to me that I wasn't talking, I looked up to see Amy smiling.

"Isn't he amazing?"

"Yes," I stammered, my smile no longer fake.

Elliott rubbed his face against my velour shirt and gurgled. He closed his eyes and went limp.

"I knew it," Amy said. "You're a natural."

I wanted to kiss her.

Three years later, after I'd given up on infertility treatments, my husband and I adopted a baby girl. A nurse placed Katie in my shaking, newborn hands and promptly left the room. It was the middle of the night, but apparently the nurse had things to do. Katie and I stared at one another in shock. Or perhaps it was awe. In either case, within an hour I knew that Amy had been right. Like all new mothers, even adoptive ones without the standard parenting classes, I did what came naturally. I held my child and loved her. It was as simple as that.

I rocked Katie for the first time and remembered how Elliott had burrowed into sleep that morning, and I'd felt a surge of pride. I was the little engine that could. I could make a baby fall asleep. I could probably change a diaper. The crowd dispersed, and I caressed his dimpled chin.

I whispered in his tiny ear, "Thank you, Elliott."

A bubble of spit perched on his lip as if poised to take flight, and I saw the glimmer of a rainbow hidden in its shiny surface.

~Cynthia Patton

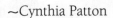

# A Dream Becomes Real

*To be pregnant is to be vitally alive, thoroughly woman, and undoubtedly inhabited.*
*~Anne Buchanan & Debra Klingsporn*

"I am going to miss being pregnant," I told my midwife as I cradled my newborn son. His sweet, pure scent tickled my nose. I kissed his soft cheek, taking in every moment. As excited as I was to hold him in my arms, there was a tinge of disappointment. My husband and I had decided that we wouldn't have any more children, and I knew that my body would long to carry another child. Pregnancy was something I was meant to do. It came so easily for me.

As my mind wandered back over the memories of my pregnancy, I wondered about people who struggled with infertility, people who could never carry a child of their own. People I might be able to help... I must be crazy.

I savored the next few months, all the while thinking there might be something I could do. It was the words my midwife said to me at my six-week postnatal checkup that started me on a wild and exciting journey.

"Helen, you should be a surrogate," said Joanne.

"I could never do that. I wouldn't be able to give away one of my own children."

A Dream Becomes Real : The Long Road  283

"There are a lot of people out there who would love a baby of their own. It would give you the chance to be pregnant again."

I blew her off. But no matter how much I tried to ignore her words, they kept fluttering back into my mind. Could I do this?

As soon as I got home, I told my husband about Joanne's crazy idea.

"John, you are not going to believe what Joanne said to me. She said I should be a surrogate."

"Well, if anyone could do it, it would be you."

Was he crazy? I was expecting him to be the voice of reason! Curiosity got the better of me. I began to do a little research, which led me to gestational surrogacy. I could carry a child for someone, and it wouldn't be biologically related to me. This was the answer I was looking for.

I found a surrogacy agency and met a lot of hopeful couples, but I didn't click well with any. I was beginning to lose hope when I was introduced to the Fassy family. From the moment Susan stepped in my door, I felt as if I had known her all my life. Hearing her story just sealed the deal for me.

"There were complications in my delivery, and before I could hold my beautiful newborn daughter, I had to have emergency surgery. That is when they removed my uterus," Susan said. "I wanted more children, but it wasn't a possibility."

I couldn't imagine my dream of having children being torn from me.

"I still have my ovaries, but what good is that without a uterus?" Susan said.

"I'll carry a baby for you," I said. That is when our journey into gestational surrogacy began.

The process went as every infertile person hopes, but few experience. "Because Susan doesn't have a uterus, the process may take more time. We have to test her to find out where she is in her cycle," the doctor said. When the doctor called the next day, we were unprepared for the results. "You are on the same cycle. This may be easier than I thought."

It was a rather easy experience, but it wasn't without its unpleasant obstacles. There were extensive tests and mandatory shots every day in an attempt to prepare my body to take on this pregnancy. I stood in the bathroom for half an hour, my shirt pulled up as I pinched my stomach, willing myself to jab in that first needle.

With each other's support, we finally made it to the transfer date. Tears ran down my face as I lay on the table. I wanted this for Susan, a chance to help fulfill her dreams. She held my hand and stroked my hair. We all held our breath as the doctor came in.

"I like to say a quick prayer before we start," the doctor said. We closed our eyes as he prayed. I was unable to concentrate because I was too busy pleading with God to help us.

The embryos were inserted, and I was tilted with my feet in the air and my head down. While I was in this position, Susan and I made plans for the future and the baby she would hold in her arms.

Four days after the procedure, I took a home pregnancy test. I had been warned against it in case of false positive results, but curiosity got the best of me. After a few minutes, there were two faint pink lines. Until they were darker, I couldn't say anything. I couldn't get Susan's hopes up until I was positive.

We had been through this journey together so we wanted to be together for the results. Six days later, we stood in my living room as I received the official news over the phone. "Congratulations," the doctor said. "You are pregnant, and your hormone levels are good."

The smile on my face gave the results away. Before I could hang up the phone, Susan and I were hugging, laughing, and jumping around. We had done it. Susan was going to be a mother again.

Our families became inseparable. When we weren't spending time with each other, we were on the phone. There were barbecues, sleepovers, and days spent just relaxing on the beach. We were not just friends, but family.

Then the big day came. It seemed only fitting to make it a family affair. Susan sat beside me, reacting to each contraction as if it were her own. With the help of my midwife, Susan's husband was going to deliver the baby. Then their daughter Alicia would cut the umbilical cord. In the meantime, Susan's mother was filming the whole experience. It was one big party.

A couple of hours into the labor, I shocked everyone. "I have to push," I said. Susan held tight to my hand, disbelieving that she was going to have a baby. A couple of pushes later, her husband delivered a beautiful, healthy boy. At my request, he placed the baby into Susan's arms. All she could do was cry as Alicia cut the cord.

Tears stung my eyes as I watched their excitement. The joy they were experiencing was enough for me. I knew I had done the right thing. Susan leaned toward me, kissing me on the head as we admired her new son.

"Look what you did," Susan said. "You gave us our baby."

Our hospital room became one big celebration. We even had a news crew joining in the party. Together we had experienced our miracle.

Each time I look at Christian, I am amazed. It is hard to believe I played a part in this special delivery. I was able to help someone experience the joy of motherhood and turn a dream into reality.

~Helen R. Zanone

# 78

# The Infertile Mother's Day

*Of all the rights of women, the greatest is to be a mother.*
~Lin Yutang

I began to resent Mother's Day altogether, a day when emotions I had stuffed away throughout the year refused to be ignored. As soon as the first Hallmark commercial aired, I longed for "The Day" to be over. Calling my mom to thank her for the piano lessons, advice, and love on this Sunday morning was always half-hearted. Driving ninety minutes to my mother-in-law's to make her day fabulous made me feel even more isolated. It should have been for me. It should have been about making my day special. I should have been getting breakfast in bed, hearing the pitter-patter of little feet coming with a sticky homemade card, and being covered in hugs and kisses.

Well-meaning people smashed my heart with their unintentional insults. "Don't think about it so much. Relax and you'll get pregnant in no time." I considered describing the unprotected sex my husband and I had had when we decided to leave things to chance years ago. Eventually, fertility drugs brought such emotional turmoil that as my friends became pregnant, their nonchalant "We weren't even trying" could send me into despair. My husband was cautious when he told me of friends and family becoming pregnant. It was never his style to discuss it, which I interpreted to mean he didn't care if we had a baby or not. He wasn't taking temperatures, counting days, assessing discharge.

Mother's Day, though, was the toughest. It was definitely the mother of all sucker punches. Though days and months were tough, there was always another day of trying, next month to hope for. Mother's Day, though, was the benchmark of how long it was taking. If I was going to have three children like I had planned, another year of a motherless Mother's Day meant coming to terms with the life I had pictured not happening.

After spending my third Mother's Day like this, I decided to have a laparoscopy, a procedure that would combat the severe endometriosis I suffered from. Since I had never had surgery before, it seemed like a serious procedure, but it was the next logical thing to try. Apparently, my endometriosis was so severe that the doctor was confident it was a major cause of my infertility.

Two months post-surgery, one miraculous pregnancy test hinted of a plus sign. I took at least five more tests. Every plus sign resulted in flutters of hope, and confirmation from my doctor left me feeling like I could fly from happiness. The pregnancy wasn't without complications, but I was determined to enjoy every moment. Who knew if I would ever get to carry another baby again? I was uncomfortable, hormonal, and exhausted, but God was I grateful.

My son arrived smack dab on his due date. A huge, perfect baby boy, he was born on that same Sunday holiday I had come to dread. That fourth Mother's Day, I received a call from my mom wishing me a Happy Mother's Day, and my mother-in-law drove over an hour to visit us. I got the cards and flowers. I got to kiss the toes that would someday pitter-patter down the hall. I covered my son with kisses, so very grateful to understand that Mother's Day wasn't actually about me, but about "us." And it was absolutely blissful.

~Julia Garstecki

# 79

# The Day Time Stopped

*I believe in prayer. It's the best way we have to draw strength from heaven.*
~Josephine Baker

The mantle clock on the brick fireplace did not chime at mid-morning on July 21st. Coincidentally, the battery-operated clock hanging on the pantry wall stopped a little before noon. Even the cuckoo clock stopped its perpetual tick-tock.

I put water on for tea and forgot it. The metallic stench of the kettle burning filtered through the house. I raised the kitchen windows and let the humid heat intrude through the screens. Shortly afterward, a fireman came, but not because of the burning kettle. He checked the water temperature from all of the faucets and peeked into my dishwasher. He checked the locks on the doors. With a grand smile, he left a scribbled report on the dining room table. And before the navy uniform slipped into the haze of the summer day, he said, "This is for the social worker from the Division of Children and Youth Services. Her name is Shaunna, and she will be here with the baby in a couple of hours."

I floated to the doorway of the spare bedroom, empty for three long years. It loomed with an echo for more than thirty-six menstrual cycles and more than 12,040 days of prayers. Empty tan walls, cleanly painted, looked back at me. No pictures brightened the room, no clothes hung in its closet, and no lamps invited anyone to visit.

The room waited, longing for a baby to bring life to its bleakness and cure the vast solitude. The room twirled in time; I dozed and daydreamed back to the past three Christmases.

•••

Snow clung to the windows. I draped festive holly across the fireplace mantle and fastened a red velvet bow to the brass fixture on the mantle clock. It chimed, the classic centerpiece illuminated by white twinkles of light. I placed my hands across my belly and smiled. Surely there would be a baby next Christmas. God was good and wonderful, I knew. The thought of a newborn by the tree or growing in my womb filled me with joy. I sat in the bentwood rocker and felt the beauty of the Christmas season. I prayed, "Lord, a baby next Christmas, please?"

The following year was fraught with visits to the infertility clinic. Marital vocabulary and conversations included words like hystersalpingograms, sperm counts and motility, Clomid, AIH, artificial insemination, and fertility calendar. I found excuses for skipping friends' baby showers. I hurried by the diaper and baby food aisles, and left the room during Pampers commercials.

The next Christmas season arrived with fragrant boughs and the red velvet bow adorning the clock's crown again. With each quarter-hour chime, I prayed, "Maybe a baby next year, Lord, maybe a baby next year." I rocked and let my tears make a white haze of the Christmas tree.

Another year passed with no hint of a pregnancy. Christmas vacation began with a blizzard. Driving through the snow, I felt like I was breaking inside. A huge lump formed in my throat, and I became angry with God. "No baby again?" I cried. "Why are you so good to others and not to me!"

"Relax!" my husband said. "There's no rush. We're fine! It'll happen when it happens."

He didn't understand. Something was wrong inside my head and my body. I could feel no pain, but neither could I feel joy. I immersed myself in a master's degree program and in music at church. I taught, wrote, developed curriculum, and kept a basal thermometer by my bed to remind my husband of when it was time for "baby-making days."

Another Christmas — no baby. The fireplace mantle and candlelit windows were storybook. I rocked and rocked and felt nothing. Nothing. Nothing. I thought the tree stared awkwardly at me. At times, I fancied it mocked me. I shivered in front of the fire and sweat in the snowy night. I felt large in my slender body. Doubtful and sad, I wanted to pray, "Maybe a baby next year, Lord, maybe a baby next year," but I felt God had abandoned me.

• • •

The telephone rang, jolting me from my nap. Christmases past flew into the blank tan walls of the spare room, and I jumped. Dazed, I answered the phone.

"It's me," said my husband. "I'm picking up a crib at the house. Ma said it's in good shape. It will be a while. Dad and I have to dig it out in the attic."

"The social worker called," I said with a bit of fear. "She said they can't leave the baby unless we have a crib."

"Don't worry," he assured me.

Miriam, a home-finder for foster care who knew of us, had called earlier that morning. "A failure-to-thrive eight-week-old boy needs bonding immediately. He's been neglected and abandoned. He was removed on Friday when a relative called and said, 'The baby's life is in danger.' He needs to be in a foster home until the parental rights are terminated. The process may take up to a year, perhaps more, but then you'd be able to adopt."

Everything became a beautiful blur. We were becoming emergency licensed foster parents with the intent to adopt. I was going to be a mother!

I went back to the empty room. Suddenly, I saw where the crib would be. I became a whirlwind of creation. I lifted a blue braided rug from the dining room and pulled the rocker into the spare room. "The baby's room," I thought with imaginative awe.

An eight-week-old baby boy was to be delivered in two hours!

The doorbell rang before my husband was home with the crib. Shaunna, a sweet woman in her twenties, stood cradling an infant the size of a newborn! Time stopped. With a full smile, Shaunna shifted the sleeping baby boy into my arms.

I really didn't know how to hold a baby. As we walked inside, she gently showed me how to hold his weak, tiny head. I couldn't take my eyes off him. Sleeping, his eyelashes drifted down to his cheeks. Only a thin layer of skin covered his malnourished body. His full lips were pursed into a pout. But when he opened his eyes… Lord, when he opened his eyes… his soul saw mine. With adoption, he would be Joseph Patrick, the son of my soul.

• • •

"You sent me my baby this Christmas, Lord. You sent me a baby this year!" Not yet adopted, he was a thriving seven-month-old struggling to sit up by himself. However, the following Christmas would be a sacred celebration of answered prayers. We signed adoption papers three days before Christmas, and he was baptized the following evening.

That Christmas the tree stood like a regal king. I fancied it honored me. White lights were diamond gems, stars of the Christmastide. I rocked and rocked and glowed like the velvet bow on the clock as it chimed. My prayers had been answered. I became a mother in three hours, the day three clocks stopped… the day time stopped to answer prayers.

~Patricia Barrett

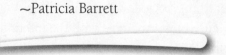

# Unfinished Business

*As your faith is strengthened you will find that there is no longer the need to have a sense of control, that things will flow as they will, and that you will flow with them, to your great delight and benefit.*
*~Emmanuel*

"I'm sorry, ma'am, but something is wrong with your baby." The specialist looked past me to the flickering screen on the ultrasound monitor, his face grim. A shot of icy fear raced through me. Moving the hand control over my enlarged belly, he paused here and there, probing my baby's tiny body. "Your baby has some severe developmental problems."

Stunned, I tried to control my voice. "Wh-what do you mean?"

"I'll send the pictures to your doctor, and you can discuss it with him. I'd advise an immediate appointment."

No, no, no! My mind whirled in shock and disbelief. Dear Lord, this just can't be happening! Not another baby! I was halfway through this pregnancy, my second. The first had ended in a miscarriage a few weeks along.

But it was happening, and I numbly went through the motions of calling my husband, sitting together in my doctor's office and hearing the technical explanations. The long and short of it was that my baby would not live more than a few days. I would deliver a stillborn.

What had happened to my simple and beautiful dream of having a baby? Pregnancy and motherhood—the whole topic felt like

Unfinished Business : The Long Road 293

a minefield to me now. You never knew when it would blow up in your face.

On another grim and frightening day, nearly ten years earlier, I had faced surgery for a suspicious mass on my ovary. I was told they would do a hysterectomy if they found it to be life-threatening; I might wake up permanently barren.

Thankfully, surgery revealed no cancer, but rather a serious case of endometriosis, a chronic and very painful condition. They were able to do repair work, but left me with a slim chance of ever having children.

I was single then, in my early thirties, struggling to trust the Lord with my heart's desire for marriage and a family. One particularly difficult day, I cried out to God for something to hang on to, some encouragement. As I read my Bible, a verse leaped off the page and into my heart: "He settles the barren woman in her home as a happy mother of children" (Psalm 113:9 NIV). So simple and to the point—husband, home, and children. I needed to trust Him to heal my body and bring about the rest.

A perfect story unfolded a few years later when I met my Mr. Right. I miscarried in the early months of our marriage, and though we were profoundly disappointed, we were encouraged I could get pregnant at all.

Two years later, I had laparoscopic surgery done to free me from the nagging pain of the endometriosis, with the hope that it would go into remission. To my astonishment, I awakened in recovery to the smiling face of my husband.

"Honey, they couldn't find any endometriosis! It was scar tissue causing the pain, and they cleaned that up. You're healed!"

Healed! God's miracle! And it was true—pain no longer defined my days, and my old enemy endometriosis was not just in remission… it was gone for good.

To our delight, I conceived soon afterward. This second pregnancy seemed normal, and we had no hint of trouble. It was during the routine ultrasound that I received the devastating news. The following days were a blur of anguish and disbelief. We cried out to God for a miracle, but when we were told that the baby had died, a pain I had never known filled me.

The delivery of our little son was very difficult, leaving my body spent and my heart deeply wounded. In the weeks that followed, a profound grief overwhelmed me. God had always been the very bedrock of my life, but now haunting questions and doubts tormented me. If He was in control, why had He allowed this to happen—why? I was forty, and it seemed that my dream for a baby had died, too.

Outwardly, I made the effort to live normally and regain some emotional balance, but inwardly I struggled in a deep and terrifying turmoil. A cold, dark depression gripped my heart, hope gone, and seemingly with it, the faith to which I had always clung. Day and night, my mind whirled with issues for which there seemed to be no answers. The agonizing months dragged on.

One day, a letter arrived from my dear mom. "When difficult trials like this happen to us, we learn to overcome," she wrote. "Your faith is God's opportunity to bring you out on top in a bad situation."

Overcoming. Somehow that idea threw me a lifeline in the maelstrom of despair. I had been blaming God, accusing Him of failing me, and yet a new thought settled in my mind: This was not an end. Rather, if I chose to keep trusting Him beyond the loss, I would keep the way open for Him to work. It would require reengaging my faith and allowing God to lead me through the process to a place of peace. A place of overcoming.

With tears of remorse, I asked God to forgive me, to heal my broken heart, and to help me trust Him again—whether or not I ever had a baby. It didn't happen overnight, but day by day the knot of pain and anger melted, leaving hope and restored peace in my heart.

Two years passed, and a fresh spring unfolded in all its green loveliness. One day in prayer, I heard God's voice, a quiet but clear question, "Do you still believe my promise?" Instantly, I knew what He meant. We had some unfinished business to take care of—His promise of motherhood given to me so long ago. It seemed as if He was saying, "Come on. It's going to be all right. You'll see."

I knew, too, what it would mean. If I still wanted a baby, my faith had to be specific—not just a general "I trust God," but faith for a flesh-and-blood baby. A frightening sense of stepping into an abyss washed over me, for I knew all too well the risk of pain and loss on this road. And yet I sensed in my spirit that it was now my choice. Could I trust Him again?

"Yes, Lord," I whispered. "I believe."

That summer, we enjoyed a mountain vacation with some family. One afternoon, they left for some sightseeing without me—I had been dealing with altitude sickness for days, or so I thought. The truth was... I was pregnant again! At forty-two, I knew this time it was God's hand, His story. No more minefields. No more crying. And again, His precious Word came to me, full of life and hope: "The winter is past; the rains are over and gone... the season of singing has come..." (Song of Solomon 2:11-12 NIV).

On a perfect May morning, I lay in another hospital bed. I was exhausted, but in my arms our beautiful baby daughter snuggled quietly, her dark blue eyes staring intently up into my face. Yes, I was the "happy mother" of God's promise, profoundly thankful for His mercy. Thankful that He didn't give up on me in the dark time, thankful that He means what He says.

Always.

~Wendy Dellinger

# Out of the Clear Blue Easy

*All human wisdom is summed up in two words—wait and hope.*
~Alexander Dumas

"Find hope and never let go of it, no matter what form it takes."

This sage advice, given to me years ago by my grandmother, lay dormant until I was in my late twenties and trying desperately to start a family. I'd always assumed it would be a cinch. After all, millions of women the world over get pregnant every day, accidentally or on purpose.

But when my husband Chip and I decided we wanted a baby, we were quickly met with discouragement and disappointment. For three long years, we battled infertility, undergoing countless tests, numerous needle pricks, and a slew of surgical procedures. We ran the gamut of assisted reproductive treatments.

And failed them all.

Throughout those dark years, I kept a variety of home pregnancy tests in my bathroom medicine cabinet. I had all the fancy name brands and several cheap ones I'd bought off the Internet. Month after month, I looked for pink lines and blue crosses, smiley faces and checkmarks. But all that ever showed up on those tests was heartbreaking stark white space.

The only test in my arsenal that I refused to try was the Clear

Blue Easy Digital. For some reason, it seemed sacred. Through every medicated cycle, every artificial insemination, and even after our first round of in vitro fertilization, my Clear Blue Easy remained untouched on the shelf. Why? Because, instead of symbols like other tests used, it spelled out the answer in bold black type.

I simply couldn't bear the thought of reading the words NOT PREGNANT, even though I had steeled myself to expect them.

In the quiet cold of a Tennessee winter, Chip and I made the difficult decision to attempt a second round of in vitro fertilization. Vigilant in tracking every single thing my reproductive system could possibly do, I spent more time with nurses and technicians than with my family and friends. Everything but my body's schedule had to be put on the back burner.

My bruised and battered stomach was evidence of the thousands of dollars worth of hormones being pumped into my body. Every day, more needles were jabbed into my veins than most drug addicts could tolerate. I even took a month-long leave of absence from my job so I could totally focus on the task at hand.

A final needle prick early on a February morning would show whether it had all been worth it.

The wait between the blood draw and the phone call from the fertility clinic was pure torture. All the prayers, all the tears, all the physical and emotional pain, all the worries over the two little embryos that had been nurtured in a laboratory and then planted in my body hit me like a kamikaze in those interminable hours of waiting.

And then the call came.

"Positive," the voice on the other end of the line said. No doubt about it. No need to hold a home pregnancy strip up to the light and squint to read the results. No need to break open another test just to make sure the first one hadn't come from a bad batch. After years of treatment, tens of thousands of dollars, and countless prayers, our persistence had finally paid off.

I called Chip to share the wonderful, life-altering news. Then I collapsed onto the sofa and wept with joy.

Later, I headed to the bathroom and opened the medicine cabinet. The Clear Blue Easy was still on the shelf. Though the expiration date printed on it had passed almost a year ago, I'd refused to throw it away. It had been a symbol of hope that one day we would have a child. Now, finally, it was time to use it.

Heart beating fast, I peed on the strip and waited the requisite two minutes. Then I held it up to the sunlight streaming through the bathroom window. Plain as day, the bold black type showed the word I had been waiting to read for more than three years: PREGNANT.

I knew there would be many obstacles to overcome in the still-fragile dream of parenthood. But in that moment, I thanked God and celebrated. The impossible had become possible. And why wouldn't it?

There's no expiration date on hope.

~Nicole R.C. Pugh

# The Master Plan

*Determine the thing that can and shall be done,
and then we shall find the way.*
~Abraham Lincoln

I was twenty-eight when I got married. Tom and I dated for five years before our big day. We had a summer wedding — a perfect time since I am a teacher. I had already earned tenure so I felt secure in my job — again, a perfect time to get married.

Who knew that I would choose to transfer to a different school district the year after we got married? Better pay and a better district were the reasons. To achieve tenure again would require four consecutive full-time years instead of just two. I had to start over, but that was okay. Having kids would be put on the backburner for now. I would only be thirty-three when I earned my tenure at this school, and we could start our family then. This was our new "master plan."

The four years went by quickly. I earned tenure and was ready to have children. I was pregnant within a year. We were excited. From the moment we found out I was pregnant, we were on cloud nine. In bed, Tom would talk to my belly and say the infamous words of Darth Vader, "I am your father!" It was cute.

Unfortunately, I miscarried at eight weeks. We were crushed. The doctors, although sympathetic, were matter-of-fact. "These things happen to a lot of women. It's not uncommon at all." I felt no comfort in those words. The doctors said to try again in a couple of months, and I was pregnant three months later. This time it was different. We put up our guard. We didn't let ourselves get excited. "Let's hope for the best," we kept telling ourselves.

This second pregnancy lasted twelve weeks. This time, the doctors ran tests and found a chromosomal abnormality. But they said there was still no reason why I wouldn't be able to carry a healthy baby to full term.

We tried to get pregnant for about a year after the second miscarriage, but were unsuccessful. We decided to give ourselves a short break from the stress of trying to conceive. "It will happen," we thought to ourselves. Deep down, I wasn't so sure.

Instead of getting pregnant, I got cancer. It was a rare type of breast cancer. Several surgeries followed by chemotherapy were scheduled. During one of my initial appointments with the oncologist, he asked, "Do you and your husband plan on having kids?" I answered, "We were hoping to." With that, he suggested I get my eggs extracted by an IVF doctor.

Several doctors informed us, "Your insurance doesn't cover this." When I asked what all of this would cost, I was told somewhere around $25,000 with no guarantee that the result would be a baby. Tom and I thought long and hard about it. Ultimately, we decided this was an "investment" worth making.

In my effort to work out a payment plan, I spoke with a woman named Lee from a certain doctor's office, and she turned out to be our saving grace. Although she verified that insurance companies don't often cover egg extraction, there were three exceptions: having cancer that required chemotherapy; being thirty-five or over and trying to conceive unsuccessfully for over six months; and having two or more miscarriages. I informed her that I actually fit into all three of those categories! She took my insurance information and fought for me. She won! Insurance would cover it!

I had to undergo two extractions, but the result was four embryos that were to be frozen for future use. It felt like a victory although I still had so much to go through. Even after chemotherapy, I had to be on medication for five years and was not to get pregnant during that time. Our dream of being parents seemed so distant. Our "master plan" needed revision.

The important thing was to fight this dreaded disease and get healthy. I wouldn't let it beat me. Chemo was hard at times, but I was one of the lucky ones. I didn't suffer much nausea, just extreme exhaustion, achy bones, and low immunity. I did lose all of my hair, including my eyebrows and eyelashes, but I continued to teach, struggling to make the seventy-five-mile roundtrip drive to work. I wore a do-rag of sorts to school, and most of my high school students and other teachers thought it was just my new fashion statement.

I made it through stronger than ever, but still my life wasn't complete. However, all that changed when my sister called me at work one afternoon. It was a phone call I will never forget. Her exact words were, "Why don't we see your doctor about making you a mom? I could be your surrogate!" I burst into tears.

The entire process took over two years, but I am now the mother of a beautiful, healthy son who was born in September 2009. I will forever be grateful for this wonderful gift I've been given. What a sister I have! I am truly blessed. It was a long journey, but the "master plan" finally happened... thanks to my sister.

~RMB McManamon

# Sixteen Pink Lines

*It is said that the present is pregnant with the future.*
*~Voltaire*

Sixteen pink lines. Eight pregnancy tests with eight positives, and sixteen pink lines. Out of tears and out of pee, I was finally pregnant.

The last several years had been filled with the ups and downs of infertility and miscarriage. My heart ached for a child I thought I would never hold in my arms. But everything changed that fateful evening when those bold and beautiful pink lines stared back at me.

"If I go to bed right now, I won't have to tell him," I told myself. "He has enough on his plate right now. I do not need to add this stress."

While pregnancy should indeed not be stressful, when you have gotten your hopes up for a child only to have the life slowly drain from your body from an unexplained miscarriage, it is difficult not to be stressed.

So I faked it. I curled up in bed, covered my eyes with our palm-tree-endowed blanket, and pretended to sleep while I prayed that somehow this embryo could develop into a happy, healthy, and wise little human.

The next morning, I tried to fake it some more.

"What's on your mind?" my husband asked.

"Nothing, nothing at all," I said, as I tried to avoid eye contact. "Coffee?"

After eight years of marriage to my high school sweetheart, I should have known I could not keep this secret.

"You look different. Anything you want to talk about?"

With all the downsizing and reorganizing going on at his work, I did not want to add to his worries.

"I took a test," I said.

"What kind of test?" He was oblivious.

"A test," I said as I wrapped my arms around my belly to give the child in my womb another embrace. "Actually, eight tests."

And for a fleeting moment, he let a smile slip across his lips. Just for a second. Then his guard came back up and he said the only words his heart would let him speak. "We'll see."

"I know, sweetie. We'll see."

As he headed off to work, I called the doctor to set up a blood test. I had been through the tests before. Last time, the first test was "questionable." Then I went for another test every forty-eight hours for the next four weeks. The pregnancy hormones that should have doubled had started slowly falling.

"What are my chances?" I would ask when the results came in.

At first, it was 70 percent, then 50/50. Finally, I received the list of symptoms so that I would know when "it was over."

Over? It was over? I always thought that was such a horrible way of describing the death of a child in a womb. "It" and "over" did not seem to come anywhere close to describing the physical, emotional, and spiritual draining that a miscarriage brings.

"Dear God," I prayed on the way to the hospital, "please let this one be different. May I please keep this child?"

Forty-eight excruciating hours later, I was back at the hospital for a second blood test and the results of the first round.

"The numbers are a little low, Jamie, but I think we have a shot. I want you to start on some progesterone, take another blood test today, and come back on Friday."

"Sounds familiar," I said.

A hug from the doctor and a poke later, I was headed to the

pharmacy for suppositories that insurance did not cover in hopes that it would save my child.

And it did.

The pregnancy was picture-perfect until the last month.

"Let me measure that again," the doctor said, as he stretched his tape across my protruding stomach. "This baby is getting really, really big. You are not gaining weight, but she is. And fast! I am going to send you to a specialist downstairs. We need a second set of eyes."

"Are we okay?" I asked.

"Yeah, you are fine, and she is fine. We just want to make sure we are staying on top of this."

I put in a call to my husband, and he met me for a special 3D ultrasound. As I lay on the bed, I watched the specialist measure every gorgeous limb on the ultrasound screen. And the numbers scared me.

Right arm: 46 weeks.

Left leg: 48 weeks.

Head: 47 weeks.

Expected weight: 10-plus pounds.

"She has a full head of hair, her organs are grown, and she is growing fast. We need to get her out. Like sooner rather than later," he laughed. "She may have teeth."

At 37 weeks pregnant, this baby was ready. Now.

We called my doctor to schedule a C-section for the next day. And at 8:32 a.m., Kimberly Anne Richardson was born. All nine pounds, two ounces of our miracle baby.

Eighteen months later, her brother, Jacob Brent Richardson, weighed in at eight pounds, ten ounces.

And the final Richardson, Aidan Kyle, was born twenty-eight months later weighing in at ten pounds, six ounces.

For a non-diabetic mother, those were some whoppers!

My babies are now six, four, and two years old. My family is my heart and soul. We have had our ups and downs along the way, but nothing in this life meets the feeling of motherhood.

I would not trade that for anything, and I have all sixteen (now faded) pink lines to mark where the journey began.

~Jamie Richardson

# Longing for a Child

*God touched our hearts so deep inside, our special blessing multiplied.*
*~Author Unknown*

Tick-tock, tick-tock... My inner clock informed me it was time to have another child. Our daughter was now an active toddler, and my husband and I were ready to complete our family. I was thirty-seven and getting older on the inside, but still full of life on the outside. The time seemed ripe to be blessed with another child. But as we all know, some things just don't work according to our schedule.

As the months began to stretch out and I had not yet become pregnant, worry began to seep in. I started to lose faith in my body's ability to conceive another child. Both my husband and I considered what life would be like with an only child. And I have to honest; it was not the picture of family that I had always considered in my head. Why could I not celebrate that I already had a happy, healthy child and loving husband? Why did I continue to obsess over my ovulation cycle and the right time to conceive each month? My months were divided into two sections—those before ovulation and those after, when I waited for the pink indicator to show I was pregnant. Of course, the little plus sign never appeared, and I would cry in disappointment.

Finally, I made an appointment with a specialist. As I sat in the waiting room with other women, I felt such a heavy and disturbing feeling in the air. These women and I all had something in common—we wanted to conceive a child—but instead of infertility pulling us together, it only isolated us. None of us made eye contact. Instead, we busied ourselves reading magazines and trying to remain detached from the whole scene. As women, we are often the first line of support for each other during crises. But in this doctor's office, there was almost a tangible feeling of shame. Women all around the world could conceive, and yet here we were unable to perform this basic rite of passage.

During my time of infertility, our close friends continued to expand their families. They would apologize to me when announcing their pregnancy. How awkward it was to reassure them that all was well when I was so sad inside. But sitting at those many baby showers only strengthened my conviction that I was meant to have another child. So after careful consideration of our finances, my husband and I raided my retirement IRA and proceeded with in vitro fertilization (IVF).

The worst part about IVF is the drugs you take to increase your rate of ovulation and the eggs that are grown in your ovaries each month. At the beginning of each month, I would receive a box filled with drugs, syringes, and needles, along with a complete set of directions for when to poke, prod, and inject myself in the stomach, arm, or buttocks. I certainly didn't look forward to the sheer number of injections that my husband gave me each day, but I always felt the need to continue.

One night during my IVF treatment, I went to our church for a healing service. It was a short mass for those who needed extra healing in their bodies and their spiritual lives. It was filled with prayers and then a time at the altar rail praying for what was on our minds. I had done all I could with conventional medicine, and now the final healing had to come from God. Only He knew the ultimate plan for my life, and it was now up to Him. I can't say that I felt an immediate healing, but I knew at last that I could find peace if a new baby wasn't meant to bless our lives.

The first round of IVF failed, and I was devastated. But we decided to try one more time. And that time, we received the good news that I was pregnant. As I went to my first ultrasound appointment, we learned the extra exciting news that I was expecting fraternal twins. Twins!

The following months were filled with waves of nausea—extra in the case of twins because of the double hormones circulating in my body.

As the pregnancy continued, there were the usual ups and downs—the good days when all went as planned, and the bad days when I was fearful and experiencing early contractions. But, through it all, I knew that God was watching these two babies and would see us through to the end. He had given me hope when I was at my lowest. My dear sweet boy/girl twins were born healthy at week 36, and my family picture was finally complete.

~K.T.

# A Letter to My Unborn Child

*Children are the anchors that hold a mother to life.*
*~Sophocles*

Dear Lola,

Today was a monumental day for me... or shall I say *us*. Today, I hatched seven eggs, one of which may be a part of you someday! In case you are confused, I had minor surgery to retrieve eggs from my ovaries and freeze them for a later time when I am healthy enough to bear children. You see, one of the most devastating things I learned about having breast cancer is that the treatment usually sends young women into menopause, leaving them infertile and not able to conceive.

Since becoming a mother has been my greatest desire for over ten years now, I was practically crippled by the news. I remember leaving the hospital that day sobbing uncontrollably and crying out to God, begging him not to take away the one thing I wanted most in life. "Isn't having breast cancer at thirty-six enough? Please, God, allow me to become a mother."

I have a fierce warrior spirit and wasn't ready to give up on my dream, so I sought the help of several fertility specialists. I must say that after my first visit, I was once again licking salty tears off my upper lip. I was completely discouraged and deflated. The first doctor said that the success rate of freezing eggs was so low that she didn't invest the time in doing it. Thankfully, she did recommend another doctor who had a reputation for being the absolute best in the field of reproductive medicine.

So a few weeks ago, I contacted this doctor and explained my desperate situation. Not only was he incredibly compassionate about my situation, but his entire team embraced me like a family member. Over the last few weeks, I have been on a very strict regimen of fertility drugs. I have spent many hours having blood work and ultrasounds done so that my body could produce the most eggs possible. I must admit it's quite exciting to look inside your body through an ultrasound machine, even if you are only looking at small black spots that are growing follicles. My IVF nurse, Peg, would shout out, "Oh, look, there's another one, and it's a big one!"

It turns out I had ten follicles present in my ovaries, and seven of them produced healthy eggs. Seven was always my lucky number! I am completely in awe of the wonders of medicine and how much more is available now to help women reach their dream of becoming pregnant. I'm so thankful there are physicians and researchers who are so passionate about this cause and making dreams come true every day.

In the meantime, you patiently wait for me, frozen in time, as I undergo chemotherapy and radiation. I will do whatever it takes to get healthy again so that we will finally meet face to face.

Love always,
Your mom-to-be

~Tiffany Mannino

# Chapter 11

# New Moms

## Second Time Around

*Children of the same family, the same blood, with the same first associations and habits, have some means of enjoyment in their power, which no subsequent connections can supply...*

~Jane Austen, Mansfield Park

# It

> *I don't believe an accident of birth makes people sisters or brothers. It makes them siblings, gives them mutuality of parentage. Sisterhood and brotherhood is a condition people have to work at.*
> ~Maya Angelou

Everyone knew Asher didn't like babies. He never tried to hide his desire for babies not to be in the church nursery, riding in strollers at the mall, or hanging out at the local coffee shop. Wherever we went, my little boy would yell with all the seriousness a two-year-old can muster, "There should not be any babies here!"

But in my heart I longed for a baby. After suffering three emotionally devastating miscarriages within nine months, I desperately wanted a baby in my arms. The empty crib in the nursery angered me more than Asher could possibly know. So while my son yelled for babies to stop crying (or smiling or existing), I sighed with resignation that his two-year-old wish seemed to be coming true.

But with the fourth conception, after I had convinced myself that my dream of a house full of children would never come true, my belly grew — and it continued to grow for a full nine months. Unlike the others, once the heart of my little Amelie started beating, it never stopped. Nausea gave way to heartburn, which turned into an outie belly button. In the final month, she gave me ankles so swollen I had to stop wearing socks.

While I managed the physical trauma of pregnancy, it became

more apparent we needed to tackle the issue of Asher's baby phobia. Attempts to convince him Baby would be a constant playmate didn't work. Our explanations of a cooing bundle of sweetness continued to fly over the top of his head. He responded by merely lowering his voice to calmly affirm his belief that babies did not belong, rather than yelling his exposition for any passersby to hear.

As the scheduled date of my delivery approached, my prayers constantly focused on preparing Asher to accept the baby who would soon arrive. We oohed and ahhed over friends' new siblings. All the library books about how great babies are passed through our home. And we still waited for his little heart to change.

We waited and waited until my due date arrived, and I finally met my baby girl face to face. I could hardly believe that I could finally hold in my arms this little gift sent from God. At the moment when the doctors pulled Amelie out and cut her cord from me, the knife cut away tension that had built up around my heart for years. My baby with a beating heart. A beautiful girl, screaming her lungs full of life. I cuddled her and cried over her and thanked God over and over that my arms were full.

And when I decided it might be time for someone else to share my joy and hold my precious bundle, I passed her around to Daddy, Grams and Grandpa. While they met Amelie, I cuddled my Asher—who seemed to have grown a foot in the few hours we had been apart—and reminded him how much I loved him.

He took it all in. The sterile hospital room, the presence of Grams and Grandpa visiting from Kansas, and Mommy in a bed. I worried that his disdain for babies would multiply now that we had one squirming and capturing the hearts of everyone he loved. But God answered my prayers.

As Grams held Amelie and gazed over her little body, Asher looked to me and asked, "Can we take it home?"

I assured him we could take the bouquet of balloons home. But that's not what he wanted to take home.

So he asked again. "No, but can we take it home?"

Scanning the room, I tried to figure out what else he wanted to take home. The new watch Aunt Becky gave him? No. The baby rattles in the bags from friends? No.

Our mutual frustration grew, and I could not figure out what he wanted to take home.

"Can we take home what Grams is holding?" he asked in frustration.

We all looked up in amazement, realizing Grams was holding Asher's little sister. And he wanted to take her—a baby—home!

Victory!

Although he wouldn't refer to her as a baby or agree to hold her, he wanted to take her home.

And that's just what we did.

~Angie Reedy

# Sea of Mother Love

*For a mother is the only person on earth
Who can divide her love among ten children
And each child still have
All her love.*
*~Anonymous*

The summer sun toasted my shoulders as I pushed my little boy on the swing. My friend, Angie, and I were at the play park. She stood behind the swings, too, and pushed her own little blond son. Both of our bellies were round with babies. I was due to deliver my second child any day, and her delivery was just a few weeks behind.

"Do you ever wonder," I asked, "if you'll be able to love another child like you love the one you already have?" It was a bold question, one that I hoped seemed more lighthearted than it was, due to the sunshine and the laughter of the little boys and the creek of the old, metal swings. But the truth was, I'd been pondering the question for months. I wondered if I could summon enough love. And I felt guilty for wondering.

Angie's arms dropped to her sides, and she let the swing coast on momentum. Her green eyes welled with tears. "Yes," she said. "I do wonder."

"Oh," I said. It was a tender moment of mom-confession. I let my son's swing coast, too. Angie and I took a seat on the grass. "It's just that I love Logan so much. It's like when he was born, my heart transformed to this sea of emotion, more deep and wide than I could ever imagine. I'm scared of not having that again."

"I understand," Angie said. "I worry about that, too."

We were silent for a moment. Then our little boys leapt from their swings. Logan rushed toward me and wrapped his summer-brown arms around my neck. "Will you push us on the merry-go-round?" he asked.

"Sure," I said.

I stood slowly, one hand on my belly. The tiny bundle rolled under my touch. I loved this child already. But would it be the same? I wondered as Logan clasped my hand in his and pulled me across the green grass.

Later that night, after we'd tucked Logan in bed, my husband and I sat on our porch swing. There was a twinge of cool in the mid-June night, and Lonny's arm slipped around my shoulders.

"It won't be long now," Lonny said. "Are you ready to be a new mommy again?"

"Ready," I said. I swallowed hard. "Hey, do you remember when Logan was born?" I asked.

"Of course," he said.

"What I mean is, do you remember when you first held him in your arms? When I first held Logan, I thought my heart would break. He was so still and peaceful. So gentle. Do you remember his thick black hair? Remember his long, tapered fingers? When he first opened his eyes, it felt like nothing else in the world. There was some new connection that ran from that baby to the center of my soul."

"Love," Lonny said, simply. "It was a new kind of love."

I snuggled into Lonny's arms and wrapped my own arms around my middle. I hoped there was enough of that new kind of love to stretch over our growing family.

By mid-morning of the next day, it was obvious that our world was about to change. We prepared to leave for the hospital when the labor pains were regular. Before I settled into the van, I caught Logan by the hand and pulled him close to me. I knelt down, the best I could, and I whispered into his ear.

"I love you, Logan. It's time to go to the hospital. We're going to meet our new baby," I said.

He looked up at me with wide eyes. "I love you, too, Mama."

I pulled him to my chest and felt his little heart beat against mine.

Later in the afternoon, our second child was born. Immediately, I heard the wail of a babe. The cry was fierce. It was filled with passion.

I caught the first glimpse of my second son as the doctor held him for me to see. The babe's tiny arms were curled to his chest. His fists were clenched. His little face was bunched and scarlet as his mouth opened and closed to swallow his first gulps of breath.

Within seconds the squalling, tiny boy was wrapped in soft blue flannel and placed in my arms. I pulled the blanket back to drink in all the details of my son. His hair was strawberry blond. His features were round. Even his hands were different from Logan's. I slipped my finger into his curled fist, and he squeezed tight.

Then I pulled his blanket back and held him to my heart. His tiny chest quit heaving, and the fierce cry subsided into a few long, hard gasps.

My son.

I held him tight. He'd just come from my body, but it seemed that when I held him close, he pulled back into a part of me. And he had. That tiny little boy, in all his newborn fury, settled deep into my heart.

It didn't take long to realize that this newly created person was completely different from my firstborn son. His labor was different. His birth was different. He looked nothing like his brother. And within the first moments of his life, I knew that his personality was all his own, too.

And I had never seen anything more lovely. His zest. His zeal. Apparent at his very first breath.

We named our second little boy Grant. And with Grant's grand arrival, the question in my heart disappeared. Could I love another child as much as I loved my first?

Absolutely. Immediately. My soul was filled with peace.

The hours rolled by that day, and I was anxious to share my son. Angie was the first friend to visit and meet our newborn babe. As she sat beside my bed with her hand on her round tummy, I longed to tell her what I'd discovered. I didn't. I knew the truth was not something that another mother could share.

A mother's heart is a sea of love, and it is deep and wide enough for all.

But like a sweet second son, that truth needed to be born.

~Shawnelle Eliasen

# I Didn't Know

*Discovering that with every child, your heart grows bigger and stronger—that there is no limit to how much or how many people you can love, even though at times you feel as though you could burst— you don't—you just love even more.*
~Yasmin Le Bon

Down the hall, I can hear my husband's muted voice as he reads a book to my three-year-old son before putting him to bed. I am sitting in my rocking chair in a dark room where slivers of moonlight seep in through cracks in the blinds, barely illuminating the room with a soft glow. Nestled in my arms is my two-week-old son, who has drifted off to sleep after nursing. I am exhausted, but I don't get up to put him in his bassinette quite yet. Instead, I examine his pudgy cheeks, his soft hair, and his tiny fingers.

I think women are universally hardwired to believe that their children are the most beautiful of all children. Even so, as I look at my new son, I decide my children really are the most beautiful in the entire world. I listen to the steady whispered breaths of my infant as I slowly rock in the chair. And I think of the friend who visited earlier in the day to congratulate us on our new arrival.

"You'll probably have an easier time with this one, now that you've already had one child," she had said.

"Well, there's a lot I didn't know before my first son was born that I know now," I answered.

"Sure," she said. "You're probably a feeding, bathing, baby-changing expert now."

After changing his share of thousands of diapers, my husband did claim to be the fastest diaper changer west of the Mississippi, but I wasn't talking about things like that. I was referring more to how I didn't know there would be days and nights that I would be so exhausted that I cried. And how I would feel like I was going insane when the baby would cry again just as my head was reaching my pillow. But I would still willingly—sometimes even joyfully—get up again to take care of him.

I didn't know that after sacrificing my career, my time, my thoughts, my energy, my money, and certainly my body, for my baby, that I would still feel like I hadn't given him enough.

I didn't know that cherished possessions, like the crystal sculpture of the place my husband and I were married, could be easily forgotten when destroyed by my toddler.

I didn't know that news stories I barely would have glanced at before my son's birth would become overwhelmingly heartbreaking as I thought of another mother's loss. Terrified, I would ask, "What if it had been my child?"

I didn't know that giving birth to a child would be a kind of rebirth for myself—allowing me to see the world again for the first time through his experiences.

But the main thing I didn't know was how mind-blowing, life-altering in love I would become. I didn't know my love for my child would surpass my love for friends, siblings, my parents, and even my husband, whom I absolutely adored. I didn't know I would stop living my life for me, and start living it for him. I didn't know I would get more joy out of his successes than I would my own. I didn't know my heart would ache so badly from loving him so much. And I didn't know that the frustrations, discouragements, challenges, and never-ending messes would be worth it.

But I know now. And I know it will be the same with my second son. I smile at my sleeping angel and tell him, "I will love you forever, baby. Forever and ever." And then I sit in the quietness a few more minutes until my husband cracks open the door. With his appearance, I know my other darling must be sleeping soundly. My husband has come to see if there is anything I need before he takes his weary body to bed.

"You good?" he asks.

I smile. "I'm good," I say. But really, I'm better than good. I'm the luckiest woman in the world because I know what I didn't know before. Again.

~Amanda Yardley Luzzader

# New Mother, Redux

*We know that birth takes a woman from one place in her life to another. The birth of a child certainly does change her viewpoint of herself and I believe her viewpoint of the world.*

~Sameerah Shareef

Years ago, I heard the phrase "no children have the same parents." At the time, I probably chuckled over the truth of the statement, but gave it no further thought, as I didn't have any children. But after the birth of my second child, that statement began to haunt me.

Poor Lukas. For the first few months of my younger son's life, that's how I thought of him. Poor Lukas. Not that there was anything wrong with him. Right from the start, he was a good-natured baby with dimpled cheeks, clear blue eyes, and light brown hair that became curly when wet. He was never colicky, rarely spit up, and didn't cry without reason. He was in perfect health. Yet for a long time, whenever I looked at him, I felt wracked with pity. Why? Because he didn't have the same mother as his older brother, Teodor.

Teo's mother was like a dream, the very picture of devotion. She spent long hours gazing at his sleeping face, bending close to him so that she could feel his breath on her skin. She kept a detailed, somewhat overwrought journal of all his early experiences, and photographed his every move. She started reading Dr. Seuss to him when he was five weeks old. She sang him to sleep and flew to his side at his first peep. Though she passed him to his father, his grandparents, and her friends readily, she always had to put her hands on her hips or find some object to fiddle with so she wouldn't give in to the urge to snatch him back. She wept at every milestone he reached and tried to ensure that he felt wrapped in peace and security every minute of the day.

Lukas's mother, on the other hand, sometimes forgot that he was there. Oh, I never abandoned him in a train station or a grocery store or anything. But all the same, there were times when I looked up from wrestling two-year-old Teo into his diapers, or sweeping up the rice he had flung on the floor, or catching him just as he was preparing to swan dive from his high chair, and was genuinely startled to see Lukas there, regarding us quietly from his bouncy seat. When he saw he had my attention, he'd break into a delighted gummy grin of complete faith, as if to say: "I knew you'd remember me eventually! I just knew it!" Poor Lukas.

Parenting books and magazines don't offer much guidance for the second-time mother. As first-time mothers, we are flooded with information on how to change a diaper, clip teeny-tiny fingernails, and deal with green poop. When we're expecting for the second time, it's assumed we already know how to do all that stuff. Most advice for the second-time mom is limited to tips on how to make time for your older child when the baby arrives. Nobody even hints that you might have trouble making time for the baby.

When Lukas was about three months old, I found myself pouring out my guilt to Felicia, a mother who had a toddler Teo's age and a baby a few months older than Lukas. "I'm a crappy mom to Lukas," I confessed. "I'm always so involved with Teo that this poor baby gets practically no attention at all." I glanced down at Lukas, asleep in my arms, oblivious to the ear-splitting whoops of Teo and Felicia's daughter Isabelle as they chased each other through the apartment. "When Teo was this age, I noticed every single thing he did. Everything. But I didn't even notice when Lukas started smiling! One day, I saw him sitting there, smiling to himself, and I thought, 'Oh! He smiles! When did that start?'"

Felicia laughed. "I know what you mean," she said. "It's so

different the second time around. When Isabelle was a baby, I really enjoyed taking care of her. Usually, I didn't even mind getting up in the night to feed her. But with Emma... sometimes I felt like she was a stranger's child that I was given to take care of in-between watching out for Isabelle." Felicia smiled at Emma, who beamed up at us from the rug, proud of her new sitting skills. "But you know what? I don't think Emma will be needing therapy because of it. This period passes. You're paying more attention to Teo right now because he's the one who needs it most. But you're still doing your job with Lukas. Look at him—he's fine."

I looked down at Lukas again and saw that she was right. He lay in the crook of my arm, his head lolling back, his sweet face blissed out on milk and sleep. There was no sign of my perceived neglect of him; there was nothing about this beautiful boy to pity. He may not have gotten the full-wattage attention that Teo received at his age, but he nonetheless had the glowing aura of a well-loved, contented baby. It wasn't Lukas who was wanting for anything. It was me.

I wanted Lukas to experience the magic of being a firstborn child. I wanted him to have parents who cheered his every blink and spent their evenings staring at him in slack-jawed wonder. I wanted this, not because it was essential for his wellbeing, but because it was what Teo had had. I didn't want Lukas to feel any less loved. But my conversation with Felicia reminded me that not only was it impossible to replicate Teo's experience, it wasn't even necessary. I still gave Lukas all the love and attention that he needed, even on the fly. Every drop of mother love goes a long way.

As Lukas approaches seven months old, I still have "poor Lukas" moments—but they're getting rarer. Why? For one thing, after months of watching Teo operate, the kid has figured out that the squeaky wheel gets the grease. If he's not getting the attention he wants or needs, he lets me know with an indignant squawk. Moreover, these days I'm more apt to think of Lukas as lucky because has something Teo never did: a loyal and loving big brother. Teo is the staunch defender of Lukas's toys, food, chair and person. When Lukas cries, Teo distracts him with a stuffed animal or a song. Once, he even heroically dragged Lukas's bouncy chair, containing a wailing Lukas, all the way into the kitchen where I was preparing lunch.

But another reason "poor Lukas" has been almost banished from my vocabulary comes from one important realization. Recently, as I watched my boys truly playing together for the first time (Teo saying "Gah!" Lukas repeating "Gah!" and both of them giggling like mad), I felt a fierce love for them that left me breathless. Bring on the lions! Bring on the bears! At that moment, I honestly believed I could have fought a wild animal and won. And that's when I knew that despite whatever inconsistent mothering behavior I'll unavoidably display in the future, Lukas and Teo will always have the same mom in one respect: They'll always have a mother who loves them beyond reason.

~Barbara Diggs

# To My Younger Son

*The world talks to the mind. Parents speak more intimately—
they talk to the heart.*
~Hain Ginott

My Dear Son,

You and your brother are my finest achievements. For some reason, the dream of parenthood did not come easily to your father and me. We fell into a category called "unexplained infertility." There was no medical evidence to show that we couldn't have a baby, but the dream of becoming parents just wasn't happening the way it seemed to be for others. There were many frustrating setbacks, losses and tears that eventually brought our family to be, and we are fortunate to have found the medical alternatives we needed to help build our family.

Your older brother was born with the assistance of a reproductive doctor who worked with us to achieve the goal of parenthood. We welcomed your brother into our family and hoped that one day we would experience the joy of the birth of a child again. We returned to this doctor to give your brother a sibling, but we were not having success. Every month brought another dose of disappointment and heartache followed by a pep talk to try and get motivated for another round of injections. We were successful before. Were we asking too much of our luck and destiny to want it to happen a second time?

One warm, summer afternoon, we thought we were going into the doctor's office to discuss a new strategy when the doctor delivered devastating news. It was his opinion that we would not have another biological child of our own. I left his office in a haze of confusion and tears. We had passed through the doors of this building many, many times, but as I walked out the doors for what would be the final time, I was overcome by a wave of emotions. I couldn't walk or breathe. I leaned against a raised planter of brightly colored flowers and wept in front of the whirling revolving doors of a busy office building entrance, only vaguely aware of the curious stares of people passing by.

After some time, I tried to drive myself home because your father had to go back to work, but at some point I realized I was driving in the wrong direction. I could no longer concentrate on the road through my tears. Turning the car onto a narrow, downtown street, I pulled into a parking space. My hands trembled as I struggled to dial the phone so I could tell your father I would wait for him to be done with work. The hours passed, and I remained in the car that humid afternoon watching life pass by in front of me as an occasional breeze drifted through the open windows. It was a brilliantly bright summer day, and the promenade near the river's edge was filled with happy activity. There were balloons bobbing in the breeze, bicycles riding by, baby strollers with the bare feet of little ones peeking out from the seats, children and adults laughing and eating dripping ice cream cones. But the doctor's words rang in my head over and over. "It is my opinion that you won't have another biological child," the doctor had said as he pushed a box of tissues to the edge of the wooden desk. Those were the odds. We were done.

After feeling the depths of despair that day, somewhere inside myself I found a renewed sense of strength and fight. That's what second opinions are for. Through hours of tireless reading and relentless research, I found a new doctor who was extremely realistic but open to working with patients who were a bit more of a challenge. Time had passed, and age wasn't on my side now to try and achieve a healthy pregnancy and birth. It was my last chance at a gamble with in vitro fertilization, and with grit and determination—and a single embryo to transfer—we did it.

You came into the world a little more than a year after that difficult day in the car, and you made my firstborn a big brother. The greatest pleasure for me is to hear the two of you laugh and talk together. It is my hope that you will always share a bond. It is the unguarded moments, when you don't think I am listening to the both of you, that make me know it was all worth it.

I love you,
Mommy

~Alice Knisley Matthias

# The Outfit

*Give your stress wings and let it fly away.*
~Terri Guillemets

"Thank Heaven for Little Boys" was delicately embroidered in cursive writing across the upper portion of the outfit, and the body of the outfit was baby blue. It was sweetness times one hundred. I hurriedly grabbed it from the metal display stand and power-walked to the register. My heart was beating wildly. The outfit resonated with the image I had been carrying around in my mind ever since the doctor said, "It's a boy!" It was as innocent as the angel who would wear it home from the hospital. But if the outfit was perfect, why was there a little voice in my head whispering to put it back?

Intuitively, I knew exactly why my insides were telling me to put the outfit back. I could hear my mother-in-law's cutting words to me three years earlier before my first child was born. "I always buy the outfits that the grandchildren come home in!" Pop! There went my balloon! For years, I had dreamed about choosing those first outfits for my children, but my mother-in-law stole that opportunity from me. And out of respect for her and my husband, I did not argue the situation. In fact, after months of anxiety and debate in my head, I thought, "I'll allow her to buy the first outfit because maybe—just maybe—I am acting selfish."

As time grew closer to my due date, I nervously waited for Rhoda, my mother-in-law, to unveil the outfit. I prayed, "Please God, let it be the most beautiful outfit in the whole world." If it turned out to be a gorgeous outfit, then some of my anxiety would be laid to rest (except for the fact that I didn't purchase it).

Much to my dismay, she waited until the day the baby was born to go shopping. She said it was because the doctors had been known to be wrong, and she didn't want to have to take it back if "she" turned out to be a "he."

Finally, after many hours of induced labor and a Cesarean birth, Autumn Leigh Dotson was born. Unfortunately, the outfit Rhoda presented at the hospital was not the magical attire I had imagined my first child wearing home from the hospital. This was to be the first journey of her life, the first journey to her new home, the first time she would be seen by aunts, uncles, cousins, and friends who would be waiting to see her when we carried her through the door! And within a few seconds, my optimism had dwindled. She pulled out an almost hot pink onesie with tiny black bow ties on it. It wasn't ugly, but plain, like drinking from a glass you thought was filled with soda, but instead was warm water. It wasn't pretty enough for my baby's first outfit. On the other hand, Autumn was a stunning baby no matter what she wore. So I sucked up my pride and proudly took my baby home in the outfit her grandma chose for her.

Three and a half years later, when I saw the perfect outfit for my second child, I raced to the register and carefully placed it on the cashier's counter. Then I heard my mother-in-law's dreadful words again, "I always buy the outfits that the grandchildren come home in!" This time, I deliberately shoved the words to the back of my mind where I put all the things I want to forget.

Then the cashier said, "You saved an extra fifteen percent today."

"It's a sign! I have to buy it now," I thought. My hand shook as I signed the check, but when I tore out the check, the corner ripped where the number and date were printed. Was this a sign, too? Was God telling me not to buy it?

Finally, I bought the outfit.

A month or so before my expected due date, Rhoda asked me if

I had bought an outfit for the baby. Timidly, I nodded my head yes, and nothing else was ever said.

April 30, 1999 arrived, and so did Nolan Wayne Dotson. He was the tiniest little thing, and I anticipated Rhoda's familiar visit with the celebrated first outfit, but packed mine just in case. However, she did not present the customary outfit.

Let's face it, mothers-in-law have a bad reputation, and even when they mean well, they come across as being meddlesome and bossy. Then there are the dimwitted and inexperienced daughters-in-law who think they know as much as, or even more than, their mother-in-law. And when you put them both together, there is sometimes a power struggle. It's been more than fourteen years since my first baby was born, and if I could go back and do it all over again, I would just give her the blessing to buy both outfits. Now that my children are older, they have never once asked about their first outfits, and probably don't even know what they wore home.

My only hope is that when I am a mother-in-law, my daughter-in-law and I will share a mutual respect for one another and won't let these kinds of issues come between us. In the end, it's the relationship that matters most — not the outfit.

~Jeannie Dotson

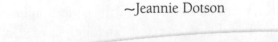

# The Second Time Around

*God sends children to enlarge our hearts,
and make us unselfish and full of kindly sympathies and affections.*
~Mary Howitt

The doctor announced my pregnancy with less fanfare the second time around. Counting the days, I figured two years and four months between the two children—perfect. My first child arrived after a long labor, but the pregnancy itself had been more enjoyable than not. We'd planned for only two children in our lives, and this time I knew more of what to expect. The magic of carrying a child was once again mine, and I intended to cherish every moment of the final childbearing phase of my life.

A mild doubt softly knocked at my conscience on my drive home, however, but I pushed it away. When I arrived in the kitchen, I smothered my toddler, Matthew, with kisses and hugs, inhaling all the marvelous mothering experiences of him. As I did, the doubt rushed in this time, crashing over my head. How in the world could I ever love another child as much as I loved this one?

Looking at the light of my life, I realized the news would alter his world forever. Not only would my world shift, but his would as well—possibly even more so than mine. Was I shortchanging him? How could I feel guilty about having another baby? But, also, how could I take this step without consideration for his needs and wishes?

"You promised Matthew all of your love," said my conscience.

A tear welled, and I set Matthew in his father's arms before excusing myself to change clothes. "Silly, so silly," I murmured in the closet. "Families have several children. I have a younger sister."

Memories of my sister didn't help. We'd fought like cats and dogs well into our college years. My memories of our fights, tears and a few spankings for our confrontations were angry and judgmental. As the elder, I'd been the quieter one, and my sibling had wielded the temper. She'd married my ex-boyfriend, stolen my car for a joyride and dented it, pilfered my clothes, accused me of being fat, and called me the goodie-two-shoes for years.

Matthew had my temperament—docile and introspective. Even at twenty months old, he showed quiet resolve. He would be two years old when his world would rock and tremble, and the attention that was his alone would be shared with an unknown entity—a person he might not like, who'd require more attention than him for a while. Guilt nagged me, and the exciting first day of a new pregnancy countdown morphed into dread.

The next step was visiting Grandma and Grandpa to deliver the happy news. Memories of the first announcement were recent enough to remain vivid, and I looked forward to the congratulations, hoping the hugs and good wishes would erase the negative niggling in my mind.

Mom and Daddy smiled and showed the appropriate delight. Mom quickly swept up Matthew upon hearing the news, showering him with an exceptional load of kisses, calling him her best angel. Her jubilation at the news didn't ring true to my oversensitive ears. I wrote off her faux effort at excitement to this being the second time around the block for me, no longer a new experience, and figured it too soon for anyone to bubble over with joy.

Watching Matthew sleep that night, I admitted the truth. Grandma held the same doubt I did. What if the second baby created more problems than delight?

This sleeping toddler was her first grandchild, and this child of perfection hung the moon in her eyes—as he did in mine. I was my mother's daughter. Love for him might fade a bit when the diapers and formula took time away from ABCs and bedtime stories. She kept her feelings to herself. I kept mine bottled up as well.

In my own bed, I shed a few self-pity tears. The deed was done, however, and I'd work twice as hard to love both, whatever the price. My conscience argued with my hormones through most of the night.

The months passed more quickly the second time around. Some things were different, others the same, but the calendar raced by. I finally called my mother and announced we were headed to the hospital. Expecting her to grab her coat and follow in her car as with the last one, she instead offered to keep Matthew and await a phone call.

Wham—the doubt rushed back at the worst moment, as Grandma exercised logic over emotion, a reaction I interpreted as protecting Matthew from what was about to happen to him. Soon back pain and gripping contractions consumed my thoughts, and I concentrated on the work at hand. Wracked with pain, I envisioned Grandma hovering over her first grandchild, determined to be the one who saved him from dejection.

Child number two came into the world quite differently than his brother's quiet entrance—spontaneous and noisy. Stephen arrived in his own way with his own style. I peered down at him and felt an unprecedented love, a love only meant for this particular person.

My love hadn't split between two sons. Instead, one glance at that tiny soul more than doubled my capacity to cherish. I understood the mothers with twins, with triplets, with a dozen children. And I better understood how the Lord loved each and every person with equal compassion and intensity.

The time came for Grandma's visit. I stood defensive and ready to justify my baby's existence as equal to his brother's. She walked into the room... and melted. Laying her eyes upon her second grandson sparked the identical understanding that had been mine in the delivery room. She ate him up in the same manner as she had Matthew in his early hours. After her visit, I cried... relieved... ecstatic at how perfect life was at this moment.

Fifteen years would pass before we discussed the silliness of our worries. The magic of childbirth is more than science; truly it is a miracle in the human capacity to love. Love cannot be restricted or measured by the number of times it happens. The second time around is just as good as the first, if not better.

~C. Hope Clark

**Chapter 12**

# New Moms

## Toddler Time

*The fundamental job of a toddler is to rule the universe.*

~Lawrence Kutner

# The Bottle Fairy

*Life itself is the most wonderful fairy tale.*
*~Hans Christian Andersen*

"You should think about weaning," the pediatrician recommended at my daughter's twelve-month checkup. At fifteen months, she urged me a little more strongly. Finally, at eighteen months, the doctor said, "It's time."

Whether or not there is a magical age for weaning, I decided to get serious; I was pregnant and wanted my daughter to be completely over the bottle before a nursing and bottle-sucking infant disrupted her life.

I read the weaning section in every baby book I had. I tried everything. After the evening routine, including teeth brushing, she could only have water from a bottle. She had milk from a cup with her meals. I also tried to eliminate her mid-morning bottle. It was supposed to be the easiest feeding to drop. Nothing worked.

My abdomen protruded more each day as my due date loomed ever closer. Finally, I came up with an idea of my own. My daughter was familiar with the tooth fairy, so I hoped this would work.

"The bottle fairy is coming," I told her. "There are new babies who need these bottles." I prepared her for a week. We counted down, crossing off each day on the calendar.

Finally, the day arrived. In the wee hours of the morning, the bottle fairy visited our house. I—er, she—packed up every single bottle. Okay, I did keep one out of sight but within easy reach if it didn't work.

"Congratulations," I told my daughter excitedly the next morning. "You are officially a toddler. Toddlers don't use baby bottles."

At first, she was skeptical. Then I helped her search the house. There were no bottles to be found. We made it through breakfast; she drank from a regular cup.

Mid-morning arrived. She sat on the couch in her favorite spot, begging for a bottle. "Well, let me check. Maybe the bottle fairy missed one."

I walked very slowly around the house. She waited, eyes dropping, hoping for that bottle as part of her morning nap routine. Eventually, she fell asleep, thumb in her mouth, waiting for me to find a bottle.

The rest of the day went fairly smoothly. She had no problem with a big kid cup at lunch, no problem all afternoon. She even did just fine with her bedtime routine.

"It can't be that easy," I said to my husband, wondering why I hadn't come up with this idea months before.

It wasn't quite that easy. The next day, settling in for her mid-morning nap, she again whined and complained and insisted on a bottle. Trying to ignore the fact that I was lying to my daughter, I promised to look once again for a bottle. I did walk around the house. I did look. But I knew what I would find. I also knew where I'd stashed the bottles.

By the end of the week, weaning basically was complete. All the books told me that the mid-morning bottle was the easiest to give up. I had never thought to question this. As it turned out, that was the time my daughter wanted her bottle the most. The other times of day were much easier. Once she learned to get through those mornings, the rest was no problem. If only I'd started with one of them, perhaps things would have gone more smoothly. But then I'd have never invented the bottle fairy. And my daughter couldn't wait for her baby brother to be old enough for the bottle fairy to visit our house again.

~D. B. Zane

# First Haircut

*Cutting Baby's hair is just a shade easier than bathing a tomcat.*
*~Stan and Jan Berenstain,* The Berenstains' Baby Book

It started out one cold morning after our son's first birthday. I had decided that it was time for Isaac to get his hair cut for the first time. Although we found his long locks cute, we had gotten a few polite comments from family members that alerted us to the fact he looked "shaggy" and "unkempt." Off we trotted to a salon that specialized in children's hair. "Make your child's first haircut memorable," it boasted. That was what we wanted, so we swaggered into the shop.

I was hoping for balloons and a parade, but instead I got a girl unexcitedly pointing to a sign that read, "Please sign in." I looked around. There was nobody in the shop, but I figured they must have lots of appointments, so I signed our son's name. The girl was sporting a nice skeleton tattoo on her arm along with her short, spiky black hair and extra thick mascara. She was sipping a Snapple while she watched a TV over in the corner. The sneer on her face did little to assure me of her ability to work well with children.

Tyler and I locked eyes with each other while we tried to communicate with our special marital telepathic abilities. "Should we go?" I tried to wiggle with my brows in Morse code. "No, too awkward to leave now," he shrugged and coughed in wordless response. I did notice him look at the door longingly. Isaac began to fidget and wanted to play. Several of the books in the waiting area were chewed around the corners. Perhaps this was done by some feral child dragged in from the wild to get a haircut, I mused.

The girl finished her Snapple and then calmly walked over to the counter. She checked the sign-in sheet. "Uh... Isaac?" she asked as she looked all around the (empty) room. We jumped up and presented Isaac to her.

"It's his first haircut!" I announced proudly.

She looked less than amused and asked, "Which chair do you want him in? We only have one for really young kids."

I quickly thought about this choice. Was it a trick question? The chair she directed us to was actually a battered circus elephant about four feet off the ground. It had a little bench for him to sit on, but no back, and the area for his feet was too shallow. It also lacked a seat belt, but I could see evidence of where one used to be. It was frayed around the edges; the feral child had already been here and thankfully escaped.

Lacking any sort of safety mechanisms, my husband bravely volunteered to hold our son in place. After a moment, the girl agreed, warning: "Don't get in the way, okay? My scissors are sharp." Yikes! Was that a threat? I suddenly began to worry for my husband's safety. I hoped he wouldn't try anything shifty. "No sudden movements," I tried to telepath to him, but he was looking away. He was on his own.

As my husband began to lift Isaac into the seat, I noticed that it was covered in hair. There were brownish hairs, blond hairs, and some others in between. Either the seat had not been cleaned for several appointments or the calico feral child running around with a well-gnawed-on copy of *Goodnight Moon* clutched in his jaw had immediately preceded us. "Could you maybe clean off the seat first?" I asked timidly. She looked inside the seat and let out a huff followed by an eye roll.

When the hair was cleared, we continued with our goal: our son's first haircut! It was already proving to be the memorable experience they had promised us. I couldn't wait to see what kinds of memories the actual haircut would provide.

She began with a few snips and then grabbed the buzz cutter. As the buzz cutter hummed away, my son started eyeing the thing with desperate concern. His little chest was rising up and down dramatically, and already his lip was starting to protrude, warning that he was about to cry. "Maybe not the buzz cutter," I suggested. She barely took her eyes off the television program she was watching as she replied, "Can't do that; have to use them."

Isaac began to cower into my husband as she came closer. When his head was completely buried into my husband's chest, the girl gave out an annoyed sigh. "I can't get to his hair." My husband tried to move away in hopes of exposing some of Isaac's head for her to work with, but Isaac's death grip coupled with my husband's security lock on his body was not providing any entry. I tried to help, but we all had little success. Isaac was wailing and trembling.

His first haircut doubled as his first traumatic experience. Someone was holding him down, another was prying his head from a safe location, and someone else was coming at him with sharp objects fashioned after implements of torture. The buzzer squealed and hummed in the background.

I tried to suggest more forcefully, "Can we try to just use the scissors?" The girl was exasperated now. "It will take longer," she grunted. She didn't look happy to be the one serving us and continued to go at Isaac with her tools. He screamed and cried and fussed, but she battled on with her task with what would have been gusto, but for the utter lack of enthusiasm.

Finally, we were done, and Isaac's face was red and wet with a look of fear. I stood shocked with my mouth open at the whole event, while my husband's face turned various shades of red. I could tell the experience of holding down our screaming son had triggered his fight or flight response. Meanwhile, the girl had brought out her most torturous instrument of all and exclaimed, "Smile!" I heard the hollow click and whine of a classic Polaroid. The flash blinded all three of us.

She gathered up some locks of hair from the floor and haphazardly plucked out the brown hairs that most obviously didn't belong to Isaac. When it seemed she was pleased with her selection of blond hairs, she taped them onto a yellow photocopied certificate. She promptly misspelled Isaac's first name and asked us how to spell "Smith" so she could get it right on the certificate.

Back in the car, my husband and I were speechless. Our son was still whimpering in the back seat. I decided that just this once I would allow him to use the pacifier I stash for naptime emergencies. He took it with a shaky hand that resembled a deprived smoker lighting up. I glanced in the window of the shop and saw the girl already back on her stool, enjoying what was left of her Snapple.

Just then, we saw a happy couple walking toward the shop with their smiling little girl. I had the urge to be a good citizen and warn them, but before I could roll down the window, my husband was speeding away. As the shop faded into the distance, the Polaroid began to slowly reveal the picture of the shock and horror that was our son's first haircut.

~Tina Smith

# ABC-CEO

*Think P.I.G. — that's my motto.
P stands for Persistence, I stands for Integrity, and G stands for Guts.
These are the ingredients for a successful business and a successful life.*
~Linda Chandler

As the parent of a preschooler, I used to jump each time the phone rang. I was certain it was a headhunter calling to fill the position she knew my three-year-old could do so perfectly: CEO of a Fortune 500 company. I had known for quite some time that my son and his preschool peers possessed the qualities we prize in our most coveted executives. Determination. Confidence. Energy. Creativity. Outstanding negotiation skills. A sense of entitlement. Am I suggesting that three- and four-year-olds could rival ambitious MBAs? You bet! Disagree, and I suspect you have never lived with one.

Let's face it, only the energy of a preschooler could enable an individual to fulfill the time-intensive requirements of a CEO. Many corporate types suffer from early morning waking. I, however, suffered from my preschooler's early morning waking. Crack-of-dawn business meetings? Not a problem for my son. He'd already eaten his cereal and logged onto the computer. So he'd have to throw on a tie... hardly a problem. Late-night dinners with clients? Can do! He was always in search of the last-minute snack, and an excuse to delay bedtime would pretty much be right up there with a ban on tooth brushing.

On occasion, I've been known to give up in the face of frustration. Not a preschooler. He or she will work diligently until finding a way to squeeze that one-inch Lego into the quarter-inch space between the refrigerator and the kitchen floor. Continued persistence matched with an unflappable sense of certainty yields a self-assured and unstoppable executive and your typical preschooler. There is a reason he believes ice cream is the only appropriate breakfast choice, and he is certain he can convince you of this, never mind if it takes him clear through to dinner. Bill Gates probably took the same approach when someone told him in 1975 that computers were a fleeting phenomenon. That's the type I want at the helm of my corporation!

Self-esteem is not a problem for the well-grounded executive or the preschooler. They feel good about themselves most of the time in spite of their eccentricities. My preschooler believed that he looked best when wearing werewolf slippers and a plastic king crown (complete with fake jewels). No one told him otherwise because it was harmless, he was happy, and it was pretty darn amusing. Kind of like the boss sporting a bad toupee or horrid perfume... who's going to touch that one?

While creativity has been responsible for the success of the most notable CEOs, it is the common denominator in preschoolers. My son once spent twenty minutes emptying my office stapler to create the ultimate "staple art" picture. He was certain that his father would worship his creation, which he did, and that my colleagues would offer him big money for it, which they did. My maternal pride flowed as I witnessed his creative and entrepreneurial talents merge.

I'll admit that your average preschooler is high maintenance. Still, his/her requirements parallel those of the Fortune 500 CEO. Chauffeur. Support staff. (My preschooler refuses to do his own laundry, shopping, meals, or correspondence.) Perhaps preschoolers are a tad less expensive (my preschooler never requested Armani), but factor in the latest in footwear expenses, and they come pretty close.

Regardless of his demanding nature, my young son, like his peers and perhaps a few business types, could be won over by loyalty and small gifts. I've always believed that corporate America could learn a thing or two from the mom of a preschooler. Negotiation. Patience. Okay, the power of guilt. I know I'm onto something because my son's preschool teacher resigned before pre-K graduation. Rumor has it that she left to become a headhunter.

~Nancy Berk

# Sleepy, Grumpy, and Dad

*Sleep is like the unicorn—
it is rumored to exist, but I doubt I will see any.*
~Author Unknown

I was pooped, plain and simple. A young mother, occupied with a household of four active little ones that I'd birthed in a six-year span, I felt my world close in on me one dreary Sunday afternoon.

"I just need to sleep," I whined to my husband. "Sleep will cure me. I crave it. I need it. I deserve it. I just want a nice, long…"

"Consider it done," he interjected.

"…uninterrupted nap."

His eyebrows darted upward as he glanced pointedly at the rain pounding on the patio. He gestured at our housebound children.

"Uninterrupted? Really?" He shook his head and gave a dry laugh. "With this crew, that's asking a lot."

If it hadn't been as tired as the rest of me, I'm sure my jaw would have clenched. Instead, I merely repeated myself, tossing the word a bit desperately over my shoulder as I scurried upstairs to bed.

"Uninterrupted. I want an UN-interrupted nap."

I fluffed my pillow, pulled a warm afghan to my chin, and curled into a ball. My eyes had barely drifted shut when I heard my red-headed toddler holler from the stairway.

"Mommy! Mommy!"

I pulled the afghan over my head.

"Mommy? Where are you?"

"I should've known this wouldn't work," I grouched to myself and heaved a sigh. But before I could toss back the covers and drag myself from bed, my husband manfully shouldered his mantle of responsibility.

"Pssst. Koy, come back down here," he half whispered, although he knew I couldn't possibly be asleep already. "Mommy's napping. If there's something you want, son, you need to ask Daddy instead. Okay?"

"Okay," said Koy, his two-year-old voice loud and agreeable.

Satisfied, I closed my eyes again.

"Well, then," my husband's voice rose as he prompted, a bit impatiently, "tell me what it is you want."

"Mommy," said Koy, plaintively. "I want my mommy."

~Carol McAdoo Rehme

# Sloppy Mommy, Little Faces

*A baby will make love stronger, days shorter, nights longer, bankroll smaller, home happier, clothes shabbier, the past forgotten, and the future worth living for.*
*~Anonymous*

I used to have some fashion sense. I knew what was hip and what was not, I knew what colors were "in" and what styles were "out." I wore hipster jeans, layered tees, flashy belts, and peasant blouses. I loved earrings and had a cute pair to match each outfit. I loved shopping at boutiques in the mall, and got excited about bringing home new accessories. I was cute.

Then I got married and started college. Slowly, without any consciousness on my part, my wardrobe started to drift into fashion obscurity. Between working, homework, classes, and new wifely duties, keeping up with modern fashion drifted more and more out of my mind. Then, I became a mommy, and all fashion sense was completely replaced by all things baby. Earrings, sandals, and color-coordination were replaced by pacifiers, baby booties, and teddy bear nursery themes. I traded my hip denim purse for a bulky Winnie-the-Pooh diaper bag. I was so busy that I didn't even notice.

By the time my second baby was born (only fifteen months after the first), my entire wardrobe consisted of over-sized T-shirts and jeans from the thrift store. I had become so consumed with my growing family that I had no idea what fashions were even "in." I considered it a great accomplishment just to be showered and dressed before noon. The nicest article of clothing in my closet was a T-shirt that said "Best Mom in the World." It actually fit me.

So, the new year came, and I decided to make some changes. As part of the "new me," I wanted to start dressing better. I was tired of looking so sloppy. So I went to Target and picked out some pretty outfits. They still weren't as hip as my clothes once were, but they were nice and actually fit me. I got them home, tried them on, and dazzled myself. It was like a new coat of paint on a ragged old room.

Yesterday was my birthday, and my husband and two toddlers and I went out to eat to celebrate. I got to wear one of my new outfits for the first time, and I felt great. I was so excited to find myself again, to emerge from the swirling sinkhole of cotton T-shirts and mom-jeans. I looked awesome.

But as soon as our food was served, I remembered why I dress the way I do. Sitting next to my two-year-old, I watched with dread as she bypassed her fork and dug right into her mac and cheese with her little fingers. Before I had a chance to wipe her cheesy hands, she grabbed hold of my arm and used the sleeve of my new black sweater as a napkin. I tried in vain to keep her hands clean and to remind her about the purpose of silverware, but as the meal went on, I ended up with more and more cheese and ketchup on my new clothes.

I looked across the table at my husband and sighed. Suddenly, I felt very sad to realize that that part of my life truly is gone. I mentally resigned myself to being a slob for life and gave up any hope of looking halfway decent. Just like that, the good feelings and confidence were gone.

Then I felt the little hand on my arm again. I looked over and saw my daughter's bright eyes and cheesy grin. "Mommy! Hi!" she squealed with delight. That little face just melted my heart. A wave of love and affection washed over me, completely absolving any sadness. I was there with my family, and that's all that mattered. I hugged that little girl as tight as I could, cheesy face and all.

I may never get the cheese out of my new outfit, but it will serve as a great reminder of the time when my daughter got complete happiness just from sitting next to me. I may be resigned to faded jeans for the next several years, but as long as I get to look at that little face, I wouldn't trade them for anything in the world.

~Julie R. Bunnell

# Flowers from an Admirer

*Think of the toddler years as a wacky and crazy—but short—
period of time.... Slow down and see past the chaos of it, and you'll see that
good things truly do come in small packages.*
~Paula Spencer

"I got somethin' for you, Mama." I smiled and looked into the big blue eyes of my two-and-a-half-year-old son. Lee hunched up his skinny shoulders and squeezed his hands tighter behind him.

"Is it an elephant?" I guessed.

Lee giggled. "Nooo..." His arms shot forward. "It's flowers!"

My breath caught in my throat. In Lee's grubby little fists were popped-off flower heads. Flower heads belonging to the petunias that had taken me most of the morning to plant. Flowers that completed my gorgeous backyard display.

"Hurry. Put 'em in a tall glass," Lee said. He was so excited about his present that I didn't have the heart to scream.

I explained that flowers needed to be attached to stems to go into a vase. Oh, well, I thought, more blooms will appear if my short gift giver didn't tromp all over the new plants. I got out a bowl, and as Lee and I attempted to get the squished petunia blossoms to float, I explained that we should leave the flowers growing outside for the hummingbirds to enjoy.

The next morning, Lee burst into the kitchen from the backyard with his arms behind his back. A grin covered his whole face. "I 'member what you said, Mama."

A trail of dirt followed my boy.

"The necks are real long. See?" Lee thrust two handfuls of petunias at me—with the roots dangling midair. "I petted all the flowers. The little honey-birds like soft ones."

I looked out the window. My floral display was covered with Lee's love. Somehow, flowers don't do well with petting, but for boosting a weary mother's spirits, you can't do better than flowers from an admirer.

~Sharon Landeen

# I Got a Boy

> *Boy, n.: a noise with dirt on it.*
> ~Not Your Average Dictionary

When I got pregnant it was exciting, but scary. I was thirty-three at the time. For most of my twenties, I didn't think I wanted children. But as I aged, I realized I did want a child. So, after three years of marriage, we were ready to try. Throughout the early weeks of pregnancy, I focused on my physical changes. I managed the nausea and weight gain and mood swings pretty well. There was also one thing I knew for sure: I wanted a girl.

Being a girl was all I knew. I am an only child and was always a girly girl. Before I got pregnant and through my early weeks of pregnancy, I did as much positive thinking and law of attraction work that one person can do. I was preparing for my girl. My mother had died in 2004, and I was ready to name my daughter Alexandra after my mother. We had it all set.

Twenty weeks of pregnancy finally arrived. Ultrasound wand on the belly, the technician gave me the news: "It's a boy!" I was in shock. As soon as I started to breathe again, I burst into tears. A boy. I couldn't believe it. The possibility of having a boy honestly never entered my mind. I cried all the way home from the doctor's office and all that night. What was I going to do with a boy? I hate sports and dirt.

Fast forward to Jackson's birth. When the nurse handed that

little bundle to me, I thought I had never seen such perfection. All I wanted to do was take care of this little boy and love him with my whole being. I felt so ashamed of myself for thinking even for a second that I wanted a girl instead of this amazing creature looking at me with his giant blue eyes. I cried tears of happiness and tears of sadness simultaneously. My son was truly a lesson from God. He knew a boy would be good for me. Girls I knew, but boys?

Oh, what a world I have discovered and grown to appreciate. Every day with my son is a lesson for me on stepping outside my comfort zone. Instead of sitting in a chair at the beach, I am chasing a boy who is chasing seagulls. Instead of getting my nails painted, I am getting my face painted to support our favorite sports team. Instead of playing with dolls, I am playing with trucks. I have made peace with dirt, dead things, living things, mystery liquids and chocolate milk on the sofa. I have learned that getting jumped on, stepped on, kicked by flailing limbs and head butts are all forms of "wrestling." I have had to get in shape to keep up with my toddler and change my wardrobe to accommodate impromptu batting practice and tackle football in the yard. I have learned not to wear flip-flops in the woods.

My son has taught me how to remain in the present moment, no daydreaming on the job. My son has taught me how to laugh at myself and at everyday experiences. Rolling down a hill can actually be fun, and water guns on a hot day can be refreshing. My son has taught me how to be more open — open to love someone else and open to love myself. He is my perpetual lesson in absolute faith in our own perfection. I am supposed to be the teacher in this relationship, but I seem to be learning something new every day. One thing I know for sure: I am so thankful I got a boy.

~Stacey Tucker

# Mixed Feelings

*Live in the moment and make it so beautiful
that it will be worth remembering.*
~Fanny Crosby

"No accidents all day yesterday for Levi... hoping for another great day today! Now, how do I start going places with him???"

I read my daughter Susan's Facebook posting and laughed aloud at the computer screen. It's begun. She is potty training my grandson. Apparently, it's been a challenge, encountering a battle of wills and a few "accidents." She's even rearranged schedules in order to stay home for long stretches of time in the hopes of reinforcing how good it feels to be dry in big boy underwear.

I chuckled as I read subsequent postings between our phone conversations. "Not a good day today for potty training. Three accidents." Another day listed, "He's just not interested. I'm going to take a break."

Susan made an announcement a week later. I read her posting, but I could hear her voice of triumph as all capital letters boasted, "LEVI NOW GOES POTTY ON HIS OWN!" I nodded in agreement as I identified with the sentiments that followed as she posted her thoughts later in the day. "It seems weird to not know he's even going until I hear the flush of the toilet." On another day, she posted, "Oh, he must've had to go, I say to myself. This whole growing-up thing is happening too fast!"

Her chronology reveals in a nutshell the mixed feelings that moms have. We have the convenience of diapers, yet the need to have our toddlers "grow up" and, in a rite of passage, move on to underwear. Potty training is the big "first" of the firsts, followed by preschool, waiting for the kindergarten school bus, all day at school, and overnights with friends. We blink, and our kids have moved from a tricycle to a learner's permit; then they ask to borrow the car when they have their license.

We anticipate, we expect, we enjoy, we celebrate, and we cry.

Convenience... independence... graduation... leaving home... becoming adults... starting their own families... and I read about my grandson. Where did time go? We live a contradiction of seemingly long days, and others when we feel as if we are standing still. We are exhausted from children who keep us up at night with earaches and then keep us up until we breathe a sigh of relief when we see their car headlights pull into the driveway.

Today, I read Susan's final post about potty training. "Why am I actually sad that my little boy is no longer in diapers???"

I commented on her post. "Because, my darling daughter, you are a mother."

~Marilyn Nutter

# Playmate Dates

*My childhood may be over, but that doesn't mean playtime is.*
~Ron Olson

Marriage is wonderful for a lot of reasons, especially because you no longer have to date. As I tossed my bouquet to all of the single gals, I also threw away the need to constantly suck in my stomach, wear make-up to bed, blow-dry my hair after every shower, and pretend like I never do "Number Two." It was such a liberating moment. Unfortunately, it didn't last.

Three years flew by, and our little family grew by one toddler. I am my son's chief playmate, but after a few years of constant companionship, I began to suspect he had grown bored with me. I couldn't blame him. Frankly, I am a little dull. My version of "Old McDonald Had a Farm" always uses the same animals. I only have two silly faces, and I'm terrible at vehicle impersonations. It was clearly time to find us a friend.

I knew exactly the type of mom I needed. She would have an open schedule and a yearning desire for adult company, as well as be respectful and tolerant of my germ phobias. Her fashion would consist predominantly of elastic, so I wouldn't have to start wearing real clothes and sucking in my (now much bigger) stomach again. And, of course, she must have a toddler about my son's age.

I plopped my son into his stroller, and proceeded to scope out the neighborhood. Apparently, I am surrounded by a million young children who are parented by a million working mothers without the time or energy to pencil me into their already hectic schedules. A couple of them put in a sincere effort to plan a play date, but ultimately their laundry was more important. I had to broaden my search.

I met a lady at the park with a child my son's age, but her slingbacks and carefully styled hair confined her to a bench (with her cell phone), leaving me to socialize with both of our children. Another lady I met was nice enough, but the runny nose she swore was teething-related made my household sick for two weeks. Pretty soon, I was handing out my number to mothers at the toy store and the market, and even posting bulletins on the Internet. Everyone responded to my desperate attempts at friendliness with big eyes and a plastered smile, but no one ever called.

Friendless and still unable to come up with more interesting animals to live on Old McDonald's humongous farm, I decided to take a break from my playmate dating. I was standing in my driveway one afternoon, trying to entertain my son with the wonders of rock landscaping, when Lisa walked by with her toddler. Lisa was a stay-at-home mom! Lisa didn't want to come onto my driveway because her son was getting over a cold, and she didn't want to share his germs! Lisa wore exercise pants and one of her husband's T-shirts, and her hair looked dirty! She was perfect. We exchanged numbers and set a date.

As with any first date, I was nervous, but still looking forward to it with eager anticipation. I had dreams of impromptu trips to the zoo together, walking our little ones to their first day of kindergarten, and splitting the cost of a limo for their prom. Of course, I was forgetting one major detail.

My son had to enjoy the date, as well. Not only was I thrust back into the dating world, but now there was an extra person with his own set of criteria. Apparently, my child wanted a friend who would share his toys without hitting, pushing, or throwing hard objects at his head. It quickly became obvious that Lisa's son was not going to fit the bill.

Sharply angled toys flew unbridled around the room, my son's sensitive skin sported red marks from aggressive squeezes, and the high-pitched sounds of consecutive tantrums permanently stole a range of my hearing. As I struggled to disguise my horror, I realized I had personally arranged the first of many chips at my son's innocence. Lisa was largely unconcerned that her child was a toy-stealing, WWE maniac. And having little experience with this type of social interaction, I was unsure of how much offense I was allowed to practice. By the end of our ninety-minute play date, I had long left the honeymoon phase and was thinking about divorce. She never called, and that was fine with me.

After spending time with Lisa's son, I was tempted to throw holy water and garlic at every toddler I saw. Even though I was frustrated and upset that such a simple task as finding a little friend for my son was turning into *Mission Impossible*, I knew that I had to keep trying. My dating days may be over, but my son has many, many more ahead of him. I reminded myself that it took time, but I did eventually find my soulmate in my husband. With a little time, a little patience, and a little less violence, I remained hopeful that we would find our playmate, too.

So, I took a deep breath and called an old acquaintance to ask if he and his daughter would like to come over to play. We didn't have much in common except for the ability to procreate, but the kids had a great time. And, really, that's all I needed.

~Michelle Civalier

# New Moms

Meet Our Contributors
Meet Our Authors
Thank You
About Chicken Soup for the Soul

# Meet Our Contributors

**Maizura Abas** was trained as an English as a Second Language teacher in the United Kingdom. She now resides in Malaysia. Maizura devotes her life to her two children. She is indebted to her husband for proofreading her creative writing pieces and loving her despite her inability to roast the perfect beef and all her innumerable quirks. E-mail her at maizura@yahoo.com.

**Rachel Allord** enjoys life with her husband and two children in Wisconsin where she aspires to live, and write, authentically. She loves to share about her family's adoption experience. E-mail her at allordfamily@sbcglobal.net.

**Alyssa Ast** is a mother to four children who works from home as a freelance writer, journalist, and author. Writing is Alyssa's passion in life along with her children.

**Erin Baebler** works with mothers who want to pursue ambitions outside of motherhood. She is also working on a book about what successful mom entrepreneurs know. Erin volunteers her time in various ways that encourage women to share their gifts with the world. She also volunteers at her kids' schools.

**Nikki Studebaker Barcus** is a licensed teacher and freelance writer who lives with her husband and their three children on an Indiana farm. She writes about the lessons God teaches her through her kids on her blog, Lessons from the Carpool Line, www.nikki-studebaker-barcus.blogspot.com.

**Patricia Barrett** is an English teacher at Foothill High School in Sacramento, CA. She has an M.Ed. and has worked as a freelance newspaper correspondent covering issues in education. Her published poetry spans over thirty years of creative endeavors. Passionate about teaching, today she inspires her students to write and publish.

**Kathleen Basi** is a stay-at-home mom, freelance writer, flute and voice teacher, liturgical composer, choir director, natural family planning teacher, scrapbooker, sometime-chef and budding disability rights activist. She puts her juggling skills on display at www.kathleenbasi.com.

**Cindy Beck**, co-author of *Mormon Mishaps and Mischief*, and author of numerous published stories, majored in entomology (insects) and graduated Sum Kinda Buggy from the University of Wyoming. She seldom shares that information, however, because then people ask her to check their houses for termites. Visit Cindy at www.ByTheBecks.com.

**Beverly Beckham** is a columnist for *The Boston Globe* and Grandparent.com. She is the author of *A Gift of Time*, a collection of essays, and *Back Then — A Memoir of Childhood*. E-mail her at bevbeckham@aol.com.

**Nancy Berk, PhD** is a psychologist, author of *Secrets of a Bar Mitzvah Mom*, and comic. She's written for More.com, Weight Watchers, and *Chicken Soup for the Soul*. A columnist for *Shady Ave* magazine, Nancy co-hosts www.WhineAt9.com — a daily blog and weekly podcast. Contact her at www.nancyberk.com.

**Amy Bourque** lives in Manchester, NH, with her husband and son. She graduated from Plymouth State University in 2004 with a Bachelor of Arts in English, and currently teaches English in Pelham,

NH. Amy enjoys skiing, photography, running, and writing. This is her first publication. E-mail her at akbourque1@gmail.com.

**Marty Bucella** is a full-time freelance cartoonist/humorous illustrator whose work has been published over 100,000 times in magazines, newspapers, greeting cards, books, the web and so on. To see more of Marty's work, visit www.martybucella.com.

**Diane Buller** received a B.A. in English from Eastern Illinois University and Masters in Education from the University of Illinois. She taught high school and college writing for more than thirty years. She lives in central Illinois where she gets to read, write inspirational nonfiction, and drink coffee.

**Julie Bunnell** received her B.A. in psychology in 2009. She lives in New York with her husband, three young kids, and two dogs.

**Martha Campbell** is a graduate of Washington University, St. Louis School of Fine Arts and a former writer/designer for Hallmark Cards. She has been a freelance cartoonist and illustrator since leaving Hallmark. She lives in Harrison, AR.

**Dave Carpenter** has been a full-time cartoonist since 1981. Besides *Chicken Soup for the Soul* books, his cartoons have appeared in *Harvard Business Review*, *Reader's Digest*, *Barron's*, *The Wall Street Journal*, *Good Housekeeping*, *Woman's World*, *The Saturday Evening Post* as well as numerous other publications. E-mail Dave at davecarp@ncn.net.

**Jane McBride Choate** received her B.S. from Brigham Young University too many years ago to count. When she's not busy being a mom and a wife, she enjoys writing and attending garage sales.

**Michelle Civalier** received her B.S. in biomedical engineering from Arizona State University in 2005. She is currently employed full-time by her toddler son. Her free time is spent working on her first novel. E-mail her at michelle.civalier@hotmail.com.

**C. Hope Clark** is editor of FundsforWriters.com by day and pens rural Southern mysteries by night. She lives on the banks of Lake Murray in rural South Carolina with her husband, their Dachshund and numerous chickens. Learn more at www.fundsforwriters.com or e-mail her at hope@fundsforwriters.com.

**Marie Cleveland** is currently a full-time wife and mother, part-time writer, occasional substitute teacher, and children's ministry worker. Besides writing devotionals and poetry, she has also written two children's books. Learn more at www.freewebs.com/mclevelandbooks.

**Dianne Daniels** is the author of the book *Mothering Like The Father: Following God's Example In Parenting Young Children*. She is a certified parent coach, and speaks to moms all over Colorado to encourage and equip them to follow God more closely in their parenting. Visit her at www.MotheringLikeTheFather.com.

**Lela Davidson** is a freelance writer and editor. Her essays appear regularly in family and parenting magazines. She lives in Arkansas with her husband, two children, and a skinny dog. Learn more at www.afterthebubbly.com.

**Wendy Dellinger** is a freelance writer who has a passion to encourage women in the various challenges of life. She loves creative pursuits, time with her husband and daughter in the beautiful Colorado outdoors, and homeschooling.

**Barbara Diggs** is a freelance writer living in Paris, France with her husband and two sons. A former corporate lawyer, Barbara now writes for print and online magazines, blogs about life as an international mother, and is working on a nonfiction book about intercultural weddings. Visit her at www.barbaradiggs.com.

**Jeannie Dotson** enjoys teaching middle school students at Powell County Middle School in Powell County, KY. Aside from writing, she loves spending time with her family, friends, and her two dogs, Gingerbread and Roscoe. She hopes to publish more writing in the future.

**Terri Duncan, EdS**, is an educator in Evans, GA. She is a devoted wife of twenty-five years to her husband Jayson and the mother of two college students, Dallas and Barret. She enjoys spending time with her family and writing. She is currently publishing her first full-length novel.

**Kim Ehlert** lives in Minneapolis with her husband and two children. Kim became inspired to pursue her childhood interest in writing after becoming a mom for the first time, and enjoys writing about her experiences as a mother of two young children. E-mail her at kimehlert@comcast.net.

**Shawnelle Eliasen** and her husband Lonny have five sons. She home teaches the younger boys. Shawnelle writes about family life and other relationships. Her stories have been published in several *Chicken Soup for the Soul* books, *Christmas Miracles*, *Praying from the Heart*, *A Cup of Comfort for Couples*, *Guideposts*, *MomSense*, and *Marriage Partnership*.

**Judy Epstein** earned a B.A. in Philosophy at Yale College and worked twenty years in TV, only to learn that becoming a mom was the hardest job on the planet... and the best. She self-syndicates her award-winning column, "A Look on the Light Side." Contact her at www.alookonthelightside.com or jepstein@mail.com.

**Melissa Face** lives and works in southeastern Virginia. She has a husband, a nine-year-old Boxer, and a new baby boy. Melissa writes regularly for *Sasee* magazine and has contributed stories to seven *Chicken Soup for the Soul* volumes. E-mail her at writermsface@yahoo.com.

**Andrea Farrier** is a very happy wife and homeschooling mother of three girls. She graduated from The University of Iowa with degrees in English and Speech Communication/Theater Arts and teaching certifications in both areas. These days she keeps her writing skills sharp by blogging at www.andreafarrier.blogspot.com.

**Malinda Dunlap Fillingim** is a hospice chaplain in Rome, GA, where she lives with her husband David and dog. She misses her daughters, Hope and Hannah, who have gone far away to college. She is trying to figure out how to fill her empty nest, but longs for the days when being a mommy was her full-time job.

**Deirdre Fitzpatrick** jokes that she "reads out loud" for a living as a morning news anchor for KCRA-TV, Sacramento. Then she goes home and "reads out loud" to her two boys. When not reading out loud, she enjoys endurance sports and has completed more than a dozen marathons and an Ironman Triathlon. E-mail her at drefitz@aol.com.

**Rhonda Bocock Franz** is an educator, senior writer for ParentingSquad.com, and writes about family, children, and cooking for websites and regional magazines. She lives in Arkansas where she enjoys walks in the woods and outings with her husband and three children. She writes on a variety of subjects at www.coffeehousemom.wordpress.com.

**Erin Fuentes** received her B.A. from Converse College and enjoys facilitating a support group for the caregivers of Alzheimer's patients. She lives with her husband, daughter, and multiple pets in Atlanta. She has a collection of children's stories. E-mail her at erinc.fuentes@gmail.com.

**Christa Gala** is a freelance writer in Apex, NC. She holds a B.A. in Journalism from The University of North Carolina at Chapel Hill and an M.A. in English and Creative Writing from North Carolina State

University. Gala lives with her husband and young son. Contact her at www.christagala.com.

**Kimberly J. Garrow** has been blessed six times as a "new mom." She is a humorist and inspirational writer featured in magazines, the *Chicken Soup for the Soul* series, author of *A Mother's Journey: Through Laughter and Tears*, and is working on a new book for moms. E-mail her at kimberlygarrow@hotmail.com.

**Julia Garstecki** received her bachelor's degree from Michigan State University, a masters degree from SUNY Fredonia in reading and is completing her certification in special education at SUNY Buffalo State College. Though working part-time at SUNY Fredonia, she prefers playing *Candy Land* with her children to folding laundry. E-mail her at juliagarstecki@gmail.com.

**Jenny R. George** lives on a five-acre hobby farm north of Coeur d'Alene, ID, with her husband and two children. She is a frequent *Chicken Soup for the Soul* contributor, and is currently working on two books. For more information about Jenny's writing, visit www.jennyrgeorge.com.

**Victoria Grantham** is a freelance writer whose work has appeared in *The New York Times*, *New York Post*, *New York Daily News* and *Downtown Express*. She lives in Manhattan with her husband, their new son and two pound puppies.

**Andrew Grossman** draws under the pen name of "Toos." His cartoons have appeared in *Reader's Digest*, *The Saturday Evening Post*, *National Enquirer*, *The Washington Post*, *Barron's*, *Stern*, the *Chicago Tribune* and hundreds of other magazines and newspapers. His work has been anthologized in numerous cartoons collections, such as *Lawyers! Lawyers! Lawyers!* and *Cats Cats Cats*.

**Patrick Hardin** is a cartoonist whose work appears in a variety of books and periodicals around the world. He resides and works in his home town of Flint, MI. E-mail him at phardin357@aol.com.

**Kathy Lynn Harris** lives high in the Colorado mountains with her son and husband. Kathy has written novels, children's books, poetry, short stories and essays. E-mail Kathy at kathy@kathylynnharris.com or read other work by Kathy at www.kathylynnharris.com.

**Katrina Rehme Hatch** received her Bachelor of Fine Arts, with honors, from Brigham Young University in 2000. She and her husband are both natives of Colorado currently residing near Kansas City. A professional mom to three small children, Katrina enjoys painting, drawing, and creating a cozy home for her family.

**Jonny Hawkins** draws cartoons full-time from his country home in Sherwood, MI. A father of three young children, Jonny's cartoons appear in hundreds of publications, his eight books and in his line of Cartoon-A-Day calendars. E-mail him at jonnyhawkins2nz@yahoo.com.

**Dawn Hentrich** received her double Bachelor of Arts from Humboldt State University in History and Religious Studies in 1999. She taught for eight years in the Los Angeles Unified School District, and is now a stay-at-home mom to Benjamin. She writes the blog www.thissideoftypical.blogspot.com about her adventures in parenting a child with autism.

**Ken Hoculock** is a western Pennsylvania-based broadcast journalist, known under the name of Ken Hawk since 1988. His works have been published worldwide since 1994. Outside of radio, his interests include bicycling, wine tasting, boating, and vacationing in Hilton Head Island, SC, with his wife Marjorie and their daughter Savannah. E-mail him at radiohawk@hotmail.com.

**Jess Holland** holds a B.A. in English and French, and an M.A. in

Curriculum and Instruction. A librarian, teacher, writer and mother, she has lived in four states and three countries. She's currently living in Texas with her daughter, husband and dogs, temporarily satisfying her wanderlust via minivan. E-mail her at wanderjust@gmail.com.

**Cara Holman** is the proud mother of Jeff, Emily and Douglas. Her personal essays and poetry have been featured online and in anthologies, including *Chicken Soup for the Soul: Count Your Blessings* and *Chicken Soup for the Soul: True Love*. Please visit her blog, Prose Posies, at www.caraholman.wordpress.com.

**Robbie Iobst** is the proud mom of Noah and happy wife of John. She lives in Centennial, CO, where she is a writer and speaker. If you'd like to get a free "Joyvotion" devotional, e-mail her at robbieiobst@hotmail.com or get to know Robbie better by reading her blog at www.robbieiobst.blogspot.com.

**Kathleen Jones** is a freelance writer and R.N. with several stories included in the *Chicken Soup for the Soul* series. This story is about her now grown daughter, the most precious gift she and her husband ever received. She hopes to tell the story of adoption to her future grandchildren. E-mail her at nesjks@juno.com.

**Lynn Juniper** worked as a customs broker for years, before quitting to stay home with her babies. She started writing a year after her last son was born. When the boys let her, she enjoys reading, writing, running, cooking, blogging and teaching piano. Visit her blog at www.windowsandpaperwalls.wordpress.com.

**Liesl Jurock, M.Ed.**, is the author of Mama's Log (www.mamaslog.com), a blog about the joys and contrasts that motherhood offers. Her work has appeared in several online publications about motherhood. She shares a beautiful life with her hubby Kevin and son Lucas in British Columbia, Canada. E-mail her at lieslmama@gmail.com.

**Danielle Kazemi** is a stay-at-home mom to two young boys who constantly remind her that a noisy house is a loving house. When not chasing after them, she enjoys reading books with a nice cup of coffee and watching television series with her husband.

**Brandy Kleinhans** cannot remember a time she didn't feel called to teach. Brandy now resides in Summerville, SC, with her husband Jeff and three children. She and her husband continue to serve children and their families, continually searching for new ways to communicate that families reconciled to God are true modern-day miracles.

**Mimi Greenwood Knight** is a mama of four living in South Louisiana with her husband David and way too many pets. She's blessed to have over 400 essays and articles in magazines, anthologies and on websites including more than twenty *Chicken Soup for the Soul* books. See more of her work at blog.nola.com/faith/mimi_greenwood_knight.

**Sharon Landeen** considers raising four children and helping bring up two grandsons as her greatest achievement. She's a retired elementary teacher and keeps young by volunteering in the local schools, being a 4-H leader, and making blankets for Project Linus.

**Kathryn Lay** is the author of articles and stories for children and adults, and more than a dozen books for children. She enjoys doing school visits and speaking to writer's groups. She teaches online writing. Check her website for more info about her talks and classes at www.kathrynlay.com or e-mail her at rlay15@aol.com.

**Pearl Lee** is a Literature student at the University of California, San Diego. In her spare time, she enjoys reading, writing and creating culinary delights. You can follow her blog at www.inanoyster.com and e-mail her at inanoyster@gmail.com.

**Aimee J. Lenger** has been married to Gil since 1995. Their son Jed was born in 2009. The family enjoys a fulfilling life in Washington

State. Aimee's interests include collecting nesting dolls, working out, journaling, reading, needlework, and confirming breastfeeding rights for women and their babies. E-mail her at lenger.aimee@yahoo.com.

**Shelle Lenssen** is a full-time working mom trying to do it all, and do some of it well. She has recently started dabbling in freelance writing. Shelle enjoys the everyday adventures of living out in the country with her husband and daughter. E-mail her at shelle.lenssen@live.com.

**Denise K. Loock's** devotions, stories, and articles have appeared in numerous publications including *Chicken Soup for the Soul: What I Learned from the Cat*. She is also the founder and writer for digdeeperdevotions.com. Her first book, *Open Your Hymnal: Devotions That Harmonize Scripture With Song*, was released in 2010.

**Amanda Luzzader** is the mother of two delightful boys and wife to her handsome husband. She received a B.S. in Family, Consumer, and Human Development from Utah State University. She enjoys writing short stories and spending time with her family.

**Tiffany Mannino** is an lifetime learner, teacher, and breast cancer survivor from Bucks County, PA. She is inspired by traveling abroad, art, music, dance, laughter, her family, and advocating for organizations that work to provide a better quality of life for women and children around the world. E-mail her at tlorindesigns@gmail.com.

**Leslie Boulden Marable** received her B.S. in Education from Lamar University. She is a third grade teacher in Tennessee. Leslie enjoys writing, traveling, genealogy, making cards, singing, and teaching. Leslie's publication credits include devotions in the *Upper Room*, plus several poems in the *The Pulse*. E-mail her at lmarable@bellsouth.net.

**Alice Knisley Matthias** lives in the New York metropolitan area with her husband, children and dog. She has a B.A. in Theater and a Master's degree in elementary education. Alice is the author of a newspaper food column as well as work in adult and children's publications. E-mail her at aliceknisleymatthias@gmail.com.

**Dawn Maxwell** is an active writer and speaker in the area of breaking generational traps and bondages. She has lost ninety-five pounds on her own personal journey in this area. She also holds a B.A. in Journalism. E-mail Dawn at ddawnmaxwell@aol.com or visit her at www.dawnmaxwell.com.

**Dena May** received her Bachelor's Degree from Southern Arkansas University. She teaches 3rd-5th grade reading in North East Texas. Dena is a member of her local Child Welfare Board, active in her church, and a past contributor to *Chicken Soup for the Soul* books.

**Tina McGrevy** lives in Springfield, OH, with her husband Charlie and their boys: Garrett, Patrick and Brennan. Tina writes about the adventures of raising sons on her blog, "taleS froM the trencheS" at www.tinamcgrevy.blogspot.com. She invites you to visit www.prisms.org for more information about Smith-Magenis syndrome.

**RMB McManamon** has earned two Bachelors degrees and her Masters of Education in Administration and is currently a high school Business Education teacher. She loves sports and is a diehard Chicago Cubs fan. She enjoys traveling with family and friends. E-mail her at rntmac@yahoo.com.

**Jane Miller** is a teacher and writer living in Pittsburgh. Her children are now ages twenty-nine, twenty-four and thirteen. She is a fellow of the National Writing Project and founded the Ruff Writers website blog, www.theruffwriters.com, for parents, teachers and librarians. E-mail her at ruffwriters@comcast.net.

Since her daughter's adoption, **Lanita Moss** has remarried and internationally adopted another daughter. She lives with her family in

Kansas, is a full-time wife, mother, and currently writes for two blogs. You can read more of Lanita's work at www.amothershood.com and www.blog.birthbypaperwork.com.

**Sarah Sweet Newcomb** is a junior high teacher and writer, living in Ontario, Canada. She focuses much of her writing on education and parenting. Sarah enjoys spending time with her son and husband, reading, blogging, and running. E-mail her at sarah.newcomb@rogers.com.

**Marilyn Nutter** enjoys being a grandmother to four and mother of three adult daughters. She is the author of three devotional books and maintains a website at www.marilynnutter.com and a blog at www.grandmothersviews.blogspot.com. She enjoys speaking to women's church and community groups and can be contacted at marilynnutter@gmail.com.

**Maria Rodgers O'Rourke** is a popular and accomplished speaker, columnist and teacher. Creator of the *Prepare Your Heart* series of devotional journals, she inspires and guides others to recognize and embrace the hidden meaning in life. Maria and her husband have two children. Visit Maria at www.MariaRodgersORourke.com.

**Mark Parisi's** "Off the Mark" comic, syndicated since 1987, is distributed by United Media. His cartoon feature won the National Cartoonists Society's award for Best Newspaper Panel in 2009. Mark's humor also graces greeting cards, T-shirts, calendars, magazines, newsletters and books. Lynn is his wife/business partner. Their daughter, Jen, contributes with inspiration, (as do two cats and one dog). Learn more at www.offthemark.com.

**Cynthia Patton** has worked as an environmental attorney, scientific editor, nonprofit advocate, and consultant. The California native lives with her daughter and a thoroughly rowdy dog and cat. Cynthia's work has appeared in magazines, anthologies, and books. She's completing a memoir on her journey to motherhood. E-mail her at cynthiapatton@att.net.

**Nona Perez** lives in rural Northern California, where she and husband, Elias, raised and homeschooled their five children, affectionately known as the Perezoo. Recent retirement from her beloved position as stay-at-home mom has afforded her more time and clear-mindedness to pen stories of her family history.

**Sharon Pheifer** resides in Ohio with her husband of ten years, Mike, and their son Max. She works in the medical field as an administrative assistant. Sharon enjoys spending time with her family, reading, and swimming. This is the first story she has written. E-mail her at sharonpheifer@hotmail.com.

**Nicole Pugh** is a librarian who received a B.A. from Ohio University in 2000, and an M.L.I.S. from the University of South Carolina in 2006. She is currently trying her hand as a stay-at-home mom in Cookeville, TN, where she resides with her husband, daughter, and two dogs. E-mail her at nicolepugh@gmail.com.

**Jennifer Quasha** is a freelance writer and editor who loves reading, and writing for, *Chicken Soup for the Soul* books. You can check out her website at www.jenniferquasha.com, and see some of what she's been doing since she went freelance in 1998.

**Angie Reedy** is a freelance writer who lives in central Illinois with her husband and two children. She delights in finding evidences of God's extraordinary greatness in the ordinary happenings of life and blogs about them at www.realreedy.blogspot.com. E-mail her at wareedy@gmail.com.

**Carol McAdoo Rehme** recognizes motherhood as her most important calling—it keeps her humble and hopping. Mother of four, she's now the delighted Grammy of eight. A veteran editor and prolific freelancer, Carol has coauthored nine books, including *Chicken Soup for the Soul: Empty Nesters* and *Chicken Soup for the Soul: The Book of Christmas Virtues*.

**Brianna Renshaw** finds inspiration for her writing on daily long runs accompanied by her daughter Makayla in her jogging stroller through their neighborhood in Scotland, PA. Every run allows her to see the world in a new way while strengthening her body, mind and faith. E-mail her at briannarenshaw@gmail.com.

**Jamie Richardson** received her B.S. in journalism and sociology from Texas A&M University in 2000. She is a stay-at-home mom to three kids, wife to her high school sweetheart, and freelance writer and editor. She is currently working on her first book. E-mail her at jamiearichardson@hotmail.com.

Besides being a proud husband and father, **Gary Rubinstein** is a math teacher in New York City. He has written two books, *Reluctant Disciplinarian* and *Beyond Survival*. This is his third *Chicken Soup for the Soul* publication. E-mail him at garyrubinstein@yahoo.com.

**Catherine Ring Saliba** graduated from the University of Vermont, was a registered nurse for over forty years, has been an actress in films, soaps and TV, is a grandmother of four, and now joyfully pursues writing. Her work has been published in professional journals, newspapers and magazines.

**Laura Sassi** specializes in children's fiction, nonfiction, and poetry. Her work has been published in *Highlights for Children*, *Spider*, *Ladybug*, and *Clubhouse Jr*. She is currently working on several rhyming picture books. She lives in New Jersey with her husband and their two "little alarm clocks."

Award-winning author, **Debbie Schmid**, has written three books; *The Beauty of Spring* and two best sellers, *Spiritual Spring Cleaning* and

*Spiritual Seasons*. Throughout the years she's been a keynote speaker and a spiritual mentor to countless women. Her hobbies include quilting, floral design and photography. E-mail her at beautyofspring2@juno.com.

Based in Ann Arbor, Michigan, **Harley Schwadron** is a cartoonist whose work appears in *Barron's*, *Playboy*, *The Wall Street Journal*, *Reader's Digest*, *Medical Economics*, many *Chicken Soup for the Soul* editions, and other books. He does a daily syndicated panel, "9 to 5", for Tribune Media Services. E-mail him at schwaboo@comcast.net or visit www.schwadroncartoons.com.

**Michelle Sedas** is author of *Welcome The Rain* and *Live Inspired* and coauthor of *The Power of 10%*. She is host of the Inspired Living Center and Cofounder of Running Moms Rock. Michelle graduated from Texas A&M University and lives in Texas with her husband and children. Visit Michelle at www.michellesedas.com.

**Julie Sharp** is currently a Personal Assistant to her three-year-old son, PJ, sixteen-month-old daughter, Analeigh, and husband, Grant. She is forever devoted to her family and first love, Jesus Christ. They are the inspiration for her writing, hope for her future, and joy in her heart.

**Dayle Shockley** is an award-winning writer whose work has appeared in dozens of publications. She's the author of three books and a contributor to many other works. She and her retired fire captain can often be found traveling around the countryside, enjoying God's handiwork. Dayle blogs at www.alittleofthisandthat2.blogspot.com. E-mail her at dayle@dayleshockley.com.

**Tina Smith** received her Bachelor of Arts in Psychology and Master of Arts in School Psychology and Counseling with honors in 2005. She enjoys writing, reading, raising her children, and hanging out with her best friend (her husband). She writes at her blog www.smashedpicketfences.com.

**Misa Sugiura** is a mother and a writer in Los Altos, CA. She blogs at www.Newsfromthetreehouse.blogspot.com. E-mail her at misamisa_1@yahoo.com.

**K.T.** is the author of two devotional books and a contributor for several *Chicken Soup for the Soul* books. She resides in South Florida with her husband and three children. She finds most of her inspiration comes from the long walks she takes each morning with her Golden Retrievers.

**Ronda Ross Taylor** lives in the Seattle area with her husband Eldon and a couple of parrots. She has two grown sons and is eager to take on the role of grandmother. When she's not writing, editing, or volunteering in school libraries, she can be found swimming at the Y.

**Becky Tompkins** enjoys working with words, both professionally — as a former teacher of English to refugees, freelance writer, and copy editor — and in her spare time. Besides reading and writing, she also enjoys learning, cooking, gardening, and spending time with her family.

**Stacey Tucker** transformed her website, www.staceylu.com, in 2010, to showcase her passion for writing. In her blog, she writes about her life experiences, hoping readers can relate. Stacey has just completed the manuscript for her first book, *Again, A Second Wedding Story*. You can contact her at stacey@staceylu.com.

**Christine White** is writer, mother, sea glass jeweler and bunny-sitter. She writes about adoption, sea glass hunting and life. She has been published in *Adoptive Families* magazine, newspapers, trade publications and websites. She believes writing is healing and truth-telling transformative. She lives with her daughter and their cat. E-mail her at Cissy_white@comcast.net.

**Mary Jo Marcellus Wyse** has an MFA in Writing from Vermont College. She currently lives outside Boston with her husband and two children.

**D. B. Zane** teaches social studies and is a writer, with work appearing in several *Chicken Soup for the Soul* books. Her hobbies include reading, gardening, and walking the dog. E-mail her at dbzanewriter@gmail.com.

**Helen Zanone** lives in Pittsburgh with her husband and three children. She is on the board of St. Davids Christian Writers' Conference. Helen is active in her writer's group. She has a story published in *Chicken Soup for the Soul: Twins and More*. E-mail her at hzanone@yahoo.com.

# Meet Our Authors

**Jack Canfield** is the co-creator of the *Chicken Soup for the Soul* series, which *Time* magazine has called "the publishing phenomenon of the decade." Jack is also the co-author of many other bestselling books.

Jack is the CEO of the Canfield Training Group in Santa Barbara, California, and founder of the Foundation for Self-Esteem in Culver City, California. He has conducted intensive personal and professional development seminars on the principles of success for more than a million people in twenty-three countries, has spoken to hundreds of thousands of people at more than 1,000 corporations, universities, professional conferences and conventions, and has been seen by millions more on national television shows.

Jack has received many awards and honors, including three honorary doctorates and a Guinness World Records Certificate for having seven books from the *Chicken Soup for the Soul* series appearing on the New York Times bestseller list on May 24, 1998.

You can reach Jack at www.jackcanfield.com.

**Mark Victor Hansen** is the co-founder of Chicken Soup for the Soul, along with Jack Canfield. He is a sought-after keynote speaker, best-selling author, and marketing maven. Mark's powerful messages of possibility, opportunity, and action have created powerful change in thousands of organizations and millions of individuals worldwide.

Mark is a prolific writer with many bestselling books in addition to the *Chicken Soup for the Soul* series. Mark has had a profound influence in the field of human potential through his library of audios, videos, and articles in the areas of big thinking, sales achievement, wealth building, publishing success, and personal and professional development. He is also the founder of the MEGA Seminar Series.

Mark has received numerous awards that honor his entrepreneurial spirit, philanthropic heart, and business acumen. He is a lifetime member of the Horatio Alger Association of Distinguished Americans.

You can reach Mark at www.markvictorhansen.com.

**Susan M. Heim** is a longstanding author and editor, specializing in parenting, women's and Christian issues. After the birth of her twin boys in 2003, Susan left her desk job as a Senior Editor at a publishing company and has never looked back. Being a work-at-home mother allows her to follow her two greatest passions: parenting and writing.

Susan's published books include *Chicken Soup for the Soul: Devotional Stories for Mothers*; *Chicken Soup for the Soul: Family Matters*; *Chicken Soup for the Soul: Devotional Stories for Women*; *Chicken Soup for the Soul: All in the Family*; *Chicken Soup for the Soul: Twins and More*; *Boosting Your Baby's Brain Power*; *It's Twins! Parent-to-Parent Advice from Infancy Through Adolescence*; *Oh, Baby! 7 Ways a Baby Will Change Your Life the First Year*; and, *Twice the Love: Stories of Inspiration for Families with Twins, Multiples and Singletons*. She is also working on a fiction book for teens and young adults.

Susan's articles and stories have appeared in many books, websites, and magazines, including *TWINS Magazine* and *Angels on Earth*. She shares her thoughts and experiences about raising children in today's world through her blog, "Susan Heim on Parenting," at http://susanheim.blogspot.com. And she is the founder of TwinsTalk, a website where parents share tips, advice and stories about raising twins and multiples, at www.twinstalk.com.

Susan is married to Mike, whose ever-present support enables her to pursue a career she loves. They are the parents of four active sons, who are in elementary school, high school and college! You can reach Susan at susan@susanheim.com and visit her website at www.susanheim.com. Join her on Twitter and Facebook by searching for ParentingAuthor.

# Thank You

We appreciate all of our wonderful family members and friends, who continue to inspire and teach us on our life's journey. We have been blessed beyond measure with their constant love and support.

We owe huge thanks to all of our contributors. We know that you pour your hearts and souls into the stories that you share with us, and ultimately with each other. We appreciate your willingness to open up your lives to other Chicken Soup for the Soul readers. We can only publish a small percentage of the stories that are submitted, but we read every single one, and even the ones that do not appear in the book have an influence on us and on the final manuscript. We strongly encourage you to continue submitting to future Chicken Soup for the Soul books.

We would like to thank Amy Newmark, our Publisher, for her generous spirit, creative vision, and expert editing. Susan is especially grateful to Amy for inviting her into the Chicken Soup for the Soul family! We're also thankful for D'ette Corona, our Assistant Publisher, who worked with us to read the thousands of stories submitted for this book and helped narrow down the list to several hundred finalists, all while seamlessly managing twenty to thirty projects at a time. And we'd like to express our gratitude to Barbara LoMonaco, Chicken Soup for the Soul's Webmaster and Editor, who always has a kind word to share; Chicken Soup for the Soul Editor Kristiana Glavin, for her expert assistance with the final manuscript, proofreading, and excellent quote-finding skills; and Madeline Clapps, for the final proofreading of this manuscript.

We owe a very special thanks to our Creative Director and book producer, Brian Taylor at Pneuma Books, for his brilliant vision for our covers and interiors. And none of this would be possible without the business and creative leadership of our CEO, Bill Rouhana, and our president, Bob Jacobs.

# Improving Your Life Every Day

Real people sharing real stories—for seventeen years. Now, Chicken Soup for the Soul has gone beyond the bookstore to become a world leader in life improvement. Through books, movies, DVDs, online resources and other partnerships, we bring hope, courage, inspiration and love to hundreds of millions of people around the world. Chicken Soup for the Soul's writers and readers belong to a one-of-a-kind global community, sharing advice, support, guidance, comfort, and knowledge.

Chicken Soup for the Soul stories have been translated into more than forty languages and can be found in more than one hundred countries. Every day, millions of people experience a Chicken Soup for the Soul story in a book, magazine, newspaper or online. As we share our life experiences through these stories, we offer hope, comfort and inspiration to one another. The stories travel from person to person, and from country to country, helping to improve lives everywhere.

# Share with Us

We all have had Chicken Soup for the Soul moments in our lives. If you would like to share your story or poem with millions of people around the world, go to chickensoup.com and click on "Submit Your Story." You may be able to help another reader, and become a published author at the same time. Some of our past contributors have launched writing and speaking careers from the publication of their stories in our books!

Our submission volume has been increasing steadily—the quality and quantity of your submissions has been fabulous. We only accept story submissions via our website. They are no longer accepted via mail or fax.

To contact us regarding other matters, please send us an e-mail through webmaster@chickensoupforthesoul.com, or fax or write us at:

Chicken Soup for the Soul
P.O. Box 700
Cos Cob, CT 06807-0700
Fax: 203-861-7194

One more note from your friends at Chicken Soup for the Soul: Occasionally, we receive an unsolicited book manuscript from one of our readers, and we would like to respectfully inform you that we do not accept unsolicited manuscripts and we must discard the ones that appear.

# Chicken Soup for the Soul

www.chickensoup.com